The Pequots in Southern New England

The Civilization of the American Indian Series

The Pequots in Southern New England

The Fall and Rise of an American Indian Nation

Edited by
Laurence M. Hauptman and
James D. Wherry

Foreword by
William T. Hagan

University of Oklahoma Press : Norman

To the Mashantucket Pequot Tribe of Connecticut

Library of Congress Cataloging-in-Publication Data

The Pequots in southern New England: the fall and rise of an American
    Indian nation / edited by Laurence M. Hauptman and James D. Wherry;
    foreword by William T. Hagan.
        p.   cm.—(The civilization of the American Indian series; v. 198)
    Includes bibliographical references and index.
    1. Pequot Indians—History.   2. Pequot Indians—Social life and cus-
toms.   I. Hauptman, Laurence M.   II. Wherry, James.   III. Series.
E99.P53P47   1990
974'.004973—dc20   90-50235
    ISBN: 0-8061-2286-2 (cloth)   CIP
    ISBN: 0-8061-2515-2 (paper)

*The Pequots in Southern New England: The Fall and Rise of an
American Indian Nation* is Volume 198 in The Civilization of the American Indian Series.

The paper in this book meets the guidelines for permanence and du-
rability of the Committee on Production Guidelines for Book Longevity of
the Council on Library Resources, Inc. ∞

7   8   9   10   11

Contents

Illustrations

Figures

Maps

Foreword

By William T. Hagan

In the fall of 1987 I had the privilege of participating in a conference on the Mashantucket (Western) Pequot Reservation in the town of Ledyard, Connecticut. Until only a few years before this, I am embarrassed to say, I had subscribed to the generally held view that the Pequot Tribe was extinct. Now I was brought face-to-face with abundant evidence that there was a flourishing enclave of Pequots in the heart of Connecticut.

Historians wrote off the Pequots after their catastrophic defeat in 1637, and two centuries later, in *Moby Dick,* Herman Melville pronounced them as extinct as the ancient Medes. To all but their immediate neighbors in Connecticut, and an occasional state official forced to recognize their existence, the Pequots had faded from the national consciousness. That was the situation until the 1970s when the western branch of this people, the Mashantucket Pequots, underwent a renaissance.

Their revival is even more remarkable considering that the Mashantucket Pequots were only one of less than twenty-five groups, out of well over a hundred, to successfully seek federal recognition in recent years. Indeed, the other four Indian groups in Connecticut, including the Paucatuck (Eastern) Pequots, were among those who have yet to establish a working relationship with the federal government.

As late as the 1960s the Mashantucket Pequots did not appear likely candidates for tribal revival and federal recognition. Three centuries earlier those Pequots who had survived the 1637 war had been relegated to a 2,000-acre reservation. Before their defeat they had been described by terms such as "rich and potent" and "stately and warlike." Now their numbers shrank as they continued to fall prey to the whites' diseases or were assimilated by neighboring populations. In 1855, Connecticut auctioned off about nine-tenths of their land holdings. By the 1940s only one family remained on the reservation. Nevertheless, the tribe's existence continued to be recognized, if reluctantly, by the state. Two of its tiny population, half sisters, fought to maintain their tribe's identity and the integrity of their 214-acre reservation.

Events in Maine in the 1970s offered new hope for Indians struggling to maintain their identity and reclaim some of their lost land. In response to a suit filed by the Passamaquoddy and Penobscot tribes, a federal judge ruled that treaties negotiated by the states, without the concurrence of the federal government, were invalid. Suddenly land titles to millions of acres of land throughout New England came under a shadow, and the tribes had found new and powerful leverage.

In the new atmosphere of the seventies the Mashantucket Pequots turned the corner. They wrote a tribal constitution and elected vigorous and politically adept leadership. With the help of the Native American Rights Fund and the Indian Rights Association, the tribe secured the legal representation and historical research needed to bring suit against Connecticut to recover the land seized by the state in 1855. After lengthy legal and political maneuvering, the Mashantucket Pequots emerged with an out-of-court settlement, endorsed by Congress, granting them federal recognition and a $900,000 trust fund. For its part the state of Connecticut ceded to the tribe twenty acres of land that included a Pequot cemetery, and pledged to spend $200,000 on roads for the reservation, now expanded to over 1,500 acres by purchases with trust funds.

The funds also would be drawn upon for economic development, and state and federal programs would be tapped, most importantly for forty units of tribal housing. Several economic initiatives were launched, not all of them successful. The most profitable has proved to be high-stakes bingo, which attracts hundreds of thousands of players a year.

But this is not just a study of Pequot successes. Readers will learn much about the process by which tribes seek recognition through the Federal Branch of Acknowledgment, its rewards and its pitfalls. And the authors are experts on the history and culture of the New England tribes. Some of these scholars were part of the joint effort to ensure that the Pequots achieved justice at the hands of state and federal authorities, a success story well worth the telling.

Preface

On October 23 and 24, 1987, the Mashantucket Pequot Tribe
of Connecticut sponsored a major conference on its reservation. The unique convocation was the first systematic and
comprehensive attempt to elucidate the history of this southern New England Indian community. Nationally acclaimed
academics—applied anthropologists, archaeologists, ethnolo-
gists, and historians—came together, invited and sponsored
by the Mashantucket Pequot Tribal Council, to help piece
together an Indian tribal history shrouded in mystery and
misconceptions and colored by myopic accounts written by
Puritan chroniclers over three centuries ago. The time was
ripe for reevaluation because the year 1987 marked the 350th
anniversary of a great tragedy in Colonial America known as
the "Pequot War," a conflict that nearly eliminated the American Indian presence in southern New England.

Although one of the Pequot tribe's major goals in holding
the conference was to commemorate solemnly the events of
1637, the Mashantucket Pequots chose this occasion to spon-
sor a meeting to reflect on how their ancestors had survived as
a people during and after their time of troubles in the 1630s.
From the beginning of the Mashantucket Pequot historical

conference project in May, 1982, the Mashantucket Tribal Council worked with the editors of this volume and a third conference organizer, Jack Campisi. They saw this conference as an opportunity to educate the public about the American Indians of southern New England. We therefore arranged for videotaping by Connecticut Educational Television in Hartford and teacher in-service credit through the University of Connecticut's main campus at Storrs, and began plans for the publication of the conference proceedings. This collection of the conference papers is intended to provide an accurate and balanced picture of southern New England American Indian life, an account that will be used at the secondary and college level as well as by specialists in the field. The editors and authors of the individual articles have consciously avoided employing the scholars' specialized terminology wherever possible.

Today, there are two separate Pequot Indian tribes in Connecticut: the federally recognized Mashantucket (Western) Pequots of Ledyard, Connecticut, and the state-recognized Paucatuck (Eastern) Pequots, who occupy a nearby landbase, the Lantern Hill Reservation in nearby North Stonington, Connecticut. These two communities had the same prehistory and history until the mid-1660s. Even after that date the two groups had similar histories and were affected by similar policies from Hartford. Thus most of the information presented in this volume, but not all, applies to the history of both the Mashantucket and the Paucatuck Pequots.

Much of the historiography on American Indians of southern New England has focused on the Pequot War of 1637. At that time the Pequots were among the most numerous and powerful tribes in the region. On May 26, 1637, in a predawn attack by an army of colonists and their Mohegan, Narragansett, and Niantic Indian allies, Mystic Fort, the Pequots' major village, was set ablaze, and anywhere between three hundred and seven hundred of their men, women, and children were burned, shot, or slashed to death. In less than an hour the Pequots' hegemony in the region was broken. Afterward they were hunted down, executed, allotted as vassals to their Indian enemies, or sold into slavery in the Caribbean. They were virtually rooted out as a people. Colonial authorities even forbade the use of their tribal name in order, in the words of their conqueror Captain John Mason, "to cut off the Remembrance of them from the Earth."[1] Thus the Pequots were in fact the first Indian nation "terminated" in American history. Their nonstatus continued for thirty years after the War of 1637.

From the age of the Puritans until well into the twentieth century, historians have largely seen Pequot history in terms of that one watershed event. A notable exception, one that traced Pequot history into the mid-nineteenth century, is John W. De Forest's *History of the Indians of Connecticut.* De Forest's book, published in 1851, has been, without doubt, the most widely circulated book treating the American Indian history of southern New England. It has been reprinted several times, influencing succeeding generations. To De Forest the Pequots were the "most numerous, the most warlike, the fiercest and the bravest of all aboriginal clans of Connecticut."[2] De Forest focused much of his attention on the War of 1637, condemning the Puritans for their policy of extermination. He also directed his attacks on Connecticut officials of the late eighteenth and early nineteenth centuries for their neglectful policies toward the Indians. Despite this sympathetic portrayal for his day, De Forest was very much a captive of the thinking of his times, seeing the Pequots, as well as other Indians, as a "vanishing race" that was somehow predestined by genetic makeup to give way to the western idea of progress:

Their gradual diminution in the period [1683 to 1844] . . . was produced by the disappearance of their brethren in the western part of the State. They were living, a barbarous race, in the midst of a civilized community. Consequently, when they were attacked by the diseases and vices of civilization, they had nothing to oppose to them but their ancient ignorance and simplicity. They were as lazy as ever, and they were besides drunken: they were as improvident as ever, and the game and fish which once supplied them had nearly disappeared. For them medical science did nothing: the couches of their sick were tended only by ignorance and indifference: intemperance and vice sapped their strength socially and individually: the annual deaths were more on an average than the annual births: some wandered to other parts of the country and joined other bands of unfortunates, and thus slowly and painfully have they faded away.[3]

It is important to note that four years after the publication of De Forest's classic, which gave further "proof" to the misconception of the Indians as the "vanishing race," the state of Connecticut illegally auctioned the majority of the remaining Mashantucket Pequot lands, leaving only 204 acres of the reservation.

Besides attempting to avoid the misconceptions of the past that have had a debilitating impact on Indian existence, contributors to this volume stress one underlying theme, namely, the maintenance and persistence of the Pequot identity over time. As Alvin M. Josephy Jr., explains so cogently in chapter 1, maintaining "Indianness" in New England is somewhat special. Their location halfway between New York City and Boston has affected the Pequots since the colonial era. "Indian Country," so visible and so identifiable in the American West, is dwarfed in southern New England by megalopolis, by one of the most populated 250-mile corridors in the country.

The Pequots and other eastern American Indians have developed and employed diverse strategies to survive, but the reader should never falsely assume that their strategems arose simply out of the Indian need to counter Euro-American civilization. Dena F. Dincauze suggests in chapter 2 that the Indians of southern New England adjusted and adapted to the ever-changing environment over the past twelve thousand years with a great deal of success, while in chapter 3, William A. Starna provides the reader with a portrait of an adaptive and vibrant native life just before the dislocations caused by "virgin-soil" epidemics and the War of 1637. Nevertheless, in chapter 4, Lynn Ceci suggests by analyzing wampum exchange that Pequots were soon to be drawn into a new global economy whether they wanted to be or not; reper-

cussions from this exchange led to increased Indian-white
tensions and nearly to Pequot ruination in the 1630s and after.

In Part Three, the heart of this book, five scholars further develop the theme of cultural persistence of Pequot identity. In
chapter 5, Laurence M. Hauptman describes the events leading to the Pequot War of 1637 and tells how contemporary
Pequots consciously and subconsciously have used the tragedy to stimulate a modern renaissance and reinforce their
separate identity from non-Indians as well as other Indians. In
chapter 6, Neal Salisbury focuses more specifically on the
critical years immediately following the War of 1637, when Pequot existence was in limbo until the reemergence of two separate tribal governments and land bases in the 1650s and
1660s. Basing chapter 7 primarily on his archaeological research, Kevin McBride describes the changes in Pequot settlement and subsistence patterns from the time of their troubles
in the seventeenth century until 1900. In chapter 8, Jack
Campisi looks at how the Pequots faced off and survived
against Hartford policy makers and their racist and paternal-
istic directives, from the Pequot War until 1970. In chapter 9,
William Simmons concludes Part Three with an analysis of the
rich oral literature that he has collected from Pequot elders,
showing the continuity and persistence of cultural traditions
down to the present day.

In Part Four of this book, Jack Campisi describes in chapter 10 the serendipitous, but significant, route to federal recognition taken by many eastern American Indian communities,
including the Mashantucket Pequots—a course that has permanently changed Indian life in New England. Then, in chapter 12, Robert Bee describes the changes in Connecticut
Indian policies during these last two decades and the new
American Indian assertiveness that has changed Hartford-
Indian relations forever. In his Afterword to the book, James
Wherry, tribal planner for the Mashantucket Pequots, looks to
the future to predict where the recent renaissance is heading
and what its implications are.

Today the Mashantucket Pequots are building for the future
and going beyond the strategies of survival described in this
book. On October 18, 1983, the United States Congress
passed Public Law 98-134, the "Connecticut Indian Land
Claims Settlement Act," which awarded the Mashantucket Pequot Tribe of Connecticut federal recognition, as well as a
$900,000 trust fund to buy land and begin economic-devel-
opment projects. The Mashantucket Pequots have built four
new housing complexes; a health center; a fire station; a
lighted softball field, which serves as both a tribal recreational
center and a tribal enterprise; and a 1,700-seat bingo hall. The
community has established a gravel industry, and begun plans
for a tribal museum. Since 1984 the Mashantucket tribal land
base has increased by over 700 percent to 1,638 acres. It is no
exaggeration to say that, with the possible exception of the Indians of Maine, the Mashantucket Pequot Tribe of Connecticut
has made the greatest socioeconomic turnaround of any Native American community in the Northeast.

The editors have worked with the Mashantucket Tribal
Council from the inception of the conference idea in 1982.
They should like to thank the council for its encouragement at
every stage of this project and for its willingness to bring
scholars with diverse points of view together in this major
endeavor.

The editors also thank William T. Hagan of the University of
Oklahoma; Francis Jennings, former Director of the D'Arcy
McNickle Center for the History of the American Indian, at the
Newberry Library; and Alden Vaughan of Columbia University,
for their participation in the Mashantucket Pequot Historical
Conference and for their encouragement of this publication project. John Drayton, Editor-in-Chief of the University of
Oklahoma Press, deserves special acknowledgment for his
helpful suggestions and his willingness to publish a book
about these remarkable native peoples far from the trans-Mis-
sissippi West.

Since the editorial process began, Lynn Ceci, one of the
contributors to this book, has died. Ceci was an excellent

scholar who was just gaining the recognition she deserved as an expert on coastal Algonquian cultures, agronomy, and on wampum in particular. She took what appeared to be small issues and turned them into significant contributions to understanding, recognized by both academic and Native American communities. Her scholarship on wampum and agronomy has inspired research by a new generation of scholars, reflected in the recent publication of the proceedings of a Ceci-directed 1986 conference on shell beads by the Rochester Museum and Science Center. She will be missed as an insightful colleague and as a friend to all who knew her.

LAURENCE M. HAUPTMAN
JAMES D. WHERRY

The Pequots in Southern New England

PART ONE

Introduction

Despite the presence of approximately 20,000 American Indians in six New England states today, popular misconceptions and a lack of accurate information persist about the
region's indigenous peoples. To many non-Indians, American
Indians may have once occupied New England but are today
merely some long lost race. Many believe that "true Indians"
are found elsewhere, most likely in the Southwest or Mexico
or Central America. Alvin M. Josephy, Jr., the noted historian
of the American Indian experience, traces the reasons for the
persistence of these damaging images and general ignorance
about Indian communities in the eastern United States. A lifelong resident of Greenwich, Connecticut, Josephy provides
personal reminiscences from his experiences of forty years. In
the process, he presents to the reader the basic intention of
this book, namely, to "help get America's head screwed on
straight *permanently* about Indians," and, at the same time,
fill a void by presenting an accurate, jargon-free history of one
of the New England Indian communities.

CHAPTER 1

New England Indians

Then and Now

By Alvin M. Josephy, Jr.

Some thirty-six years ago, when the world was younger and more innocent, when American Indians were considered the private property of anthropologists, missionaries, museum keepers, and BIA bureaucrats, when the general non-Indian population knew that all Indians were vanishing and that those who had not yet disappeared were children who could not manage their own affairs or understand that termination and the melting pot were best for what some historians and fiction writers called "bucks" and "squaws" and "papooses"—in those radiant, innocent days, I wandered into a museum in my hometown of Greenwich, Connecticut, and was informed, regretfully but authoritatively, by a curator who had the mournful look of an undertaker, that all Indians in Connecticut were extinct.

It was, indeed, sad news, but there was no doubt about its truth because for decades the knowledgeable experts at the museum had been reassuring hordes of wide-eyed Greenwich school children that there was no longer any danger of their being scalped by skulking savages in their state. There might be rattlesnakes still in the backcountry woods along the Mianus River—and in a glass cage the museum *did* have a live

5

monkey that looked pretty scary and smelled up the whole
building—but there were no more red men. Or women. Or
children. As proof, the museum possessed a thumb-worn, yel-
lowing old photograph mounted on a card. It had been taken
in 1908 and showed rather blurrily a bandy-legged, little old
man named Uncle Amos, or something like that, who was
barefoot and had been digging clams on a beach on Long Island Sound. Underneath it, someone had written—not casually, but in bold capital letters that proclaimed a portentous
turning point in history—CONNECTICUT'S LAST INDIAN. So there
it was. 1908. There was no use asking what tribe he had be-
longed to. No one at the museum seemed to know anything
about that. Maybe he was a Squaxin. Or a Squawxin. Or a Pequot. *That* sounded right. The Pequots had once lived in Connecticut. Somewhere. Of course, he couldn't be a Mohegan,
because James Fenimore Cooper had written about the last
of them sometime around the Revolution.

At any rate, like Greenwich's school children, I accepted the
doleful intelligence and turned my interest to the western states
where I knew there were still reservations and real live Indians.
Imagine the shock I experienced, therefore, when one summer evening, while attending the Miss Indian America pageant
at Sheridan, Wyoming, I heard the master of ceremonies in-
troduce a lovely young Indian contestant from Greenwich,
Connecticut! I could scarcely believe what I had heard. But
there she was—sandwiched among Arapahos, Crows, Sioux,
Navajos, Comanches, and others in feathers and beautiful
beaded gowns—a living Indian from my hometown! Needless
to say, I lost my composure and could scarcely sit through the
rest of the ceremony. When it ended, I bolted down from the
grandstand to the arena and sought out the young lady. It
turned out that she was actually of Mohawk ancestry, but lived
in Greenwich and commuted daily on the old New Haven Rail-
road to a thoroughly unromantic job in New York City.

However, it was largely through her that I was very soon set
aright about that matter of extinction. There *were* proud descendants of the original peoples, not only in various parts of

Connecticut, but all through New England. And there were very many of them. In the following months and years I was privileged to get to know them—to observe their efforts to carry on their traditions and heritage and values, as well as their struggles for justice and rights. And I also saw the ignorance, indifference, neglect, and prejudice with which they had to cope.

By profession, I was a journalist and not an academic historian. I was equally interested in today and yesterday. And the thing I suddenly wanted to know very badly—back there in those days of innocence—was, how come? How come there was so much ignorance and misinformation about Indians among the non-Indian population? Clearly there was a huge communications gap that insulted and harmed Indians and thwarted their quest for justice and rights—and at the same time insulted and harmed non-Indians also, stunting and twisting their minds with falsehoods, stereotypes, and prejudice that robbed them of the great Indian heritage that they too might have shared and from which the entire country and world could have benefited.

One answer, opening my eyes very quickly, was close at hand. I happened in those years to have been an editor at *Time Magazine* in New York, and one day I proposed our doing a story on Indians—I think about Indian museums and powwows in New England. It was shot down at once, and I learned with a start that all of Time, Incorporated's publications had an absolutely and seemingly unbreakable policy against running any stories about Indians anywhere in the country. It is hard to believe it today, but Henry Luce and some of the top editors at the company intensely disliked Indians and had a low regard for them as newsworthy subjects. For some reason, Mr. Luce referred to them as "phonies." That was a new one to me, and unfortunately I never learned what he meant. Possibly he believed that the Indians were Chinese, whom he admired, and resented that the Indians did not agree with him about their ancestry. Whatever the cause, I noted thereafter that whenever a correspondent in the field suggested a story on Indians, the query was simply crumpled up and thrown in the wastebasket. By edict, both *Time* and *Life* virtually blacked out information about Indians. Over a long period of years, the edict prevailed, to my knowledge violated only once by these most influential print organs of communication, when *Life* pictured a winter airdrop of food to isolated and starving Navajos. But even then, that story focused on the good Samaritans who were dropping the food, and they, of course, were not Indians.

Happily, in the 1960s, when Indian assertiveness began to make front-page headlines—and when the jewelry counter at Saks Fifth Avenue to the hippie pads at Haight-Ashbury, Indians were "in"—the policy at Time, Inc. crumbled. On July 2, 1971, the editors finally threw in the towel altogether and devoted an entire memorable issue of *Life* to Indians, whom the American non-Indian people had at last discovered. But before that period it had become obvious to me and to many others that Time, Inc. was not so unique. Elsewhere among the media, there were not necessarily blackouts, although it might have been better if there were; instead—among newspapers, magazines, radio, television, books, and movies—untruths, half-truths, stereotypes, distortions, and unreality continued to rule the day, as they had for generations. Naturally, it continued to affect adversely the lives and needs and aspirations of the Indian peoples of New England as surely as it did those in every other part of the country.

There were additional factors contributing to the communications gap. If a media person—a so-called molder of public opinion—wished information about Indians, where could he or she turn? Rarely to the Indians themselves, because few media people knew any Indians, let alone which ones to talk to, and besides, their own ingrained stereotyped thinking got in the way. They knew—because they had been taught to know—that Indians were unreliable and would give out misinformation anyway. What they wanted was some central, reliable Indian public relations office, staffed and run by *non-Indian* experts, and there was none. So they called all over the

place, accepting and printing large hunks of more misinformation from unknowledgeable people at museums, Indian-
interest organizations, state government offices, libraries, and
the Bureau of Indian Affairs—in short, from people who were
used to doing all the talking for and about Indians, whether or
not they knew what they were talking about. For the media
person, it was a grueling and frustrating experience, and usually ended up with that person hoping devoutly that he or she
would never be assigned to another Indian story, or would
never again be hit by the great idea of fashioning a magazine
article or a television documentary on contemporary American Indians. And for the Indians themselves, it was more in-
sults, more misinformation, and more harm.

There were other, more obscene problems that *particularly* affected the status of New England Indians. Possibly because of the influence of anthropologists, who were respected
scientists employing a learned jargon that sounded like the Ten
Commandments, even if it defied the average person's com-
prehension, Indians acquired that widely held image of being
dead as arrowheads—and not only that, but somehow or
other they were mixed up with, in a curious and thoughtlessly
degrading way, birds, dinosaurs, and other subjects of natural
history. In bookstores frequented by the general public, for in-
stance, books about Indians usually ended up on shelves and
tables with books about trees, mushrooms, and insects. And
why not? Undoubtedly, the book industry got its cue from museums, large and small, everywhere in the country, that treated
Indians as a facet of natural, rather than human, history, lump-
ing them among bugs, stuffed animals, and fish. I need hardly
remind anyone that this kind of categorizing exists even today
in the great natural-history museums in Chicago, Los Angeles,
Denver, New York, Washington, D.C., and elsewhere, and is at
the heart of the recent struggle by the Museum of the American Indians in New York to avoid the politicians' efforts to bury
it among the meteorites, African mammals, and butterflies of
the American Museum of Natural History.

For generations the persistent image of Indian tribes as

dead peoples hit the Native Americans in New England very hard, because in New England the average non-Indian truly believed the image. Elsewhere the continued presence of large reservations made most people aware that, while Indians were vanishing, they hadn't yet quite said their final farewell. But in New England few urbanites, suburbanites, or exurbanites could assert that they had ever seen an Indian, much less thought about one. There are always, of course, exceptions to generalizations. There were always non-Indians in New England who stopped by to visit Indian-owned museums like that of the Tantaquidgeons, people who knew that certain blocks and neighborhoods were inhabited by "families" who called themselves Indians but didn't wear feathers and looked and dressed and wore shoes like everyone else and therefore probably weren't real Indians, and people more or less familiar with the fact that within their state were still clusters of Indians, some large, some small—Pequots, Gayheads, Narragansetts, Penobscots, and so forth—whom bigoted neighbors and acquisitive developers and corporations could push around without fear that it would get in the papers. But more common throughout New England were those like the museum curator in Greenwich, who, along with practically every other non-Indian in populous Fairfield County, had not the foggiest notion that within a few miles a cohesive group of Paugussets, with roots going back to long before the arrival of the first Europeans, still lived proudly and kept their Indian heritage alive near—of all places—Bridgeport.

No, back in those innocent days, it was a rare non-Indian who knew that there were still Indians living on Indian land in New England. Such ignorance kept the Indian communities there even more submerged, powerless, and neglected than those on reservations in the West. The events of history, as well as the long passage of time since the era when the New England tribes loomed large in the daily affairs of the invading Europeans, contributed mightily to the blithe ignorance. The most commonly held notions of New England's Indians, I would venture, were those of the McGuffey Readers' textbook

versions of the times of the Pilgrims and Puritans—of Massasoit, Squanto, King Philip, and Thanksgiving. It all happened
so long ago, and it was over and done with in those dim, fuzzy
colonial days to which nobody can relate anymore—ancient,
mythical history. Why, George Washington and George Custer
hadn't even been born yet. In those misty, unreal years, the Indian tribes of New England were smashed, rendered powerless, cut up into little pieces, assimilated by Dartmouth College, enlisted as harpooners of *Moby Dick,* and finally overrun
and smothered out of existence by non-Indian cities, factories,
and waves of European immigrants who had never heard of
the New England Indians, had never seen one, and who just
assumed they were as dead and vanished as those quaint Pilgrims in high hats who had eaten turkey and cranberry sauce
with them and then chased them out to Wyoming. So stereotype fed on stereotype, and if there were any Indians whom the
museums were displaying as dead-and-gone peoples, they
were sure to include the New England Indians.

At the same time, most historians and free-lance writers
who were interested in Indian-white history, and who might
have been of considerable help, showed little or no interest in
the history of the New England tribes. It was as if the nineteenth-
century historians and popular writers had written everything
there was to say about the New England Native Americans.
So, instead, they mostly researched and wrote about the western tribes, and the southern tribes, and the midwestern tribes.
The New England colleges and universities were even more
negligent. They had no interest in *any* Indian history, or Indian
studies, or Indian students. Even Dartmouth, whose chroniclers gave the nation the impression that the college had been
founded for the education of Indians and that Eleazar Whee-
lock was still instructing them on the campus at Hanover, New
Hampshire, had long since pulled down the shutters against
Indian applicants. When an Indian youth applied for admit-
tance and was sent to a Dartmouth alumnus for the custom-
ary personal interview and screening, the awkwardness and
humiliation were horrible to behold. After two steadying belts

of whiskey, the shocked alumnus would be forced to tell the young Indian that he wouldn't be able to keep up with his fellow freshmen, or that he just wouldn't fit in, and advise him that the government ran schools especially for Indians, and that he undoubtedly would be accepted by, and be more comfortable at, one of them. Of course, that was precisely what the Indian didn't want. But it did not matter. Almost inevitably, that's where he ended up—off with other Indians in a BIA school that landed him nowhere.

All these factors contributed to what I called the communications gap—and lest I convey a one-sided impression, it sometimes ran both ways. On the whole, in that period before the 1960s, Indians were not only unversed in the procedures and methods of utilizing the dominant society's organs of mass communication to tell their side of things, but had little or no access to them. Moreover, most Indians were so used to what they termed the white men's lies and cockeyed notions about them that they had a fatalistic feeling that, no matter what they might try to do to straighten the record, the whites preferred to have their heads screwed on backwards and would go on telling each other what they chose to believe. Rather than be frustrated or angry, many Indians resigned themselves to the inevitable, and let off steam by finding humor in the idiot white man's forked tongue, even deliberately feeding misinformation to pesterous whites and then laughing like hell about it among themselves.

Of course, it helped to save their sanity and no one could blame them, but the gap persisted, unperceived and neglected by many people who should have known better. Still a journalist at *Time* in the late 1950s, and thoroughly concerned about the abundance of error and untruth that was injurious to both Indians and non-Indians, I tried to do a little pioneering work toward rectifying the situation in addresses I delivered at an American Society for Ethnohistory Conference in New York and the 1959 annual convention of the National Congress of American Indians in Phoenix. The ethnohistorians, who were then relatively few, were, of course, not activists and not about to help take on American public opinion. The NCAI, as expected, knew well what I was talking about, printed my sermon, and circulated it among its member tribes.

As it turned out, the Indian peoples themselves were on the eve of a great explosive period in their relations with the rest of the American population. Led in large measure by young Indian activists from every part of the country, including New England, who had had enough of untruths, injustices, and silent suffering, they themselves—temporarily, at least—closed the communications gap with a bang. In the course of the momentous events that began in the 1960s, the Indians of New England returned to full public view, some of them joining in solidarity with Indians from other parts of the country to assert the dignity, pride, and spiritual strength of their traditional Indian values and tribal heritages. As participants in the panorama of conferences, workshops, powwows, marches, demonstrations, confrontations, social and spiritual ceremonies, claims and rights cases, and demands for self-determination and sovereignty that at last began to enlighten the non-Indian world and to erode stereotyped thinking, the New England tribes played a stunning role, not alone by what they, too, demanded, but also by opening non-Indian eyes to the bewildering discovery that they still existed. Long assured to have vanished, they taught the nation the lesson that Indians did not intend to disappear and that even after three hundred years of every sort of pressure, adversity, neglect, and relegation to obscurity, Indians possessed a wondrous spiritual strength and determination to survive and to continue to be Indians.

It is not my purpose to review the 1960s and 1970s, when many non-Indians began to be straightened out about the Indian past and present, when Indians began to use the media to communicate to mass audiences, when universities groped and stumbled toward accepting Indian students and establishing courses in Indian studies, when aspiring historians in droves turned to researching and writing books about Indians, and when Indians were "in," even with fashion designers and sophisticated collectors of fine arts. But as one example in which the Indians themselves, working with the help of non-Indian friends and supporters, raised abruptly and by many notches the level of non-Indian awareness of Indians and understanding the truth about Indians, I remind you of the shock waves that radiated out from the Maine land claims case of the Penobscots and Passamaquoddies. In a real sense, that was history coming back to haunt the nation, but, equally significant, it was a landmark moment in the course of Indian-white relations. Until a short time before, it had been the tradition of most non-Indians in Maine to ignore the soul-searing prejudice, discrimination, deprivation, and injustices endured by the Maine Indians, who could expect little, if any, interest or protection from the state government. Many remember a brutal episode in which non-Indian hunters bullied and committed murder in an Indian community, apparently certain they had nothing to fear from Maine justice. Well, no more. Thanks to the Penobscot and Passamaquoddy claims fight, non-Indian perceptions and attitudes toward Indians experienced what one might term a rapid evolution for the better in Maine.

From the Indian victory in that state, from other claims and rights cases pursued at sacrifice and with difficulty by the Mashantucket Pequots and other tribes here in New England and elsewhere, have come many beneficial changes for the present-day Indians and their children and children's children. Among those developments have been increased knowledge about Indians by non-Indians, and a heightened and more widespread desire to learn more and to know the truth.

But all, we know, is still not well. Too much of the Indian world still endures deprivation, neglect, prejudice, injustice, and all the other terrible hangovers from history. And too much of the non-Indian world is still scornful and indifferent, the unknowing victim of continuing ignorance, misinformation, and stereotyped thinking. In fact, it is fair to say today that Indians are no longer "in," that too much of the dominant society has abandoned the interest it had in Indians when Indians were making news, and that the communications gap may again be as wide as it was before the 1960s.

One sees evidence for this conclusion on every hand. One would think, for example, that by now the educated molders of our public opinion would know that before 1492 the North and South American continents were not great empty wildernesses, but were inhabited by tens of millions of people. Yet only a few days ago, the op-ed page of the authoritative *New York Times* casually informed its readers that before Columbus, the entire so-called New World was inhabited by only hundreds of thousands of people. It is not funny, for it, too, feeds the misinformation that leads people to accept false and damaging assumptions injurious to Indians, and also to erroneous judgments concerning a tribe's right to ancestral lands and resources.

If the communications gap is again wide and troubling, as I think it is, then who today will be able to do something about it? We learned in the 1960s that the Indians themselves were effective communicators about their peoples, and they still are. Today there are many talented Indian authors, poets, playwrights, painters, film makers, and other creative artists, many with national and international reputations. Their works, usually based on Indian themes and on their own tribal heritages, have strong educational impacts on non-Indians and on American culture as a whole. What I miss is not being swamped by Indian historians. Where are they? There are a few in the nation, but not yet anywhere near enough. The country needs them, to join with their non-Indian colleagues and provide the perceptions, insights, and inherited knowledge of their own people's lives, values, and spiritual foundations that few, if any, non-Indian historians can satisfactorily furnish, try as they may. I and others look forward to the Mashantucket Pequots and other tribes encouraging the development of Indian historians who will enrich the knowledge and understanding—and, yes, the appreciation—of Indians among non-Indians and will enhance their own people's pride in their heritage as Indians and tribal members.

At the same time, I am not denigrating the role or work of the non-Indian historians. Simply because they do not write about their own people does not devalue the importance or worth of what they continue to contribute to scholarship and knowledge. I hope you will forgive me if I make a special, personal plea to them, as well as to emerging Indian historians. To help close the communications gap, I hope that more of them will consider the urgent need to write not so much primarily for students and for their academic peers, but for the general public, Indian and non-Indian alike—for the great mass of American readers who will welcome history that is accurately told but also well told. I think that at this late date, we are obligated to use our pens and typewriters and computers to help get America's head screwed on straight *permanently* about Indians. I hope that Indian and non-Indian historians, working alone or together, will reach out to ever-widening audiences. It can't hurt trying, and it might do a lot of good.

PART TWO

Southern New England Prehistory and Early Pequot History

Avoiding technical jargon, Dena F. Dincauze provides a general overview of the prehistory of southern New England using a cultural terminology geared to the nonspecialist. Some 12,000 years ago, Paleo-Indian hunters began the colonization of southern New England. These "Pioneers" and their successors in the region were regularly challenged by the changing environment. Beginning about 8,000 years ago, that "Pioneering phase" gave way to the "Settler period," which included several epochs, when larger populations lived in more visible groups and moved less frequently. Between 4,700 and 2,500 years ago, with a moderation of winter climates, vegetation characteristic of areas farther south became established in southern New England, enlarging the store of edible foods. Social environments, and with them increased ceremonialism, began to overshadow natural environments as the definitive characteristics of habitats. Around 3,000 years ago, trade and exchange relationships increased and ceramic technology arose marking the beginning of a "Later Settler phase." Beginning about 1,000 years ago, with a significant amelioration of climate, maize cultivation was introduced into New England, marking the start of the "Farmer," or Late Woodland,

17

period for the last few centuries of prehistoric time. Dincauze concludes her survey by emphasizing that, by the time the Europeans had entered the region, the climate had deteriorated and harsher winters and shorter growing seasons were more characteristic than had been the case a few centuries earlier. Thus the prehistory of southern New England, as Dincauze carefully shows, was marked by flexible strategies on the part of native peoples adapting an ever-changing environment.

William A. Starna provides the reader with a clear ethnographic portrait of Pequot Indian lifeways before the War of 1637. For southern New England Indians subsistence activities in the Late Woodlands and early historic period centered around horticulture. They supplemented their economic existence by hunting, gathering, and fishing. Starna describes these economic activities as well as the sociopolitical life of the Indians. He concludes his survey by emphasizing the disastrous impact of European-introduced diseases on native peoples in the region, a factor that "recast the structure and form" of Indian life forever.

As Starna suggests, the conquest of the Pequots was achieved in part as a result of a biological catastrophe—epidemics of immense proportions, affecting all American Indians. There were other factors as well, including economic dislocations and significant changes in the ecology of New England. Lynn Ceci, however, focuses on the economic side of early Indian-white contact. She describes how a distant region of eastern North America became intertwined with the new global economy, or world-system, of Europe in the seventeenth century. In the process of becoming part of Europe's mercantilist system, the Pequots, with their access to and plentiful supply of wampum, soon became the focus of the English colonial authorities who wanted to control this increasingly important North American commodity. Thus, Ceci sees wampum as one of the major reasons for the growing tensions and conflicts between Puritan and Indian in colonial New England, giving rise to the War of 1637.

CHAPTER 2

A Capsule Prehistory of Southern New England

By Dena F. Dincauze

Human colonization of the area now called southern New England began about 11,000 to 12,000 years ago, sometime after the melting of the last great glaciers and the draining of most of the large glacial lakes. By that time, with the exception of the coastal regions, the landforms that are familiar to us today had achieved essentially their modern characteristics, although their vegetation and the animals that lived on and among them were different. In southern New England 11,000 years ago the forests were composed predominantly of northern species of trees—spruces, pines, birches, and alders—and the trees were not notably dense, being more common in the valleys and lowlands. Tundra vegetation grew among and beyond the trees, especially in the uplands, where the soils were thinner and drier. People shared this landscape with mammoths and mastodons, caribou, and beaver. Bones of the latter two species have been found in the remains of human camps, but we have no direct evidence that people here were hunting or eating the large elephants. Smaller mammals, such as foxes, martens, and hares, must have been more plentiful than any of the larger species, and could have been useful sources of meat and warm fur for clothing and bedding.[1]

19

These first peoples to come into the landscape are known only by their household trash and the edged stone tools that they left behind them. No human remnant of this age has been found in New England (probably none have survived), and of course, no record of their language or thought has come down to us. Archaeologists call them, for convenience of reference, "Paleoindians." In order to humanize them and to emphasize their considerable achievements, I will call them Pioneers.[2] Clad in their caribou-skin clothing, carrying infants and household goods and thrusting spears with elegantly shaped points of colorful stone, these are the people who first gave names to the landscape, who explained its special areas and vistas in terms of their own cosmology, and who first explored and exploited its riches for human purposes.

The Pioneers were skillful practical geologists, zoologists, and botanists—they had to be both clever and well informed in order to maintain themselves in the new land. The climate was warming as the Ice Age drew to its close, and the glaciers melted back into northern Canada. Southern New England may have had warm summers, but the winters were much more severe than they are in this century, so that people had to be especially hardy and alert to equip themselves and to feed themselves through the cold season. The lowlands now near and under Long Island Sound and extending to Massachusetts Bay would have been the warmest and surely the lushest areas; remarkably, the remains of the Pioneers in southern New England are relatively scattered and insubstantial in comparison to more-clustered and spectacular sites farther north. Near the northern edge of southern New England, in what is now Ipswich, Massachusetts, large encampments have been found and are now under study to learn what they can tell us about community life. Most of the southern sites are small, yielding only a few artifacts. They are interpreted as having been occupied only briefly by small numbers of people, perhaps extended family groups who were frequently on the move. It was rarely easy to be Pioneers.[3]

As the climate warmed and the soils deepened, the vegeta-

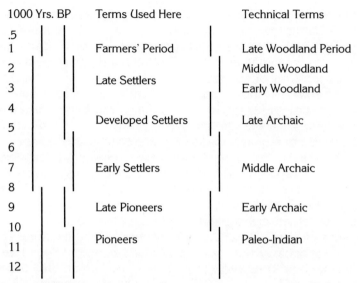

1000 Yrs. BP	Terms Used Here	Technical Terms
.5		
1	Farmers' Period	Late Woodland Period
2		Middle Woodland
3	Late Settlers	Early Woodland
4		
5	Developed Settlers	Late Archaic
6		
7	Early Settlers	Middle Archaic
8		
9	Late Pioneers	Early Archaic
10		
11	Pioneers	Paleo-Indian
12		

Fig. 1. Comparison of cultural terminology with that standard in the archaeological literature.

tion changed. Forests became denser, as pine and oaks succeeded the spruce. Tundra shrubs gave way to berry bushes
and grasses. More diverse plant foods and plant resources
certainly became available, but large hooved animals for meat
became less abundant. The mammoths and mastodons had
become extinct just about the time that the Pioneers arrived in
the area. The contribution by human hunters to that extinction
is a matter of lively debate. Caribou soon drifted north, following the retreating tundra. In the leafy forests, moose and then
deer became the largest herbivores, while bears competed directly with people for berries and fish. Hunting moose and
deer required strategies different from those for taking caribou
and, perhaps, elephants. The large northern encampments,
which reflect the need for numbers of hunters to drive and kill
herd animals, disappear from the archaeological record about
the time that the caribou left the area; a causal connection

here is very likely. People, however, did not abandon the area. While some may have followed the caribou north, it is clear from a scattering of stone weapon points of novel forms, dating from the centuries between 10,000 and 8,000 years ago, that people continued to live in the forest clearings along the river banks and inland ponds. We know very little about the life-styles of these people, but we may at least consider them Pioneers, since the changing environment must have challenged them regularly to discover and to innovate.[4]

The scant traces of the Pioneers in turn challenge archaeologists to interpret the forms, frequencies, and distributions of stone artifacts in terms of human lives and livelihoods. To do so, archaeologists use information and techniques developed in many other sciences; thus the study of the Pioneers, and the results of that study, are heavily influenced by the natural sciences of geology, botany, climatology, and paleontology. Even oceanography has a role to play as we try to map the coastal lowlands and shores, all now under water, of these ancient times. The chronology is provided by radioactive clocks, read from the minute traces of radioactivity that all living things acquire in the course of their lives and that gradually run down after death. Ancient pollen, recovered from lakes and bogs, can be interpreted to approximate the plant communities of former forests and forest edges. Climate is inferred from the vegetation and from astronomical theory and calculations that measure differences in the intensity of solar radiation caused by the varying shape of Earth's orbit and the tilt of the planet as it swings around the Sun. Domestic structures are inferred from the spacing of cold campfire ashes and from the clusters of stone tools and the debris created during stone shaping. We can trace the stones to their sources to infer something about the movements of the people who acquired and transported them. The tools themselves carry evidence, in the form of characteristic wear patterns, of the uses to which they were put; and so we know that hides were cleaned and cut, and presumably tailored, and wood and fibrous plants were processed for food or artifacts. We have only imagination to guide us, however, as we try to picture what the clothes, houses, and tool handles looked like, or how people wore their hair and decorated themselves.[5]

By about 9,000 years ago summer temperatures were near their postglacial peaks, but winters were colder than now. Such seasonal extremes must have taxed people's ingenuity, but the archaeological record indicates that within a thousand years they were thriving in southern New England. Sometime in that millennium (by 8,000 years ago) they passed from the Pioneer phase to what we might call the Settler period, when larger populations lived in archaeologically more-visible groups and moved less frequently. Tool kits included specialized equipment for a large range of tasks, including axes for heavy wood-cutting and adzes for shaping wooden implements and structures. Weapon points of stone were, on the whole, smaller than before, had stems for hafting, and were produced in much larger numbers. They continued, however, to reflect what can be considered the norm for southern New England—cultural contacts predominantly to the south along the piedmont and seaboard lowlands. With postglacial sea levels still reduced compared to those of today, the coastal zone was wider, and until about 6,000 years ago people could walk dry-shod from Cape Cod to Martha's Vineyard and Nantucket, no doubt hunting deer, rabbits, turtles, and birds on the way. The locations of their major campgrounds and some chemical evidence indicate that 8,000 years ago fish were providing an important component of the diet. Spawning shad were probably the attraction at the major falls along the larger rivers. The shad harvest could have supported large numbers of people for a few weeks in the late spring, and we can assume that people took advantage of this resource to schedule festive gatherings where they would visit with friends and relatives, make new acquaintances, and exchange news and gossip about people, politics, and resources. From this period we still know little about the forms of clothing or houses, or whether there were boats (very likely), or just how the seasonal round of activities and camp moves was managed. For convenience, we can refer to the period between 8,000 and 5,500 years ago as the Early Settler period, although this long time span may be subdivided when more is known about many details of life.[6]

Dramatic changes occurred within the next millennium; the Developed Settler period between about 4,700 and 2,300 years ago is the richest time span in the archaeological record as we now know it. From the few features between 4,700 and 4,000 years ago, we have evidence of several kinds of houses; facilities, such as the Boylston Street fishweir in Boston; elaborate graves and cemeteries; woodworking tools probably used to shape dugout canoes, among other useful things; and clusters of activities and structures that deserve at least the name of seasonal villages. The villages stood in clearings in forests where the trees were much like those of today, with many kinds of nut trees adding important protein and fat to the human diet and supporting deer, squirrels, and turkeys that were also very good to eat. Hickory nuts seem to have been especially plentiful, or at least, they were collected in abundance and were brought back to campsites and villages where we find their charred remains today. Life seems to have been good, and perhaps relatively easy at this time; the populations expanded to create an archaeological record so extensive that, during the first half of this century, it was mistakenly thought to be the remains of the people living here when the Europeans came. We know better now, from careful excavation into the layered trash heaps that are the shell middens along the coast. The middens reveal the order in which different kinds of trash were deposited and permit archaeologists to understand the sequence of appearance of various tools, and how and when they were supplanted by other tools developed for somewhat different purposes.[7]

How are we to understand these changes in human terms? It is possible to argue that they are all interrelated and that they are integrated aspect of the same situation. With some moderation of winter climates, vegetation characteristic of areas farther south became established in southern New England, enlarging the store of edible foods. People had less need of

travel to obtain the plant and animal products necessary for
their sustenance, and so they moved less often and less far.
This decreasing mobility permitted an increase in population
because people temporarily limited in their physical capabili-
ties—the ill, the wounded, the pregnant, mothers of small children—were not forced to be frequently on the move. To an
extent, an increasing population itself limits the mobility of the
constituent groups, at the same time making it possible to invest additional labor in the gathering and preparation of local
resources. All these changes meant that communities became somewhat larger, more numerous, and more localized.
Territories were probably better defined. In turn, relative sed-
entism meant that some things people needed were to be
found only in the territories inhabited by other communities,
so that it became more than ever necessary to establish trading and marriage relationships beyond one's own group. We
can see some of that in the archaeological record, with the
widespread distribution of some relatively rare raw materials.
We can also see the increased localization of communities
and activities in the intensive use of local stones, in the increasing diversification of tool forms and tool-kit contents
across time and space, and in the appearance within these
centuries of storage pits for keeping food for future use. Presumably, storage pits reflect some production of surplus beyond immediate needs, to supply people staying in the vicinity
past harvest time.

By 4,500 years ago in southern New England, social environments had begun to overshadow natural environments
as the definitive characteristics of habitats. With the need to
maintain good relationships with other communities that controlled access to essential raw materials, and with far-flung
relatives who could help out in times of shortage, people had
to invest more time and effort in social activities to ensure the
continuity of those relationships. These new needs may help
to explain the remarkable increase in ceremonialism attested
to in the archaeological record of these centuries. Ceremonialism is inferred from the existence of a large communal house

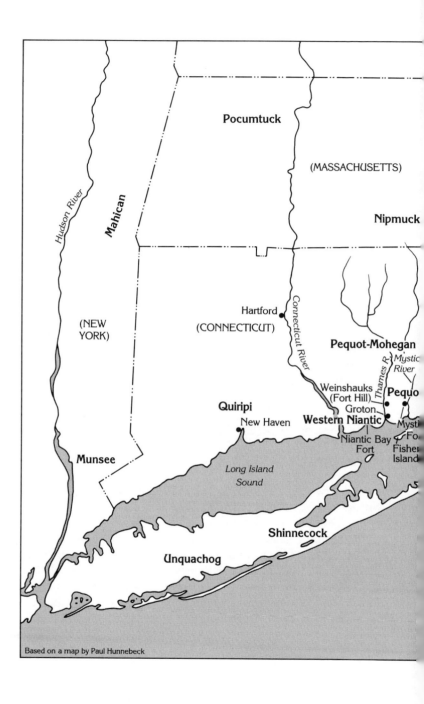

Based on a map by Paul Hunnebeck

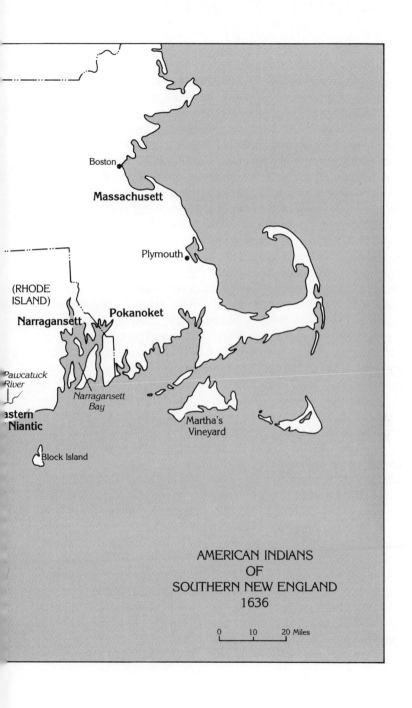

Boston

Massachusett

Plymouth

(RHODE
ISLAND)

Narragansett   **Pokanoket**

Pawcatuck
River

*Narragansett
Bay*

astern
Niantic   Martha's
Vineyard

Block Island

AMERICAN INDIANS
OF
SOUTHERN NEW ENGLAND
1636

0   10   20 Miles

in the Wapanucket village on Lake Assawompset in Massachusetts, and even more clearly from the elaborate burial rites
that show up there and elsewhere in this period. By 3,500
years ago there were large and elaborate cemeteries in many
parts of lowland southern New England. They testified, by the
impressive social costs invested in artifacts, effort, and time, to
the importance of the activities associated with their construction and use. Ceremonialism was well established by 4,500
years ago as a significant means of resolving social tensions
and for creating a humanly defined harmony in the world.[8]

Around 3,000 years ago, trade and exchange relationships
apparently increased toward the west; in central New England,
objects showing styles typical of New York state became increasingly common. In Connecticut and Rhode Island, however, both weapon points and the new ceramic pots show a
continuance of the traditional ties to the southwest along the
coastal plain. At this same time, there seem to have been important changes in the distribution of people over the landscape, as sites in the uplands were smaller and less numerous
than they had been. Whether such changes reflect the effects
of the climatic cooling of the time, an increased efficiency of
exploitation in the lowlands, or social dynamics we cannot yet
perceive is still a matter of debate and research, as, indeed, is
the reality of the "change" itself, which could be an artifact of
uneven data collection or misidentification of sites.[9] What is
evident, however, is that the newer arrangements, with larger
sites in the lowlands, reflect spatial distributions and trade relationships that endured into the historical period. Thus it is
convenient to separate a Late Settlers period from the Developed Settlers period to call attention to the importance of the
new conditions.

The appearance of ceramic technology about 3,000 years
ago was once thought to mean that farming began, but we
have no evidence that such was indeed the case in southern New England. Ceramic vessels replaced the older carved
soapstone cooking and storage vessels, the necessary skills
being introduced apparently from both the coastal plain on

the south and from the Great Lakes area on the west within a century or so of each other. The new technology relieved the need to obtain the heavy and expensive stone vessels from the few places where soapstone could be quarried and shaped. Anyone with the necessary skills could shape vessels from the widespread clay deposits laid down throughout the region in the ancient glacial lakes, and fire them to useful hardness. The changing shapes and decorative motifs of ceramic vessels are intently studied by archaeologists to provide a chronological sequence for archaeological sites as well as some ideas about the community affiliations of the potters.[10]

In some places it appears that the Late Settler settlements reflect even less mobility than before. Large base camps may have been occupied for most of the year by some members of the community, while others went out to gather resources on behalf of all.[11] After about 2,000 years ago, elaborate burials became infrequent, and large cemeteries absolutely rare. Also rare or absent from the archaeological record as we know it now are the remains of domestic or other structures. Wig-wamlike structures there must have been, but archaeologists have not been able to find their traces. Large shell middens along the shores indicate the regular utilization of rich coastal and estuarine food sources. The relative stability of sea level during the past 3,000 to 4,000 years has preserved the late middens, whereas earlier ones have been washed away or covered by the rising sea.

About 1,000 years ago there was a significant amelioration of climate, expressed in warmer winters and longer growing seasons. Then, or sometime after that, maize cultivation was introduced in southern New England. Whether squash pre-ceded maize here, as was the case on the west, is not known, nor do we yet know whether beans came then or somewhat later. Maize cultivation by means of hoe horticulture appears spottily in the regional archaeological record from this time on, so that we may define the last few centuries of prehistoric time as the Farmer period. The hilling of maize plants with hoes is a North American technique, not an introduction from

Mexico, as were the domestic plants themselves. With corn and hoes apparently came triangular arrowpoints and ceramic vessel shapes that were rounder than the earlier ones and that had thinner walls. At this time unquestionably, though not yet evident in the archaeological remains, came the corn ceremonies and the calendrical lore that regulated the timing of gardening activities and mobilized the labor necessary to clear land, keep down the weeds, and plant and harvest the crops.[12]

We cannot clearly see any dramatic changes in settlement distributions or size coincident with the adoption of maize horticulture. Garden crops probably provided only dietary supplements, rather than economic staples. The crucial difference would have been the seasonal abundance of harvested crops and the addition to the larder of plant foods that could be dried and stored for use in the hungry times of winter. There is no direct evidence that wild foods became less important or that their collection was any less fundamental to the seasonal round. Still, burning to clear fields and improve hunting grounds must have changed the natural vegetation and landscape to a degree; pollen studies are beginning to reveal those changes. The proximity of good light soils for tilling must have become important in decisions for locating the major settlements, but those soils were reasonably common in the areas long favored for large sites. No doubt, over time, the match between available garden soils and population size became a more important consideration, and we may expect that the institution of long terms for the leaders, the sachems, can be traced at least to the Farmers' period, when the need for institutionalized dispute resolution would have been strong. The varying quality of soils may have accentuated the regional differences in population densities, sociopolitical organizations, and characteristic resource emphases that we saw emerging in the Developed Settler period. An unresolved issue among archaeologists is the extent to which coastal communities relied upon domesticated crops.[13]

Possibly reflecting the intensifying regional contrasts in subsistence strategies is the strictly coastal distribution, to date, of large communal burial pits dating from early in the Farmer period, or possibly just before it. These ossuaries are fundamentally unlike the older Settler cemeteries, being composed of the remains of many people deposited together in a large pit with a minimum of grave goods. The Settler sites had exhibited differences between individuals in rites and grave accompaniments. In the Farmer period these were suppressed; the community alone was differentiated. We do not know the specific intent of the people who constructed the ossuaries, but the pits clearly reflect a community structure and a communal value system different from those of the Settlers, and possibly different from those of contemporary peoples in the uplands, where there is no evidence of ossuaries. Clearance of land for farming, and the crops themselves, created locally distinct landscapes and changed the relationships between human communities and the natural world around them. Gardens attracted nonhuman diners, which had to be kept away from the crops by energetic hunting, devious trapping, or effective spells. Manipulation of the natural world was intensified, and we can assume that these new relationships had some effect upon religion and community structure.[14]

By the time the Europeans intruded into the region that we know as southern New England, the climate had deteriorated, with harsher winters and shorter growing seasons than had been characteristic a few centuries earlier. Because of this, we cannot accept the English and Dutch narratives describing native horticultural practices and reliance upon cultivated crops as representative of the preceding times. Certainly, changes had occurred since the crops were adopted; just as certainly, reliance upon them was always tempered by circumstance. The degree to which knowledge of wild foods remained an important element in regional culture is demonstrated by the captivity narrative of Mary Rowlandson, who traveled with refugee and war parties throughout the winter of 1675–1676. She describes, with a mixture of disgust and grateful respect, the remarkable dietary resourcefulness of the people deprived of their harvest and their intimate knowledge of emergency foods. Hunger was not unknown to the Farmers.[15]

Whether the intergroup hostilities the English and Dutch described were characteristic of precontact social relations is unclear. There were aspects of the new relationships between people and land and between communities that could have spawned hostility and aggression; however, we must resist trying to read the archaeological record in terms of the historical record because we have found very little evidence of the latest prehistoric period, and because we know extreme biases exist in the historical record. The biases were not only the Europeans' failures to understand or respect the local people; they also include the changed social and environmental conditions that separate the sixteenth and seventeenth centuries from earlier times. The devastating European diseases eliminated significant portions of the native populations, even entire communities, probably requiring major realignments in the political, economic, and religious realms of culture. History and *especially* prehistory is not given to us—we must earn it by diligent, imaginative, respectful, and honest inquiry into the remains available to us.[16]

CHAPTER 3

The Pequots in the Early Seventeenth Century

By William A. Starna

The Pequots, or as they are commonly referred to in the anthropological and historical literature, the Mohegan-Pequots, occupied the Thames River drainage basin for some time prior to European contact. Because of the similarities between the names "Mohegan" and "Mahican," early writers assumed a late prehistoric migration by the Mohegan-Pequots to eastern Connecticut from the Hudson Valley of New York state; nevertheless, they are closely related, both culturally and linguistically, to other Algonquian-speaking people residing in southern New England, and thus, appear to have developed in place from a common origin.[1]

While it is impossible to define precisely their former territory, the Pequots, in general terms, seem to have exerted influence over, and exploited the resources of, a large area of land. The Pequot land base began at West Niantic, near New London, Connecticut, and ran northward along the divide between the Connecticut and Thames rivers to approximately the headwaters of the Thames, then eastward to the present border between the states of Connecticut and Rhode Island, then south along this border to the coast. By historic times, the Pequots had expanded their holdings to the eastern end of

Long Island. The total extent of this territory was some two thousand square miles.[2]

Although Giovanni da Verrazano made the first recorded visit by a European to southern New England in the spring of 1524 by sailing into Narragansett Bay, it was not until the early seventeenth century that any mention is made of the Pequots. They first appear in the record as the "Pequatoos . . . the enemies of the Wapanoos," having probably been observed in 1613–1614 on the Thames by Dutch sailors under the command of Captain Adriaen Block (for whom Block Island was named); however, regular contacts between the Pequots and the Europeans, both Dutch and English, did not begin until the early 1630s.[3] By this time the Pequots had apparently gained control of the Connecticut Valley as far north as Windsor and of eastern Long Island, their domination here and elsewhere having been gained primarily through warfare. During this early period of European exploration and trade, Indians throughout southern New England exhibited very similar cultural patterns or lifeways, adapted as they were to a coastal or seaboard ecoregion, its hardwood forests, and its plant and animal communities.

The more traditional view of southern New England holds that fully developed horticulture communities were present before contact, which included sedentary village life, high populations, and sociopolitical complexity. Others maintain these characteristics, excepting horticulture, were primarily a product of European contact. More recently, archaeologists have suggested that small, semipermanent settlements and an increase in the degree of social and political complexity may have occurred fairly early in coastal areas, independently of horticulture. A final perspective is that Indian cultures were in transformation, shifting toward a more complex adaptive system by the first years of the seventeenth century.[4]

For the Pequots, not unlike other groups in southern New England, subsistence activities centered around horticulture. Hunting, gathering, and fishing provided supplemental foods derived from the very rich environments of inland lakes,

streams, tidal marshes, estuaries, the forests, and the ocean.[5]
In cultivated fields scattered here and there about their settlements were grown varieties of corn, beans, squash, and tubers, specifically, the Jerusalem artichoke. Tobacco was also
grown. The design and layout of garden plots among the Indians of southern New England were similar. Generally, an
area was selected and cleared of vegetation by cutting down
and burning brush and trees. Ashes from the burning would
have provided needed soil nutrients. Once an area was cleared,
earth mounds or hills were constructed, spaced generally four
or five feet apart. In these hills were placed kernels of corn and,
later, beans, so as to allow their vines to use the growing stalk
as a pole. Squash, gourds, and tubers were planted in the
spaces left between the corn hills. Hoes for cultivation were
manufactured from the shells of horseshoe crabs, clams, the
scapulae of deer, or turtle carapaces.

Archaeological research and documentary sources indicate
that a great variety of vertebrate fauna were exploited by Indians of the area, an activity carried out by men. A partial list
includes white-tailed deer, bear, raccoon, opossum, eastern
cottontail, gray squirrel, porcupine, gray fox, weasel/mink,
meadow vole, deer mouse, muskrat, and beaver. Avian fauna
included duck, turkey, Canada goose, brant, common loon,
and others. The Pequots also fished Atlantic sturgeon, striped
bass, scup, tautog, striped sea robin, sheepshead, sandbar
shark, tomcod, skate, and cunner, to name but a few. Among
marine mammals hunted were the gray seal and harbor seal.
Turtles and otter were also a food source. Shellfish varieties
collected were bay scallop, quahog, long clam, Virginia oyster,
whelk, blue mussel, boat shell, and many others.[6]

Wild plant resources, whose availability varied with season
and locality, were exploited by the Pequots. In the spring and
summer could be found any number of plants to be used as
greens or potherbs or for seeds. The summer also provided an
abundance of wild fruits including strawberries, blueberries,
blackberries, elderberries, currants, and others. Butternuts,
walnuts, acorns, hickory nuts, and chestnuts were collected in

the fall. These could be dried or roasted and stored for use over the winter. Roots and tubers were collected throughout the year, although they seem to have been mainly a winter resource.[7]

From all indications, the planting, cultivating, and harvesting of domesticated plants were carried out principally by women. Tobacco, it seems, was grown only by men. The collecting of wild plant resources was also probably accomplished by women. Hunting was a male activity, as it was throughout southern New England and elsewhere in the Northeast. Fishing may have been a communal activity, although various associated tasks were performed as prescribed by the sexual division of labor.

Information specifically describing Pequot settlements is limited; nevertheless, by employing extant sources and analogies from other, better-known regions of southern New England, a rather detailed picture emerges. Large villages, whether fortified or otherwise, do not seem to have been the rule among the Pequots or, for that matter, anywhere in southern New England. Instead, small villages of ten to twenty houses, hamlets, farmsteads, or simply isolated dwellings were most common. The settlement pattern is best described as dispersed, with habitation sites shifting from place to place over a year (or season). Such a settlement pattern evolves as an expression of subsistence activities or the subsistence round; that is, relatively frequent moves were predicated upon the availability of food resources such as fish, wild plants, mammals, and domesticated crops. Thus, populations would be essentially semisedentary, shifting their locations seasonally. The following discussion outlines generally the movements of Pequot populations throughout the course of a year.

Summer appears to have been a time of lessened mobility and relatively minimal dispersion. Early observers describe either individual houses or small farmsteads surrounded by cultivated fields. From these locations the occupants made short and relatively brief trips to fishing or plant-gathering stations. For example, people of Nemasket in southeastern Massachusetts appear to have journeyed up to fifteen miles from their farmsteads to the seacoast to harvest lobsters.[8]

Once the cultivated crops were harvested, Pequot populations began a move away from the coast and other exposed locales, retreating to inland forests and well-protected areas where they prepared to spend the winter.[9] In the orthodox view, this was the time when populations were most concentrated, although not entirely sedentary; however, archaeological research carried out in the Pequot area has failed to identify the large inland sites that are to be expected if such concentrations did, in fact, take place.[10] What instead prevailed were relatively isolated Pequot settlements representing small seasonal camps of households rather than task-specific locations of what have been termed "logistically oriented groups."[11] In the spring Pequot households moved out of the winter settlements and established fishing and fowling camps. After they shifted from those stations, the summer farmsteads were again occupied. Small camps were established in the fall to take advantage of nut and other vegetable resources before the inland dispersion of populations for the winter. Thus the seasonal round was completed.

Dwellings at these seasonal habitations varied somewhat. The most commonly occurring house is the wigwam, or round house. The generalized shape of such a dwelling approaches that of a hemisphere or dome having a round or oval floor plan. These structures were constructed with a framework of saplings fixed in the ground, which were bent or bowed over and lashed together. This framework was then covered with woven mats or bark sheets. The woven mats were made of flag leaves, rushes, or cattails, or, infrequently, bark. Such houses were easily and quickly constructed or dismantled, and were moved from place to place with apparent ease. Overall dimensions varied. Generally, these structures were nearly circular in floor plan and had diameters of ten to sixteen feet. Measurements taken from two mid–eighteenth-century oval wigwams show diameters of about seventeen by twelve feet, and fourteen by nine feet, and heights of approximately six to ten feet.

The occupants of such houses were small social units; for example, nuclear or extended families. This agrees with the settlement-dispersion behavior, or settlement system, discussed above, where family groups moved throughout their environment exploiting a variety of resources during a year.

The second type of dwelling found among the Indians of southern New England is the longhouse. This structure, which was essentially oblong or roughly rectangular in outline, varied considerably in size. Most sources describe long houses as being anywhere from fifty to two hundred feet long and up to thirty feet wide. The house frames were similar to those of wigwams and were covered in much the same manner. From the historical accounts, it appears that small or medium-size long houses functioned as domiciles for large or extended family groups or lineages. The largest structures may have had a dual purpose, functioning as both a communal dwelling and a place for ceremonies and rituals. Ethnohistorians have suggested that high-status individuals, such as sachems, may have occupied such a large house.

Early accounts provide precious little information concerning the social and political organization of Algonquian-speaking populations living in southern New England. When such information exists it poses problems. From the outset, many European observers were indifferent to or simply ignored patterns of sociopolitical organization. When such issues are mentioned, it is clear that the subtleties and complex nature of these systems were beyond the grasp of Europeans and, for the most part, escaped them. The result is a series of descriptions or interpretations that are often misrepresentations and oversimplifications. A strong bias is generally demonstrated by the application of misleading and inaccurate analogies to European social and political systems.

The village or hamlet appears to have been the basic sociopolitical unit among the Pequots and other Indian groups in southern New England; however, current research indicates that the concept of the household as the center of economic activity—the primary economic unit—is the most appropriate model with which to interpret the function of small seasonal camps present in the lower Connecticut Valley and its environs at contact. This is in contrast to traditional views, which hold that it was in the villages or hamlets that subsistence activities and the redistribution of goods were organized and operated. This recent interpretation of the archaeological data may ultimately bring into question conventional wisdom that holds that the nuclear or extended family was the basic household social unit during the farming season, while the lineage dominated social activities during the winter population aggregations.[12]

Patrilineality seems to have been the rule among the Pequots and others in southern New England, although there was an apparent trend toward bilateral kin groups and possibly matrilineal groups.[13] What this means is that kin relationships or descent were traced through the male line, but with a trend toward recognition of kin on both sides of the family; through both the mother's and the father's line and, in some cases, only through the female's or mother's line.

There remains considerable confusion regarding kin recognition in the literature. For example, Lewis Henry Morgan, the "father" of American anthropology, was informed by a Narragansett woman that descent among the Pequots and the Narragansetts had originally been in the female line.[14] Others have concluded that some southern New England groups were matrilineal during late prehistoric times and that the system was then modified to "conform to the patrilineal bias of the English colonial authorities."[15] There are no depictions of this situation for the Pequots. There is, however, good evidence from the region that certain political offices were inherited patrilineally. Whatever the case, it is certainly true that the Pequots and adjacent groups were under considerable social stress when they were first described by European chroniclers. They had suffered significant and rapid mortality and population decline as a consequence of smallpox, influenza, and other European diseases. In addition, they were being encroached upon by European colonists and their economic system, and were generally in a state of social upheaval. Thus, it is no wonder that hard and fast rules regarding social structure are not easily applied to these Indian populations.

Postnuptial residence patterns are even more difficult to ascertain. There are no clues in the literature that would indicate where a couple would reside following marriage, with the possible exception of high-status families. Archaeologist Bert Salwen notes that early in the postcontact period, high-status individuals practiced a patrilocal postnuptial residence pattern. Generally, however, an ambilocal pattern was the rule.[16]

In some cases, the social organization of southern New England groups has been described and interpreted as if it were far more codified than it may, in fact, have been. For example, anthropologists have identified three basic divisions in Wampanoag society: "(1) the sachem and members of the 'royal family'; (2) ordinary members of the community; (3) resident nonmembers (generally captives of war) who acted as servants." They have also described "true hereditary social stratification" and "class" structure in the region, even though there is little compelling evidence to suggest the existence of stratified societies anywhere or at any time in the Northeast.[17]

The Pequots were probably organized into what Elman Service calls "lineal tribes."[18] Fundamentally, a lineal tribe is characterized by a lineal descent structure, either matrilineal or patrilineal, a social structure composed of lineages and clans, and recognition of status differences. Marshall D. Sahlins has defined such a structure:

The tribe is a constellation of communities and relations between communities. The main elements of this structure are in substance major groupings of kinsmen. Descent groups in particular often comprise the nucleii of tribal sections; certain types of descent groups can provide a framework for the entire tribal organization.[19]

The definition of community here is "the largest grouping of persons in any particular culture whose normal activities bind them together into a self-conscious, corporate unit, which is economically self-sufficient and politically independent."[20] For the Pequots, communities functioned within the social confines or parameters of the small villages, hamlets, and farmsteads.

Tribes are also unstratified societies; that is, there is an absence of clearly defined social strata in the sense of the division of a society into separate, homogeneous, but unequal levels. Such unstratified societies differentiate roles and status positions.

The historical descriptions of the social organizations of southern New England Indians, and other data, suggest that the Pequots were an unstratified, ranked society. Such a social structure is characterized by a limited number of valued or high-status positions, some of which are ascribed, that is, inherited, while others are achieved. Thus in a ranked society there will be relatively few positions of high status, and the vast majority of the population remains "ordinary" members of the community. It is noted that "ranking does not involve an evaluative judgment of 'better' or 'worse,'" rather, it is more concerned with questions of "more" and "less."[21]

First and foremost of the high-status positions among the Pequots, and other Indian populations in the region, was the position of sachem (or sagamore). Although these offices were commonly held by men, female sachems were not unknown. The position of sachem was hereditary, following the male line. This does not necessarily mean that a father would pass down the position to his son, which no doubt did occur, but that the office was held by men who were related patrilineally.[22]

Sachems were civil officials, providing communities leadership on a day-to-day basis. Although they were vested with authority to lead or govern, power was held within segments of their constituency, for example, by councils of elder men or the patrilineage that had appointed them, and also by coun-

cils of women. A sachem's influence was maintained largely
through his own persuasive abilities. These were coupled with
what was perceived as his generosity, manifested in his giving
of gifts and providing for indigent members of his tribe. At the
same time, in many of the early historical accounts there are
references to "tribute" or "gifts" being paid or bestowed to a
sachem. This same behavior, observed by Roger Williams,
was interpreted as being part of a political system that Williams described as "monarchical," a misleading conclusion.[23]
What was seen by Williams and other Europeans was, in fact,
part of the system of reciprocity. Such gifts were exchanged
among groups and individuals within a community within a
prescribed framework of ritual and ceremony. The primary
concern in this sort of exchange is to fulfill social obligations
and to gain prestige in the process. For example, a Pequot
sachem incurred an obligation by accepting gifts given to him
in the form of "tribute" or other goods. He, in turn, might re-
ciprocate by granting the gift giver some request. In the same
fashion, by redistributing items of wealth or goods—food
stuffs, for example—to his constituency, a sachem might
achieve political support for his leadership decisions and position. Power and authority relationships are reciprocal agreements. Therefore, instead of participating in "monarchical"
system, or one marked by vassalage, such as is often described in the early historical documents and repeated by historians and anthropologists, the Pequots functioned within a
sociopolitically reciprocal political structure. There appear to
have been status differences among or between sachems,
which perhaps were linked to "chiefly" or senior lineages. How
those status differences affected the Pequot political organization is not known.

Of the other categories of high-status positions, two require
mention. The first is the *pniese.* These were individuals who
realized a particular supernatural vision during an ordeal, a ritual that involved physical and psychological deprivation and
the drinking of infusions that altered consciousness. Once
having had the vision, the pniese was regarded as a special

person, one of status and considerable importance and influence. Such individuals functioned as a sachem's counsel, took part in decisions regarding war and peace, and apparently were integrated into and operated within the reciprocal system of the sachem.[24]

A second position of high status was the *powwow,* or shaman. Shamans are part-time magico-religious specialists who act as intermediaries between the physical and spiritual worlds. William Simmons has observed that "because of their access to a range of spirits both within and outside of themselves the *powwows* advised the *sachems* in decision, but the inspired role of shaman and the hereditary role of *sachem* did not overlap generally in one individual."[25]

Although there was a clearly identified individual in a single position of authority in each Indian community in southern New England, such a person's jurisdiction was in no way absolute. Decision making and the operation of government was based on consensus. Each sachem received counsel from other high-status individuals, including the pnieses and powwows. In addition, influential or well-regarded warriors had input into the political process, along with members of the community, such as elders and other respected persons, who formed councils or caucuses. At all of those levels, reciprocity drove the process. The outcome was a village-oriented, autonomous, consensual government.

There undoubtedly were multivillage alliances throughout the region. The precise patterns of these relationships is not known. It is true that soon after contact extensive alliances formed, often under the leadership of a single powerful sachem or several sachems; nonetheless, anthropologists Ted Brasser and Dean Snow suggest that precontact sociopolitical units were very small, usually at the level of the small villages, hamlets, or farmsteads discussed here. The larger units that formed in the historic period were essentially a response to organizational needs developing from the fur trade and contact with European state-level governments.[26]

European-introduced diseases disrupted the prehistoric

cultural systems that had operated in southern New England and, of course, elsewhere in the Americas. This disruption took place very early in the contact period, so that secure reconstructions of pristine Indian societies, based upon the extant contemporary documentation, are virtually impossible. Consequently, any ethnographic sketch undoubtedly reflects, to a degree, the effects of European contact.

From the outset it is important to note that Indian populations were not disease-free before their encounter with Europeans. For example, tuberculosis and treponematoses (syphilis) were not uncommon, along with other diseases and disease agents. The list of New World diseases also included bacillary and amoebic dysentery; viral influenza and pneumonia; various arthritides; various rickettsial fevers; various viral fevers; American leishmaniasis; American trypanosomiasis; round worms; bacterial pathogens, such as streptococcus and staphylococcus; and salmonella and other food-poisoning agents.[27] Added to that list were a variety of parasites; blastomycosis, which is difficult to diagnose distinct from tuberculosis; anemias; and dental pathologies.

In general, however, Indians were comparatively healthy, and the diseases they suffered from were relatively benign. In fact, early accounts by Europeans frequently comment on the well-being of Indian populations. Repeatedly, and often with amazement, chroniclers depict Indians as robust and healthy individuals unusually free from any apparent physical defects or deformities. Nonetheless, there is consensus among paleopathologists that at contact, hunting, gathering, and horticultural populations such as those in southern New England suffered from chronic nutritional deficiencies and attendant diseases marked by Harris Lines in long bones, and linear enamel hypoplasias and other microdefects in teeth, along with other skeletal indicators.[28]

Although Indian health care systems were in place and functioning at the advent of European exploration, they were of little use in stemming the tide of disease. These systems generally had emerged from a broad base of herbal medicines and curing rituals used to fight prehistoric disease and disease processes. Against maladies such as those introduced by Europeans they were often ineffective and, indeed, in some instances counterproductive and deadly. For example, sweat baths, a means by which disease might be purged, and the attendant human behaviors associated with their use, actually spread the disease viruses and dehydrated people who were already ill. The situation was a difficult one.

With the Europeans came community infections unknown in the Americas. These included smallpox, measles, malaria, yellow fever, chicken pox, whooping cough, scarlet fever, diphtheria, plague, cholera, poliomyelitis, and others.[29] According to demographer Sherburne Cook, aside from minor and local outbreaks of already established contagions, two pestilences of wide, severe, and epidemic proportions struck New England Indians in the early years following European settlement. These episodes stand out as particularly destructive, and indeed, there does not seem to have been a complete or even notable recovery from their lethal effect. The first was the so-called "plague" between 1616 and 1619.[30]

Several theories have been forwarded concerning the nature of this infection. Two theories suggest that the illness was bubonic/pneumonic plague or smallpox. A third possibility suggested is yellow fever, although this is unlikely since the disease persisted throughout the year and it is doubtful that a mosquito-borne infection could survive a New England winter. Another possibility recently proposed by researchers is viral hepatic disease, hepatitis A. This is a strong hypothesis supported by compelling arguments.[31] Whatever the disease was, it devastated populations all along the coast of New England from the Kennebec River, and perhaps Penobscot Bay in Maine, south to Narragansett Bay. It does not appear to have crossed over to Indians west of Narragansett Bay. Thus apparently the Pequots were spared.

The next major epidemic struck New England in 1633. The disease was smallpox. This epidemic and its offshoots were so widespread as to become almost universal. There is little doubt that it struck the Pequots.[32] After the decade between 1630 and 1640 smallpox and other introduced diseases were never absent among the Indian populations of eastern North America. At short intervals, epidemics flared and reached new Indian tribes or attacked the nonimmune younger generations in areas that had previously experienced the disease. At the same time, indigenous pathogens such as tuberculosis and syphilis, along with other disease conditions exacerbated by contact and changing social and environmental conditions, appeared in increasingly virulent forms.[33]

Mortality rates from smallpox and other illnesses striking epidemiologically pristine Indian populations were appallingly high. A conservative estimate of disease mortality, based upon comparative data, is set at 55 percent. Others have provided estimates ranging up to 95 percent. Although these figures may sound excessively high, they are nonetheless accurate when applied to specific cases.[34]

The Pequots numbered about thirteen thousand persons just before contact. After contact and the effects of European diseases, but before the Pequot War of 1637, their population had been reduced to some three thousand individuals, indicating a mortality rate of 77 percent. Following the War, this number was further diminished to one thousand.[35]

Virgin-soil epidemics and warfare also had disastrous sociopolitical and religious implications. Besides high rates of mortality, there were precipitous drops in fertility and disruptions in the socialization process. Ideological systems were now under severe stress while individual Pequots in the affected populations were unable to complete even the most routine tasks such as farming, fishing, preparing meals, or collecting firewood and water.[36] Thomas Morton, writing in 1637, provides a catastrophic picture of the havoc and tragedy produced by disease:

But contrary wise in short time after, the hand of God fell heavily upon them [the Indians], with such a mortall stroake, that they died in heapes, as they lay in their houses and the living; [sic] that were able to shift for themselves would runne away, & let them dy, and let there Carkases ly above the ground without buriall. For in a place where many inhabited, there hath been but one left alive, to tell what became of the rest, the livinge being (as it seemes) not able to bury the dead, they were left for Crowes, Kites, and vermin to pray upon. And the bones and skulls upon the severall places of their habitations, made such a spectacle after my comming into those partes, that as I travailed in that Forest, nere the Massachusetts, it seemed to mee a new found Golgotha.[37]

The high rates of death opened leadership positions that probably could not be filled in traditional ways. It is likely that competition increased, while contention for status and leadership positions was already altered by the Indians' involvement in the fur trade. Thus, Indian politics in southern New England were recast in structure and form.

The early years of the seventeenth century signaled only the beginning in the history of Indian-white relations in southern New England. Ravaged by disease, increasingly dependent on and affected by the European economic system, beset by righteous missionaries, and participating in an ever-widening scale of warfare, the Pequots could only surmise the future.

CHAPTER 4

Native Wampum as a Peripheral Resource in the Seventeenth-Century World-System

By Lynn Ceci

The focus on how one small strategic resource, wampum, functioned within the expanding world-system provides a perspective for understanding frontier processes in one part of the Northeast. Reconstructing the economic, political, and social connections between peripheral suppliers and core consumers offers a new, broadly based interpretation of the major events of the history of each category, traditionally studied as separate native and colonist cultures. Thus the seventeenth-century southern New England–coastal New York frontier, like frontiers everywhere, is really about human relationships and economic contest.

Though the name has been applied generically to all varieties of shell (and nonshell) beads, wampum properly refers to the particular type of white and purple shell bead seen in the famous wampum belts of the Iroquois. This belt wampum, called "true" wampum by some,[1] is distinguished from all others misidentified as such by three traits: species, shape, and size. White wampum beads are "sliced" from the narrow inner pillars, or columellas, of two marine species, the small northern whelks *Busycon canaliculatum* and *B. carica,* which are especially abundant between Cape Cod and coastal

New York. Purple wampum is cut from purple segments of the more widely distributed hard-shell clam, or quahog, *Mercenaria mercenaria*. Wampum is tubular in shape, well finished, and smooth from grinding down the columellas. Mid–seventeenth-century wampum beads average 5.5 mm in length and 4 mm in diameter; the tiny bores drilled with European metal awls average 1 mm.[2]

The origin of wampum has been the subject of inquiry and debate for a century or more. Researchers working with limited archaeological evidence and the late-dated belts in existence have concluded the wampum bead type was historic, dated to around 1600 A.D.[3] Others, misapplying the name to all types of shell beads, concluded wampum was prehistoric.[4] Overlapping the historic and prehistoric estimates are Iroquois traditions and myths linking the appearance of "original" wampum to the period of tribal formation (ca. 1400–1605 A.D.).[5]

Shell beads from archaeological sites primarily in western New York state indicate that, although marine shell beads were present as early as the Late Archaic period (ca. 2500 B.C.), the first small tubular white beads to meet the three criteria for wampum were recovered from more recent Middle and Late Woodland sites (ca. A.D. 200–1510). The average length (7.6 mm) and diameter (5.2 mm) of these beads fall within two standard deviations of those for seventeenth-century belt wampum; the average for stone-drilled bores (2.4 mm) is significantly larger. The dates for this prehistoric form of wampum on inland sites correlate well with new radiocarbon dates on and associated with prepared columella bead blanks from village sites in coastal New York. Together, the inland and coastal findings provide archaeological evidence for both "proto-wampum" and the appropriate bead blanks, and no less importantly, for the existence of an inland-coastal exchange network for marine shell in the Northeast before European contact.[6]

Inland sites of the Seneca Iroquois in western New York occupied after contact yield European trade goods associated with increasing numbers and types of marine-shell beads.

These include white wampum beads statistically indistinguishable from seventeenth-century belt wampum; average bead length (6.7 mm) and diameter (4.7 mm) fall within one standard deviation, and the bores, now drilled with metal awls, are smaller (1.96 mm). This postcontact wampum was woven into small strips, bracelet-size, by the late sixteenth century, and into larger widths or small belts containing white and the first purple wampum by the early seventeenth.[7]

The most dramatic change in wampum assemblages occurs on two Seneca sites—the Power House and Dann sites—dated circa A.D. 1640 to 1675, where the number of beads and large broad belts increases sharply. For the Power House site as many as 250,000 wampum beads have been estimated, besides eight belts; and an estimated 100,000 beads and fifteen belts were at the Dann site. Those estimates, stretched to include those for the other Iroquois tribes of the period (Cayuga, Oneida, Onondaga, Mohawk), mean that millions of wampum beads flowed into the Northeast interior by the mid-seventeenth century. Those millions were made from shell gathered, processed, and carefully finished primarily by Algonquian bead makers along the coast of southern New England and New York.

In the late fifteenth and sixteenth centuries a new European world economy came into existence. The charting of new routes around South America and Africa by Portuguese navigators in this period expanded not only the geographic size of the known world but also the knowledge of economically valuable resources accessible to European merchants. This expansion and the worldwide exploitation of resources that followed, in effect, transformed the European social system to a "world-system." At the heart of this social and economic world-system lay the European "core"; the "periphery" included the raw-material zone and, beyond that, the external zone still outside the influence of the system. This model makes the study of small regional cultural systems and events inadequate without reference to the larger overarching world-system to which they were linked.[8] The bounded culture or isolated society usually studied by social scientists, anthropologist Eric Wolf has argued, is a "bundle of relationships" abstracted from its connections to the "world of human kind." Similarly, the historian O. Zunz has insisted that social history is "connected history" that links "everyday experience to the large structures of historical analyses and major changes of the past."[9] Wampum and its role within the North American periphery of the European world-system demonstrates the value of this approach.

Portuguese navigators were among the first to chart the North American Atlantic Coast. Records left by Portuguese and later explorers commonly include, in addition to navigational data, surveys of resources potentially profitable to core sponsors of the voyage, for example, furs, slaves, minerals, timber, and so forth. While codfish taken from the rich fishing banks off northeastern North America was the first important resource to exemplify expansion of the world-system into the region, furs obtained from native peoples on shore became the second and, very quickly, the more important one. The sixteenth century, in short, can be viewed as the period when the Northeast and its natives who hunted, prepared, and offered skins to Europeans gradually evolved from a zone external to the world-system to a periphery within.

One may trace this frontier process by examining the archaeological evidence on sites of sixteenth-century native fur-suppliers, such as the Seneca Iroquois already mentioned. One may also trace the process through the cartographic evidence of maps revealing the economic geography of profitable resources. Of the many early New World maps that yield such evidence, only three will be cited here to illustrate the expansion of the world-system into northeastern North America. The first is the 1569 Mercator World Map, one of the most influential in the history of map making. The section depicting the North American Atlantic coast (tilted northeast due to misunderstood magnetic readings) reveals the extent then known of coastal regions where fishing and fur trade activities were brisk. This surprisingly early map provides details for the interior (for example, the Appalachian Mountains and long rivers

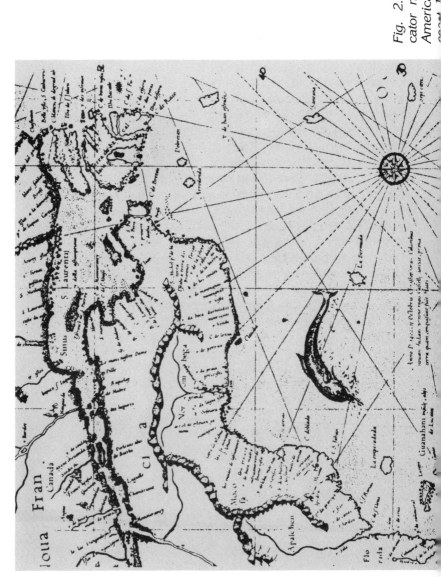

Fig. 2. Gerard Mercator map of North American Atlantic coast, 1569.

that Europeans had either explored or learned of from native informants). The northeastern river identified as "r. grande" at about 41°N must be the Hudson River (40° 42' N) because the island "Claudia" on the east is Block Island. The "castle" drawn next to this and other rivers may be taken to represent palisaded settlements where Europeans could expect to meet native inhabitants, as other maps of the period show more clearly.[10]

The second map, a 1610 survey done for King James I of England, is thought to show the new data gathered by Henry Hudson in 1609.[11] The section for southern New England and coastal New York shows the river mouth at the correct latitude and, on either side, the ethnonym "Manhatan" for the Indians with whom Hudson had traded; Long Island still appears as part of the mainland. The purpose of his voyage under the Dutch East India Company flag, Hudson later confessed, was not to explore but to make a profit by exchanging "merchandize for furs."[12] Indeed, details of his itinerary indicate extensive trading for furs with natives, many of whom already possessed European goods. Importantly, at the head of the Hudson River, where better-quality furs were available, local natives gave Hudson ten or more "stropes of beades."[13] Given the date, the location, and the value natives placed on them, it is not unreasonable to infer that the "stropes" were woven widths of wampum, not unlike those recovered on Seneca sites for the same period.

A third map, the 1614 "Carte Figurative," executed only a few years later, reveals the great transformation brought about by Dutch commercial interests. Dutch fur traders had been active in the Northeast, including central New York, since 1600 or earlier, and in each year after Hudson's venture, but it was not until skipper-merchant Adriaen Block explored the local coast in a small shallow-draft yacht that the insularity of Long Island was discovered along with the area's many estuaries and inlets. To serve the interests of his sponsors at the core of the world-system, Block marked key locations in the new Dutch territory ("Nieu Nederlandt"), for example,

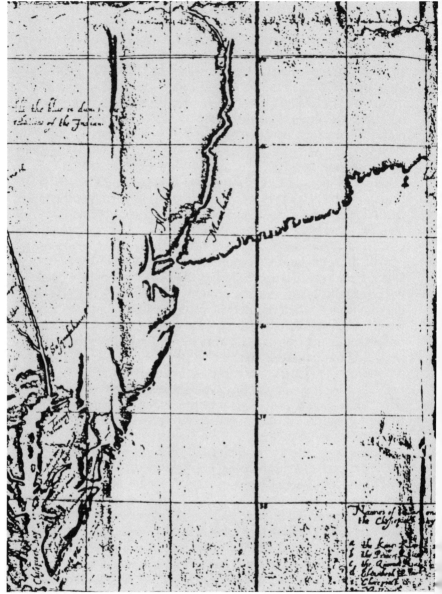

Fig. 3. Section of the Velasco map of 1610 showing southern New England and coastal New York.

the trade post up the Hudson River and, by anchor symbols, coastal anchorages such as Lower New York Bay and Narragansett Bay. More mysteriously, he also marked fourteen Xs offshore between the Connecticut River and Fishers Island Inlet and at Narragansett Bay, points where wampum, it may be inferred, would have been available. Block also charted ethnonyms for coastal Algonquian and inland Iroquois peoples who, in later documents, are clearly identified as suppliers of wampum and furs. This very act of first naming lands and communities in itself can be seen as an extension of the world-system. Although the "Pequats" and "Sennecas" he named, for example, may have existed as ethnic communities centuries before, and perhaps even were linked in a regional exchange system in 1614, their cultures were transformed now by virtue of their significant economic and social relationships within the Dutch world-system.[14] In short, the Block map represents the conjoining of this new northeastern economic periphery to the European core, and it was a layout for extracting profitable raw materials from the natives he named.

That valuable resources in one zone could be exchanged profitably for cheap shell beads from another was long known to Portuguese, Dutch, and English middlemen who transported shiploads of East Indian cowries (Italian, *porcellana*) to West Africa for gold and other goods. Although the Dutch are usually credited with the discovery, or invention, of the wampum-for-furs exchange system, there are hints that French traders along the southern coast of New England between 1604 and 1607 had also learned of the special value of the small, tubular columella beads from natives there, who wove them into chains, necklaces, bracelets, and armlets. The French learned that these beads (*porcelain*) were "esteemed more highly" than trade goods by northern fur suppliers, who would buy them "very dear."[15] Other Europeans who traded in the interior may have realized the beads' potential as an exchange commodity simply by observing how precious wampum was to the Iroquois. Indeed, wampum is linked to the founding of the Iroquois League itself because Deganawidah

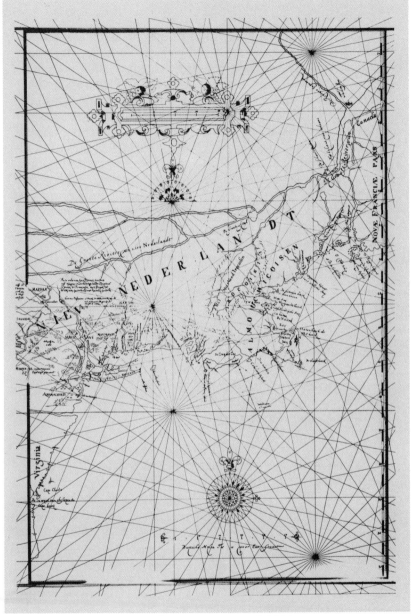

Fig. 4. Adriaen Block's "Carte Figurative," 1614.

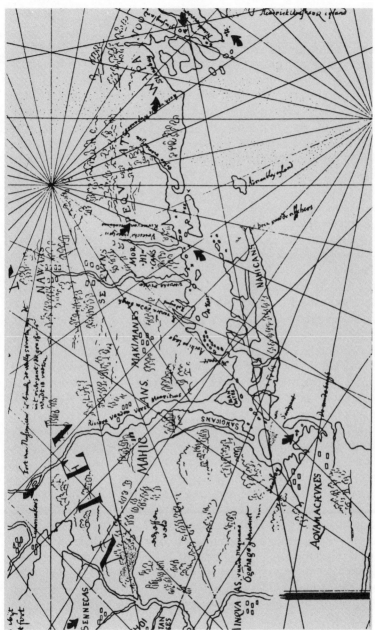

Fig. 5. *Detail of Adriaen Block's "Carte Figurative," 1614.*

established peace among the tribes based on reciprocal exchange of wampum.[16] So powerful was the desire for wampum among the Iroquois that the Dutch called it "the source
and the mother of the beaver trade."[17] A final possibility is that
the coastal beadmakers themselves initiated the wampum-
for-furs exchange in order to acquire furs from inland sources
to trade for European goods on the coast, especially after
local fur-bearing species were depleted. After all the word
wampum (or *wompam*) was Algonquian, as were the names
for purple wampum (*suckauhock*), the columellas used for
white beads (*meteauhock*), and the purple "eyes" used for
purple (*suckauwaskeesaquash*).[18]

Although the Dutch word for wampum, *zeewan,* is mentioned in a 1622 account, details of the trade secret were not
revealed until 1626, when Secretary de Rasieres, stationed at
the Dutch West India Company (DWI) trade port on Manhattan, explained them in a letter to the company directors. De
Rasieres planned to forward a "thousand yards of *sewan*" to
the company's upriver trade post for the Indians, who came to
the Dutch "for no other reason than to get *sewan*." With additional supplies of "duffles," a coarse textile of growing importance in Holland, he would know "how to get wampum" to
stock the upriver post and prevent Indians from going to
competitors.[19]

What De Rasieres outlined is a trade triangle. First, manufactured goods—here cloth but elsewhere other trade goods—
were sent by European investors to the wampum-producing
zone and exchanged for wampum. Second, the wampum was
transported upriver and exchanged for furs. Third, the furs were
shipped back to investors and sold at great profit. DWI records
outline the three legs of this triangle and, in particular, the itinerary of company sloops between Narragansett Bay ("Sloup-
bay") and the Dutch post upriver at Fort Nassau, or Castle Island—points shown on the 1614 map. The records also indicate
the profitability of this commodity chain in the rising number of
furs shipped back to Holland each year. By 1632 the English

had learned that the annual worth of the furs was 20,000 English pounds (about 200,000 guilders); in 1633, Dutch cargo worth 31,000 guilders would return 143,125 guilders.[20]

Curiously, the biggest European competitor was introduced to the scheme by De Rasieres himself when he sold about fifty English pounds' worth of wampum to the Pilgrims at Plymouth in 1627.[21] They followed his advice to try this commodity in their own trade with fur suppliers in northern New England, and within a few years their "dependence" on the wampum trade made them active seekers of supplies. For the Pilgrims, indebted by 1,800 English pounds to the London sponsors of the *Mayflower* voyage and in need of European supplies, wampum proved profitable (more so than the labor-intensive maize commodity traded earlier), and the Pilgrims' trade balance improved.[22]

The growing competition between the Dutch and English for wampum supplies may partly explain the steadily rising costs of wampum and furs after 1627.[23] But competition also came from native entrepreneurs such as the Pequots, whose geographic location between coastal wampum and hinterland furs (and between the English colonists and the Hudson River) placed them in a monopolistic position. Their production and control of wampum supplies from less-powerful coastal bead makers, English observers wrote, made them "rich and potent" by 1627, and a "stately warlike people" by 1634.[24] Clearly, the function of wampum among northeastern natives had shifted from gift-giving and reciprocal exchange to a more capitalistic market exchange which, in turn, engendered intertribal competition and conflict.

But wampum's function for colonials also changed. Small, durable, and backed by the steady worth of beaver in European markets, confidence in wampum was sufficient to make it acceptable as coinage or cash in lieu of scarce hard coin from Europe.[25] This critical use of wampum as a legal tender "minted" by natives sets the economic stage for the antagonistic events that followed. The European settlers, isolated from their core support, had to gain control of their local currency and the commodity basic to their fiscal stability and profitmaking.

For reasons that contemporaries and historians since have pondered, a series of relatively minor incidents beginning in 1634 became the excuse to punish the mintmasters and extract wampum payments. In one case there was the death of a Dutch trader who had ransomed a Pequot sachem, Tatobem, for wampum, then killed him despite the payment.[26] In another, the killing of an English wampum trader on Block Island in 1636 by the Narragansetts precipitated an English military campaign resulting in the killing or wounding of fifty-three Pequots, a fine of "1000 fathom of wampom for damages," and the taking of children as hostages.[27] The following year, a few months after wampum was declared legal tender at three beads per penny, war was formally declared on the Pequots.[28] Within two months 1,500 Pequots had been driven out of their settlements or slain, according to a report by the English Captain John Underhill. In the infamous May 1637 attack at Mystic, Connecticut, Underhill indicated that four hundred Pequot "souls" were burned or shot within a half hour. To charges that the attack was too "furious" and unmerciful, Underhill cited scripture and the "word of God" as justification for killing non-Christians.[29]

Historians such as Francis Jennings, Neal E. Salisbury, and Alden T. Vaughan have debated the origins of the Pequot War, producing numerous writings on the subject, evaluating and weighing the blame of English colonist and Indian alike. Historian Henry Steele Commager suggests that the Mystic attack represented a simple act of terrorism, "deadly violence against random and innocent victims," to bring about quick and complete capitulation by enemies perceived as large, powerful, and in possession of critical resources.[30] The evidence seems to add an economic motive to English intentions.

With conquest of Pequot land and control of other bead makers, the value of the English pence doubled to six beads per penny.[31] The future stability of that rate was gained by controlling the quantities of wampum in circulation after the 1638 Hartford Agreement stipulated the tributes to be paid by all Indians who harbored or were assigned Pequot refugees: "one fathom of white Wampum for the Pequot man, and half a fathom for each Pequot youth, and one handlength for each male child."[32] Other bead makers, frightened by attacks on the Pequots, dared not disobey. There were also threats to seize their possessions and their children as hostages and to deport "Runaway Pequots" overseas.[33]

These wampum tributes and fines paid by Indians for sundry "crimes," scattered through many records, are generally ignored or considered incidental.[34] Nevertheless, the records do indicate that payments between 1634 and 1664 to English colonists amounted conservatively to over 21,000 fathoms of wampum—almost 7 million beads. This total means that beads worth about 5,000 pounds in English currency entered colonial coffers during this period, more if double-valued purple beads were included. Thus, a second outcome of the Pequot War was, in effect, the partial underwriting of New England colonization costs by the conquered natives. A third outcome was the creation of a new, more advantageous English trade triangle, one that began on this side of the Atlantic with free tribute wampum gained without trade goods, and ended with credit—including final payment of the Puritan indebtedness—and badly needed supplies from Europe.[35]

Other economic results of the Pequot War could be cited, such as the expansion of English settlements across conquered Indian agricultural territories claimed and mapped earlier by the Dutch, and ultimately, the conquest of Dutch New Amsterdam in 1664 through the manipulation of wampum money supplies and tributes to outbid the Dutch for furs. The Dutch, following the English example, hired Underhill and other mercenaries, and attempted to exact "contributions" by attacking local bead makers from about 1640 to 1645, but the DWI Company and Dutch colonists were weaker and less able to coerce local bead makers, who were already tributary to the English controlling wampum-production sites.[36]

Table 1. Wampum payments by New England–
Long Island Indians, 1634–1664

Year	Payment (fathoms)	Worth[a] (English £)	Wampum Beads[b]	Source
1634	400		132,000	Winthrop 1908 I:140
1635	?			
1636	1000		330,000	Winthrop 1908 I:186
1636	6000		1,980,000	Speck 1919:59
1637	220		726,000	Winthrop 1908 I:212, 228, 231
1638	30		9,900	Winthrop 1908 I:226, 271
1638?	60		19,800	Pulsifer 1859 I:102
1639	50		16,500	Winthrop 1908 I:299
1640	0.5		165	Trumbull 1850:52
1641	?			
1642	?			
1643	65.5	£15	21,600	Winthrop 1908 II:143
1644	56		18,480	Winthrop 1908 II:159–160
1644	100		33,000	Ferguson 1935:23
1645	2000		660,000	Pulsifer 1859 I:44
1646	1300		429,000	Pulsifer 1859 I:74
1647	608.5		200,805	Pulsifer 1859 I:102, 107
1648	?			Trumbull 1850:164
1649	1937.5		639,375	Pulsifer 1859 I:145
1649	87.3	£20	28,800	Winthrop 1947:344
1650	308		101,640	Pulsifer 1859 I:168
1650	126.5	£29	43,065	Pulsifer 1859 I:169
1651	312		102,960	Pulsifer 1859 I:207
1652	?			
1653	343.5	£78 14sh 6p	113,364	Pulsifer 1859 II:107, 108
1654	?			Pulsifer 1859 I:130, 132
1655	552		182,160	Pulsifer 1859 II:142, 154
1656	215		70,950	Denton 1845:66
1657	242		79,860	Pulsifer 1859 II:194
1657	3054.5	£700	1,008,000	Pulsifer 1859 II:180
1657	560		184,800	Trumbull 1850:303
1658	180		59,400	Speck 1919:58
1658	164		54,120	Hazard 1794:387
1659	168		55,440	Pulsifer 1859 I:226
1660	739		243,870	Pulsifer 1859 II:249, 250
1660	43.6	£10	144,000	Trumbull 1850:362
1661	?			
1662	?			
1663	80		26,400	Speck 1919:59
1664	40		13,200	Speck 1919:59
	21,043.4		6,944,349	

[a] Payment cited as worth in English £, converted to fathoms at 6 beads/pence (£ = 20 shillings = 240 pence)

[b] The 6-foot (1.83 m) fathom = approximately 330 (5.5 mm) wampum beads

For the conquered coastal Algonquians, the Pequot War brought drastic change. Absorption of their land and labor into the colonial economy accelerated the breakdown of cultural traditions and relationships within and among coastal communities. Coerced to pay "acceptable" wampum according to coinage standards, they produced millions of almost uniformly sized beads for Iroquois fur suppliers. For the Iroquois, in contrast, still located at the edge of the periphery, it was the period of greatest prosperity, a golden age, when great quantities of tribute wampum reached their villages and were woven into belts. By the end of the seventeenth century, however, the Iroquois too would be attacked as the fur frontier moved west. Wampum now made on colonial lathes would follow the new periphery.

Pequot Survival

The Pequots faced their time of troubles from the War of 1637 onward; nevertheless, the Pequots survived. In Part Three of this book, five authors explain how and in what ways the Pequots' identity persisted from 1637 to the early 1970s.

Laurence M. Hauptman describes the origins of the War of 1637 and the war of extermination directed at these Indians. The Pequots did survive with remembrances of what had befallen them. Hauptman shows how contemporary Pequots, as is true of other victims of genocide, make use of their great tragedy to deal with the contemporary world they live in. Today's Pequots are state-building, redeeming their nation after three hundred and fifty years of living in a diaspora. Their relationships with their Indian and non-Indian neighbors are still significantly affected by the horrors of 1637. To Hauptman, the past is a present reality that helps fuel a modern rebirth of the Pequot tribe.

In Chapter 6, Neal Salisbury focuses on the forty years between the War of 1637 and King Philip's War. Salisbury sees the unifying theme of this period as economic: for more than two decades after the War of 1637, wampum from New England, which had been previously controlled by the Pequots, supported Iroquois diplomacy and ritual while the Mohawks contributed decisively to the balance of power in the Puritan colonies. These exchange networks constituted a countervailing tendency toward peace and stability in southern New England. By emphasizing the role that the Mohawks played in New England during this period, Salisbury—in the words of Alden Vaughan—reminded the reader "that political boundaries are almost always arbitrary and that the inhabitants of northeastern North America three and a half centuries ago paid little attention to lines drawn on imperial maps as they pursued their own military, economic, and social interests." While Salisbury gives us an overall framework for events during this fragile peace, he also traces the establishment of the two Pequot reservations in Ledyard and its environs—the Mashantucket in the mid-1660s and the Paucatuck in the mid-1680s—as well as the developing Pequot-English alliance that came to fruition in King Philip's War between 1675 and 1677.

Kevin A. McBride analyzes the changes in the Mashantucket Pequot Reservation community between 1667 and 1900. McBride, an archaeologist, makes use of a wide range of sources including oral history and the colonial records of Connecticut. He gives the reader a clear picture of the Pequot population; the number, locations, and size of villages and forts; the number and distribution of sachems; the location of cornfields; hunting and fishing strategies; social and political organization; housing styles and patterns; and the roles of Pequot women. He shows how each changed over time.

Importantly, McBride's article also demonstrates another side of Pequot survival. The Mashantucket Pequot Ethnohistoric Project is unique since it is the only major archaeological undertaking in the United States exclusively funded by an American Indian nation. Thus, contemporary Pequots, in their modern experiment in state-building, see the value of working closely with academics to uncover and elucidate their past.

Jack Campisi, who drafted the Mashantucket Pequot Fed-

eral Acknowledgment Petition, traces Pequot-Hartford relations since the late seventeenth century. He shows how the Pequots survived increasing pressures. In 1674 there were three
hundred male Pequots. Their few warriors joined with the English against the Wampanoags and Narragansetts in King
Philip's War as part of a survival strategy and out of economic
necessity. During the eighteenth, nineteenth, and twentieth
centuries, the Pequots, through their tribal council, frequently
challenged the authority or honesty of their "overseers" and
asked for their dismissal. Pequot political leadership survived
among core families and respected elders, who often were
women. These leaders took steps to protect their land base
and direct tribal affairs; nevertheless, they at times found
themselves powerless, as in 1855 when the Connecticut General Assembly passed the act that provided for the sale of the
bulk of the Mashantucket Pequot Reservation without tribal
consent. The Pequots clung to a tenuous tribal existence in
part because of money from this sale and from revenues from
their major cottage industry, basketry, which declined after
1900. By 1935 only forty-two Pequots remained, of whom
only nine lived on the reservation. Because of the efforts of two
sisters, Elizabeth George Plouffe and Martha George Langevin
Ellal, from the 1930s onward, the Pequots held onto their
shrinking land base. In the 1970s descendants of these two
women began the tribal political, economic, and social revival
that is continuing today.

   In the concluding Chapter 9 in Part Three, William S. Simmons, a folklorist of the New England Indian experience, turns
our attention to Pequot oral literature. Legends float in a kind
of twilight between what may really have happened and what
people believe to have happened, but convey one generation's
interpretation to the next; they open our eyes to the insiders'
point of view. Folklore is a basic, essential part of the historical
record of New England Indians, and conveys the spirit of the
culture when other phenomena, such as language, have long
disappeared. Simmons captures the enduring quality of Pequot culture by carefully analyzing the stories he has collected

from both Mashantucket and Paucatuck Pequots. The texts that he has assembled convey, among other things, a special sense of place, ancient medicinal beliefs, and commonly held Pequot lore, encouraging a better appreciation of these Indians' culture.

CHAPTER 5

The Pequot War and Its Legacies

By Laurence M. Hauptman

The Pequot War of 1637 is one of the most important events in early American history. It was the first serious conflict between colonizers and the indigenous populations in New England. The War, which nearly exterminated one of the most powerful Indian groups in New England, opened southeastern Connecticut to English colonization and established English hegemony over the Indians of southern New England, allowing future Puritan missionary endeavors in the region.[1] Some historians have even suggested that the War was the major turning point in the history of Indian-white relations in colonial America because it marked the end of a great opportunity to see if Indians and whites "could live with themselves, each other, and the land."[2] Some historians have interpreted the conflict as a rationalization of racial violence toward Indians in general and as the basis for later arguments for manifest destiny.[3] Moreover, in a recent account, one prominent historian states that the War created exaggerated tensions and dysfunctional behavior in one community, Wethersfield, contributing to the Puritans' excessive concern over witchcraft and leading them to persecute witches from the 1640s onward.[4]

The Pequot War has produced vociferous debate by those

69

interpreting the event.[5] Interpretations have followed historians' changing views of Puritanism, the Indians of New England, and the nature of Anglo-Indian relations. In more recent
years the new methodology of ethnohistory has provided
new insights into the conflict. Nevertheless, historians have
disagreed about every facet of the War, including its origins;
the Puritan and Indian motivations, conduct, and aims during
the battle; the racism and the economics involved in Puritan
Indian-policy decisions; and the relationship of the Pequots to
their Indian neighbors.

This essay was conceived in 1982 and 1983 after discussions held in Ledyard, New Paltz, and Philadelphia with
Richard ("Skip") Hayward, tribal chairman of the Mashantucket Pequot Tribe of Connecticut. I can vividly recall one
meeting held at the Mr. Pizza Restaurant with Chairman Hayward and ethnohistorian Jack Campisi. After discussing a
general outline for a conference on Pequot history as well as
its educational aims, Chairman Hayward began to shift the
conversation to the English colonial army's burning of Mystic
Fort in 1637 and the decimation of his people during the
battle and the ensuing war. I was fascinated by the discussion.
At a time when the contemporary Mashantucket Pequots were
experiencing a revival and achieving federal recognition, Chairman Hayward was sincerely concerned and inquisitive about
the tragedy that befell his people nearly 350 years earlier. We
three sat and reflected upon the Pequot historical experience,
comparing and contrasting the events of 1637 with incidents
of genocide in the twentieth century. Although we did not
discover any specific or universal truths, the discussion did
prompt me to shift from Iroquois research and read more
about the Pequot War.[6]

Consequently, I decided to focus on how contemporary Pequots make use of the tragic events of 1637 to build their
modern-day tribal existence. Historians and anthropologists
visiting today's Mashantucket Pequot community get the distinct impression that these terrible past events are still very
much a present reality to these Indians. The ways in which the

Pequots, who are always conscious of the War of 1637, commemorate this tragedy, interact with both their Indian and
non-Indian neighbors and build the modern-day community,
are similar to other survival experiences after genocide.[7]

In the early years of the seventeenth century, the Pequot Indians had fifteen villages in southeastern Connecticut, located
along the coast between Niantic Bay and the Pawcatuck River
and along the Thames and Mystic rivers. One of their two
main villages was Mystic Fort, situated on the Mystic River; the
other was two miles southwest at Fort Hill overlooking Noank.[8]
At approximately the time of the initial European penetration
of southern New England, the Pequots were also expanding their territory and their trade networks, as far west as
present-day Hartford, to the coast between New Haven and
Charlestown, Rhode Island, and to eastern Long Island and
the environs of Block Island.[9]

In 1632 the Pequots made their first recorded contact with
Europeans, and in the next five years these Indians' lives were
to be transformed beyond recognition by European policies
and by Indian intratribal and intertribal politics. By 1633 both
the English and the Dutch were already seeking trade advantages on the Connecticut River. During the winter of 1634–
1635 the English established Pyquag (now Wethersfield), and
in 1635 they built Fort Saybrook at the mouth of the Connecticut River. In 1636 the inhabitants of three Massachusetts
Bay towns migrated to the Connecticut Valley—Watertown to
Wethersfield, Dorchester to Natianuck (Windsor), and New-
towne to Saukiog (Hartford). In the same year Springfield was
established as an English outpost on the Connecticut River.
Importantly, in the mid-1630s the Pequots and Narragansetts
became involved in a war for domination of southwestern New
England, while at approximately the same time a major smallpox epidemic hit the same region.

A murder in 1634 was to cast a long shadow and to set in
motion a series of events that culminated in the Pequot War.
Tatobem, a Pequot sachem, was captured and later killed by
Dutch traders, even though the Indians had paid to ransom

him. In retaliation, the Pequots attacked the Dutch trading
post, The Hope, in the lower Connecticut Valley near modern-
day Hartford. Soon after, John Stone, a Virginia trader, was
murdered by Indians, most probably by Western Niantics, a
lower Connecticut River tribe that paid tribute to the Pequots.
In order to bring peace to the Connecticut Valley, Sassacus,
the new Pequot chief sachem, worked out an accord with
Massachusetts Bay officials. The Pequots agreed to hand over
Stone's killers, to allow English purchases of land and settlement in the Connecticut Valley, and to pay a substantial in-
demnity of four hundred fathoms of wampum, forty beaver
skins, and thirty otter skins. In return, the Puritans promised to
send them a trader. John Oldham, the English trader sent,
was subsequently murdered off the shores of Block Island.[10]
Although the Indians in the environs of Block Island were
Eastern Niantics and Narragansetts, the English retribution for
the murder of Oldham fell heaviest upon the Pequots.

   In August, 1636, John Endicott organized a punitive expedition against the Pequots, which soon became the first military
attempt by the English to expand their power over the Indians
of New England. Endicott sacked Block Island and then, with
ninety volunteers, sailed into Pequot Harbor. He demanded that
the Pequots hand over Stone's and Oldham's killers and that
the Indians provide one thousand fathoms of wampum tribute,
as well as Indian children to be held as hostages to ensure
a future peace. After a brief skirmish and looting, the Puritan army departed for Massachusetts Bay, leaving the newly
established English towns in the Connecticut Valley susceptible to the brunt of Pequot reprisals. Nevertheless, the Pequots were weakened by an internal crisis and the political
in-fighting between Sassacus and his rival Uncas. The Mohegans, under Uncas's leadership, soon joined the newly formed
anti-Pequot alliance of English and Narragansetts.

   On April 23, 1637, the Pequots attacked Wethersfield, destroying much property, killing nine English settlers, including
three women, and taking two young girls as prisoners. This attack became the excuse for a full-scale Massachusetts and

Connecticut colonial war of extermination against the Pequots. Just before dawn on May 26, 1637, an army of English
soldiers led by Captains John Mason and John Underhill,
along with Mohegan-Pequots under Uncas and a contingent
of Narragansetts and Eastern Niantics, assaulted the Pequots'
eastern fort on the Mystic River. This attack, which occurred
while most of the Pequot men were away, resulted in the
deaths of between three hundred and seven hundred women,
children, and old men. Many of the Indians were killed when
Mason ordered the wigwams burned. The English and their
allied Indians surrounded the village and cut down those trying to flee. During the massacre, which lasted less than an
hour, all but seven Pequots perished. Two Englishmen were
killed and twenty wounded, while twenty Indian allies were also
wounded. Captain Underhill later reflected on the events of
that day:

Captain Mason entering into a wigwam, brought out a firebrand,
after he had wounded many in the house. Then he set fire on the
west side, where he entered; myself set fire on the south end with a
train of powder. The fires of both meeting in the centre of the fort,
blazed most terribly, and burnt all in the space of half an hour. Many
courageous fellows were unwilling to come out, and fought most
desperately through the palisades, so as they were scorched and
burnt with the very flame, and were deprived of their arms—in regard the fire burnt their very bowstrings—and so perished valiantly.
Mercy did they deserve for their valor, could we have had opportunity
to have bestowed it. Many were burnt in the fort, both men, women,
and children. Others forced out, and came in troops to the Indians,
twenty and thirty at a time, which our soldiers received and enter-
tained with the point of the sword. Down fell men, women, and children; those that scaped us, fell into the hands of the Indians that
were in the rear of us. It is reported by themselves, that there were
about four hundred souls in this fort, and not above five of them escaped out of our hands. Great and doleful was the bloody sight to
the view of young soldiers that never had been in war, to see so
many souls lie gasping on the ground, so thick, in some places, that
you could hardly pass along. It may be demanded, Why should you
be so furious? (as some have said). Should not Christians have more

Based on a map by Paul Hunnebeck

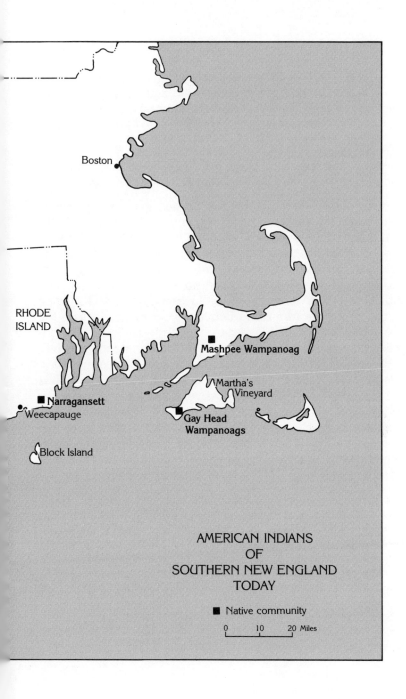

Boston

RHODE
ISLAND

Mashpee Wampanoag

Martha's
Vineyard

Narragansett
Weecapauge

Gay Head
Wampanoags

Block Island

AMERICAN INDIANS
OF
SOUTHERN NEW ENGLAND
TODAY

■ Native community

0   10   20 Miles

mercy and compassion? But I would refer you to David's war. When a people is grown to such a height of blood, and sin against God and man, and all confederates in the action, there he hath no respect to persons, but harrows them, and saws them, and puts them to the sword, and the most terriblest death that may be. Sometimes the Scripture declareth women and children must perish with their parents. Sometimes the case alters; but we will not dispute it now. We had sufficient light from the word of God for our proceedings.[11]

Many of the Pequots not in the fort during the conflagration were captured, killed in skirmishes, or executed in the months that followed. Others were enslaved, assigned to the "protection" of colonists or to Indian leaders—Uncas, the Mohegan; Miantonomo, the Narragansett; or Ninigret, the Eastern Niantic—or sold into slavery and sent to Bermuda and the West Indies. The War formally ended in September, 1638, when sachems for the remaining Pequots were forced to sign the Treaty of Hartford, also called the Tripartite Treaty. By the humiliating provisions of that accord, the Pequot nation was officially declared to be dissolved. Even the use of the designation "Pequot" was soon outlawed by colonial authorities.[12] Thus the Pequots—viewed as aggressive, bellicose, and blasphemous, even satanic, by the English in the Connecticut and Massachusetts Bay colonies—were almost erased from history. According to a Puritan account of 1643, divine intervention had saved New England and had punished the Indian transgressors:

And in the war, which we made against them [the Pequots], God's hand from heaven was so manifested that a very few of our men in a short time pursued through the wilderness, slew, and took prisoners about 1,400 of them, even all they could find, to the great terror and amazement of all the Indians to this day; so that the name of the Pequots (as of Amalech) is blotted out from under heaven, there being not one that is, or (at least) dare call himself a Pequot.[13]

What befell the Pequots in 1637 and afterward clearly fits the most widely accepted definition of genocide, one set by the United Nations Convention on Genocide in 1948:

In the present Convention, genocide means any of the following acts committed with intent to destroy, in whole or in part, a national, ethnical, racial or religious group, as such:

(a) Killing members of the group;

(b) Causing serious bodily or mental harm to members of the group;

(c) Deliberately inflicting on the group conditions of life calculated to bring about its physical destruction in whole or in part;

(d) Imposing measures intended to prevent births within the group;

(e) Forcibly transferring children of the group to another group.[14]

Modern Pequots use this tragedy to overcome tragedy. They see their present-day successes as the long culmination of holding actions and survival strategies developed over the centuries. The War of 1637 is thus indelibly marked in the contemporary Pequot's psyche and has influenced nearly every phase of the tribal renaissance over the past decade and a half. Moreover, Pequots can hardly escape their past even if they try, since their reservations date from the mid-1660s and the site of the Mystic Fort is only ten miles down the road from the reservation. The Pequot cemetery also contains the bones of ancestors who rebuilt the community after the Pequot War. Many of their non-Indian neighbors in southern New England, as well as their Indian neighbors—the Mohegans at Norwich and Uncastown, Connecticut, and the Narragansetts at Saunderstown, Rhode Island—are the descendants of people who enslaved and nearly annihilated them in the seventeenth century.[15]

You can visit the Mashantucket Pequots and witness for yourselves the tremendous strides that these native peoples have achieved in the past decade and a half. Until the early 1970s the state of Connecticut had overseers and the vestiges of a colonial administration to supervise the affairs of the Pequots. As late as 1976 the Pequots had only 213.9 acres of land. Today the Pequots have over 1,600 acres as a result of lobbying, conscious public-relations initiatives, the efforts of sympathetic non-Indian politicians, such as the late Governor

Ella Grasso, Congressman Sam Gedjenson, and former Senator Lowell Weicker, and the energetic leadership of the Mashantucket Pequot Tribal Council.[16] In less than a decade they
have built four housing complexes, a health center, a fire station, a lighted ball field, and an 1,800-seat bingo hall; established a restaurant and gravel industry; organized a major historical conference; and begun plans for a tribal museum. It
may truly be said that they have started to rebuild their ancient
homeland—from two women clinging to a shrinking land base
and living there three decades ago, to a modern computerized
tribal government with nearly 150 people on the payroll.[17]
Mashantucket Pequot tribal members regard the Mashantucket Pequot Historical Conference, the museum, curriculum
development, archaeological exploration, ethnohistorical research, and historical preservation as nation building. What
may appear to casual observers as a Pequot "edifice complex" is really a master plan, state-building in its grandest
sense. The Pequot diaspora is now over, redemption is at
hand, and a new future is planned after 350 years of tribal
misery.[18]

Mashantucket Pequot council members are not overly concerned with the ritualistic side of life, but are pragmatic leaders
interested primarily in tribal survival. By providing land, housing, health care, and economic activity on the reservation, they
are fostering the gradual return of other Pequots. By attaining
federal recognition for the Mashantucket in 1983, they have
eased this return, have generated pride, have taken their right-
ful place in Indian country, and have ensured Pequot survival
by establishing a federal-Indian trust relationship. By building
a museum with a major focus on the Pequot life of the seventeenth century, by sponsoring an historical conference, and by
developing curriculum materials sensitive to the Pequot perspective, they are revising the earlier English colonial portraits
of Pequots as the "children of Satan," correcting the generally
held view that all Pequots were exterminated, celebrating Pequot survival, and teaching great moral-historical lessons

about the genocide of 1637. By building networks of support through cooperating with federal, state, and local officials in tribal planning endeavors and raising $20,000 from tribal bingo for the United Way of Southeastern Connecticut, they have countered the long-held historical view that their Pequot ancestors were bellicose and bloodthirsty Indian imperialists who had to be "taught a lesson" by the early English colonists at Mystic Fort in 1637.[19]

A visitor to the Mashantucket Pequot Reservation receives the impression that the events of the seventeenth century are very much alive in the community partly because of the tribe's extensive sponsorship of archaeological and ethnohistorical research. The Pequots' use of the tools of applied anthropology may be unique for an American Indian community in the United States.[20] Visitors in the tribal office complex soon find themselves discussing nearly every aspect of Pequot history— from the War of 1637 to Pequot genealogy, to Indian whaling stories, to the prominent modern-day Pequot Elizabeth George, to changes in Indian life over the past two decades. When walking on the reservation, the visitor sees the touchstones of tribal survival all around, from the Old Homestead, or Beehive—the oldest house on the reservation—to the new facilities built during the last decade.[21] I am not the only visitor to be impressed by the rootedness of Pequot existence and the continued importance of the War of 1637. When anthropologist Ethel Boissevain visited Mashantuckets before a research trip to Bermuda in 1976 to ascertain what happened to Indians sold into slavery in 1637, the contemporary Pequots in Ledyard expressed keen interest in the research and gave her a message to bring to those on the island: "Invite them to come back and join us here."[22]

There are other indications that the events of 1637 still shape the Pequot world. Today, for example, Pequots appear to have closer ties to Massachusetts Wampanoags and Maine Passamaquoddies and Penobscots than their immediate Mohegan and Narragansett neighbors. Thus modern Pequots cannot completely forget the Sassacus-Uncas rivalry, the Mohegan-English alliance in the War of 1637, and the subsequent enslavement of the Pequots.[23]

Diverse peoples around the world have commemorated their tragedies and sought land, money, and respect as compensation for injustices. At times these same peoples are criticized for a morbid preoccupation with tragedy; nevertheless, they have persevered and have constructed memorials to the victims, established museums, held conferences, prepared special study programs, encouraged research and created research centers, and institutionalized their genocide by holding an annual memorial day. Except for a memorial day, the Pequots have followed the same course.

On October 18, 1983, President Ronald Reagan signed a bill awarding the Mashantucket Pequot Tribe of Connecticut federal recognition and creating a trust fund to allow Pequots to purchase land.[24] The *New York Times,* one of the nation's leading newspapers, carried the following headline about the tribe's achievement: "Pequot Indians Prevail in Battle Begun in 1637."[25] The Pequots arose out of the ashes of Mystic Fort, and their world view has been conditioned by that fact. Yet, despite the immediate assessment expressed in the *New York Times*'s headline, only time will tell if the Pequots' present experiment in nation-building is permanent, whether it will completely counter the effects of the centuries of tribal history since the War of 1637.

CHAPTER 6

Indians and Colonists in Southern New England after the Pequot War

An Uneasy Balance

By Neal Salisbury

Historians have had difficulty discussing native-settler relations during the period between the Pequot and King Philip wars. For one thing, they have been unable to establish a unifying framework for the period from 1637 to 1676. Alden Vaughan divided Indian-white relations between the wars into four categories: political-military, legal, commercial, and missionary. These are neat semantic distinctions, but they overlap repeatedly because they do not reflect reality. Francis Jennings focused primarily on political-military and missionary relations, subordinating legal relations to those two aspects and overlooking commercial relations altogether. Both historians also have difficulty interpreting the period: they depict the Narragansetts and Niantics as always on the brink of war with the colonists, yet none of those scares developed into war. When war finally broke out again between Indians and English, it initially involved the Wampanoags and Plymouth, who had previously enjoyed the oldest intercultural partnership in the region.[1]

In order to explain these paradoxes, historians need to rethink the assumptions they bring to interpretations of native-settler relations in the mid-seventeenth-century. Rather than focusing solely on the issues that fill the official colonial records and the writings of elites, they need to pay more attention to the processes of everyday life. And rather than looking only at intraregional relationships, they need to consider those between New Englanders and people outside the region. After all, "New England" was the invention of the English colonizers: its boundaries had no meaning to the Indians. By so widening the inquiry, a very different picture emerges.[2]

From the end of the Pequot War of 1637 through the early 1660s—the space of an entire generation—a New England economy flourished that differed markedly from that which emerged later in the century. The era was one in which natives participated fully by producing goods for export, providing support services and land to settlers, and by consuming imported goods. Although deprived, to one degree or another, of the complete political autonomy of the presettlement period, the Indians' land bases continued to provide their subsistence needs while they participated in reciprocal exchanges with other Indians as well as with the English. In this sense their relationships with the colonists at midcentury should be termed ones of interdependence rather than dependence. But the terms of these relationships differed sharply from one locale to another depending on the extent to which the two peoples competed for the same resources, particularly land.

Direct contact with farming settlers was minimal for those interior Indian bands engaged in large-scale fur trading. As immigrants filled up the area around Boston in the early 1630s, English traders moved their posts inland, positioning themselves on major water routes. Of these, the most successful were the Pynchons, father William and son John, who moved from Roxbury to found Springfield on the Connecticut River in 1636. Ethnohistorian Peter Thomas has shown how the elder Pynchon declined to join the new Connecticut Colony, instead preferring political ties with the more safely distant Massachusetts Bay. As a result, he was made a magistrate over the Connecticut Valley with virtually dictatorial powers to match the economic power he brought in the form of capital and trade connections. The Pynchons traded cloth and other goods not only for pelts but also for land for themselves and the town at Springfield, maize to supply their employees, and wampum— in heavy demand both by Indians throughout the Northeast and by currency-hungry settlers. During the peak *recorded* years between 1632 and 1658—the volume in years pre- ceding was probably higher—John Pynchon's shipments of beaver pelts alone weighed nearly 14,000 pounds, bringing gross profits of nearly £7,000. While insignificant compared to that of the Dutch on the Hudson or of the French on the St. Lawrence, Pynchon's volume made him one of the wealthiest and most powerful men in New England. For the Pocum- tucks, Norwottucks, Woronocos, and Agawams of the middle Connecticut Valley, direct contact with the Pynchons brought the power and prestige that came from overseeing the flow of goods between southern New England and Indians on the north and west.[3]

For other native bands, colonization was a more mixed blessing. The Mohegans in Connecticut, the Narragansetts and Eastern Niantics in Rhode Island, and the Pokanoket Wampanoags in Plymouth likewise served as intermediaries between the networks of indigenous exchange and English accumulation. But whereas their fur-trading counterparts re- sided beyond the pale of English settlement, these groups lived in greater geographic and social proximity to the new- comers and therefore were tied more closely, politically and legally, to colony governments. Besides dealing in furs, they furnished their new neighbors with wampum, use rights or quitclaims to land, and labor services, for example, guiding cattle drives, hunting wolves, and building fences.[4] In return, the Indians received a wide assortment of cloth, metal, and glass goods, which they employed for both ritual and utili- tarian purposes.[5] At the same time, they were subject to legis- lation that restricted certain subsistence activities that might interfere with activities of the settlers, and which segregated them socially from the colonists.[6]

In spite of such impediments to their autonomy, tribes of

southern New England—Mohegans, Narragansetts, Niantics, and Pokanoket Wampanoags—were the most formidable native groups in the mid-seventeenth century. Each not only retained a substantial land base for itself but also used its relationship with a colony government to maximum advantage in its dealings with other Indians. While the rivalry between the Narragansetts and Mohegans was in part an expression of that between Rhode Island and the United Colonies (Massachusetts, Connecticut, Plymouth, and New Haven), its roots were in a struggle that began early in the century, before the arrival of the settlers, among native groups over trade with the Dutch.[7]

The range of choices was narrowest for those Indian communities most removed from the centers of the fur and wampum trade—in eastern Massachusetts, where English settlement was most concentrated, and on geographically isolated Martha's Vineyard. Puritan missionaries such as John Eliot in Massachusetts Bay and the Thomas Mayhews, senior and junior, sought to convert these Indians not just to Christianity but to a "settled" way of life based on household production of food and handicrafts and the explicit renunciation of native customs and beliefs.[8] But the most tangible effects of such conversions, as far as most colonists were concerned, were not theological nor cultural but material. "Praying Indians" were induced to part with substantial portions of their land and to provide the unskilled and semiskilled labor of themselves and their children to English merchants and employers.[9]

At the same time, the missionaries served as protectors against even further losses of land and other abuses from English neighbors, from tribute-demanding Indians of other bands, and from powwows and other leaders in their own bands who resisted pressures to convert.[10] This protection afforded a communal core around which these Indians were able to maintain and reconstruct familiar social relationships. Leadership in praying Indian communities generally remained in the same lineages as earlier. Converts continued their familiar subsistence rounds, and they exchanged many of the pieces of clothing and the agricultural, carpentry, and sewing implements that they received to encourage their "civilization" with other, non-Christian natives. They were buried with these items and other personal possessions of both Indian and European manufacture.[11] Even their "conversions" to Puritanism, undertaken in response to the failure of shamans to prevent or adequately explain disease, epidemics, and the collapse of the older social world, were often less permanent and more syncretic than the missionaries wished.[12]

Despite the sharp differences in their political and economic situations, natives throughout southern New England countered political domination and expansionist pressures by capitalizing on the colonists' needs for goods, services, and markets. As a result, they maintained their subsistence economies as well as their communal identities. But the new conditions also brought change. By the late 1630s the epidemics, the "Great Migration" of English settlers, and the Pequot War had depleted and scattered native communities. Inequalities in population and in access to pelts, wampum, European goods, and English favor put pressure on norms of reciprocity among both individuals and groups. Individual natives made a point of displaying European cloth, glass, and metal goods in life and in death—in their graves—to signify their roles as agents of intercultural exchange. These tendencies were certainly reinforced by the English insistence on dealing with individual leaders, rather than entire groups, an insistence that helped propel such individuals as Massasoit of the Pokanoket Wampanoags and Uncas of the Mohegans to positions of prominence.[13] In this setting, native bands had to combine numbers, geographic position, and political savvy in order to survive. Particularly impressive were those whose group identities had been most seriously threatened by the events of the 1630s—the Mohegans, Pequots, and Massachusetts. By using the protection afforded by their English patrons, these groups rebounded from humiliation and near-extinction to reemerge as distinct entities during or after the Pequot War.[14]

Native settler exchanges also enabled certain Englishmen

to become intercultural mediators and to consolidate their standing in settler society. By trading cloth from England and wampum from New England's south coast for pelts, land, and maize, the Pynchons reinforced their positions both as inter-colonial and overseas traders and as regional political leaders. Though an ordained minister, Roger Williams also traded with Indians. After he was exiled from Massachusetts Bay in 1636, he used his trade connections to help construct the unique re-lationship between New England's strongest Indian alliance and Rhode Island, its most independent colony. Another trader, Thomas Mayhew, Sr., had acted as factor for London mer-chant Matthew Craddock in the 1630s at Medford, Massachu-setts. In the early 1640s, Mayhew purchased two competing English-held patents for the island of Martha's Vineyard. There he reestablished his family's lost manor of Tisbury and began preaching to the island's fifteen hundred Indian inhabitants. John Eliot, minister at Roxbury, learned the Massachusetts language from an Indian slave and then began preaching to surviving bands in eastern Massachusetts. As a result of his efforts, English funds and goods began pouring into New En-gland in support of missionary endeavors.

Thus southern New England in the mid-seventeenth cen-tury was crisscrossed by a maze of exchange networks involv-ing both natives and settlers, characterized by both reciprocity and profits, and carrying a wide range of goods and services produced by both indigenous and European peoples.[15] De-spite the pervasiveness of those networks, the precarious bal-ance of power that emerged in southern New England after the Pequot War was not simply an intraregional affair. It also involved outsiders—Abenakis, Mahicans, and, above all, Mo-hawks. The recorded Mohawk role began during the Pequot War. After the Mystic Fort massacre, the Mohawks captured and executed the sachem Sassacus and several dozen other Pequots seeking their support, allying instead with the Nar-ragansetts. In so doing, they sealed the fate of the Pequots and their replacement by the new colony of Connecticut as a major power alongside the Narragansetts on Long Island Sound.[16]

The Pequot War had no sooner ended than tensions developed between the Narragansetts on the one hand and Massachusetts Bay, Connecticut, and their Mohegan allies on the other. One bone of contention was control over the distribution of wampum. The colonists sought wampum in part as a substitute for scarce English currency, but for all parties, wampum served as a symbolic expression of allegiance. Since the English were attempting to colonize the region, they sought to subordinate the Narragansetts and other natives to themselves by extracting tribute in the form of wampum payments. To the Narragansetts, however, such payments were gifts freely presented to potential allies with the expectation that they would be reciprocated. During the 1640s the commissioners of the United Colonies discovered time and again that the Narragansetts and their allies had given substantial amounts of wampum to the Mohawks while defaulting on payments to the English, and that the Mohawks had expressed support for the Narragansetts against the colonists.[17] The commissioners assumed that these presentations represented gifts exchanged by the Narragansetts for Mohawk military support against the English colonies. That the Narragansetts were hostile to the United Colonies was indisputable, but their hostility stemmed primarily from the commissioners' efforts to reduce, with the aggressive assistance of the Mohegans and their sachem, Uncas, the Narragansetts' land base and political autonomy.

Only in 1651 did the commissioners finally acknowledge the importance of the Mohawks to the colonies' welfare. The occasion was their rejection of a proposal by New France for an Anglo-French military alliance against the Five Iroquois Nations. Gabriel Druillettes, the French emissary, argued that recent Iroquois attacks against the Abenakis and Sokokis represented an immediate danger to English trade on the Kennebec River and a future threat to the colonies themselves.

The commissioners rejected the proposal. Not only did they have no quarrel with the Mohawks and no desire to precipitate one, they recalled that during the Pequot War the Mohawks "shewed a small Respecte" toward them and had maintained amicable relations since. To make war on them now would only risk alienating the New England allies of the Five Nations and endanger both English settlements and Puritan mission-ary efforts among the Indians.[18]

Three years later, when the United Colonies again felt pro-voked by the Narragansetts, Roger Williams reminded the Mas-sachusetts General Court of just how important the Mohawk-Narragansett connection was to the peace and stability of colonial society. These "are the two great bodies of Indians in this country, and they are confederates, and long have been, and they both yet are friendly and peaceabl[e] to the English," Williams argued. If the colonies went to war with one without making sure of the loyalty of the other, they would surely be defeated.[19]

While the Iroquois fought the Beaver Wars in the north, the Mohawks constituted a source of peace and stability in south-ern New England. Close Mohawk ties to the Narragansetts and to the Pocumtucks and other Connecticut Valley bands gave the United Colonies pause in their efforts to reduce Narragan-sett power and influence on Long Island Sound. As we have seen, the wampum that flowed from New England via the Mohawks to the other Iroquois tribes was a principal compo-nent of this connection. But, what flowed the other way besides the Five Nations' reputation for ferocity? In repudiating Druil-lettes' proposed alliance against the Iroquois, the commis-sioners maintained that "liveing att a distance from the Sea," the Mohawks "have littel entercourse in these parts."[20] Yet that claim was belied by other evidence that the commissioners presumably did not wish to publicize, especially in New France.

Two of the most active centers of Indian-English trade in the mid-seventeenth century were the Massachusetts portion of the Connecticut River Valley and Narragansett Bay. At both locales, English traders obtained furs from Indian allies of the Mohawks in exchange for European goods.[21] Given the amount of wampum that was passing from these groups to the Mohawks, the Iroquois were almost certainly reciprocating with skins obtained in the Beaver Wars. These skins kept the New England fur trade alive longer than the local beaver population alone could have done. The English merchants were by no means unaware of the Mohawks' commercial importance. From the time of Springfield's establishment in 1636, the Dutch traders at Albany had decried the Pynchons' success in diverting Mohawk and Mahican trade to Connecticut.[22] Indeed, John Pynchon was later involved in a series of efforts to establish an English post on or near the Hudson. And for most of the 1640s, Richard Smith actually directed his Narragansett Bay operation from a home in New Amsterdam, where the Mohawks' commercial role was well understood.[23]

Although native exchanges were being integrated ever more closely with colonial commerce, the period from the 1640s through the mid-1660s was one of relative stability in Indian-white relations and even of increased political maneuvering for many bands. Despite the warnings of some colonists during the 1650s of complacency in the face of growing anti-English sentiment and strength among some south-coast and Connecticut Valley natives, there were no significant shifts in colonial policies for more than another decade.[24] The very real tensions between the Narragansetts on the one hand and the United Colonies and Mohegans on the other never developed into war because they were offset by the exchanges of furs, wampum, and European goods linking English traders to the Narragansetts and their allies and, through them, to the Mohawks. In the face of the recurrent war scares so often emphasized by historians, these exchange networks constituted a countervailing tendency toward peace and stability in southern New England. So also, for a time, did the availability of land to satisfy the immigrants. This is not to suggest that English land hunger disappeared after the Pequot War. On the contrary, a market in land had developed that encouraged geographic mobility and speculation, much of the latter by merchants and wealthy gentry on a scale modest by English standards, but substantial in the New England context. Behind these developments lay the land hunger that had impelled the settlers to migrate in the first place. But this expansion took place on land obtained from Indians in the 1620s and 1630s or—on a more limited basis—from client bands thereafter, rather than as a result of additional military aggression.[25]

The termination of native-settler coexistence after 1660 had several causes, but certainly one was the virtual extinction of the local fur-bearing animal population because of commercial overhunting. As a result, southern New England natives were reduced to roles as middlemen in the fur trade between the English and Indians north of the region. Already, merchant-gentry traders such as John Pynchon, John Winthrop, Jr., and Richard Smith had begun selling and renting land procured from fur-poor Indians to whom they furnished credit and supplies, and from whom they obtained agricultural surpluses and timber products for export. At the same time, Pynchon and other New England traders sought to establish direct contacts with the Mahicans and Mohawks of New Netherland to circumvent those New England natives who had formerly served as their intermediaries.[26]

The decline of the Indians' roles as fur producers was accompanied by a decline in the demand for their wampum. The success of their overseas trade had brought New England's merchants a long-sought influx of English currency, leading the colonies to cease accepting wampum as legal tender. The merchants thereupon dumped their remaining reserves in New Netherland, where wampum still prevailed, in exchange for furs and Dutch goods. With a scarcity of guilders and an abundance of severely devalued wampum, New Netherland was beset with debt and inflation, and its merchants were unable to obtain sufficient supplies of goods to trade with their Dutch clients. The resulting decline in Iroquois demand for the beads undermined both the Dutch merchants and the New England Indians who had previously supplied them.[27]

As the ties that bound them to the Iroquois and English weakened, the Mohawks' former allies in southern New England and on the lower Hudson drew closer to their fellow Algonquian-speakers on the north—the Sokokis of the upper Connecticut Valley, the Abenakis of Maine, and the Montagnais of the St. Lawrence Valley—all of whom were allied with the French against the Five Nations. As a result, the cycle of highly destructive raids and counterraids that characterized Iroquois relations with these more northerly Algonquians expanded southward, beginning in 1622, and included the Pocumtucks, Norwottucks, and other middle Connecticut Valley groups. With the English conquest of New Netherland in 1664 and the escalation of Anglo-French imperial rivalry, the conflicts among Indians in the Northeast became more closely linked to those of the Europeans. Although severe tensions on each side made the actual conflict far more complicated than this, the basic configuration pitted Iroquois and English against the French and most other Indians south, east, and north of the Five Nations. For the southern New England groups that had previously traded and been allied with both English and Mohawk, the new configuration left them dangerously exposed to those erstwhile friends and isolated from any powerful source of outside support.[28]

Besides the Indians' declining commercial roles and their vulnerability to great-power rivalries originating outside the region was the filling of the demographic vacuum in which the earlier coexistence had flourished. The founding settlers were mostly families headed by parents who were between the late twenties and the early forties in age. The children of these migrants were generally very young; indeed, most were born in New England itself. Relatively few became husbands or wives in households independent of their parents' in the late 1640s and 1650s. But with marriage for New England men delayed until their mid-twenties or later, and with the settlers' high fertility and extraordinarily low mortality, a powerful backlog of potential households was created that began to be realized in the 1660s. Combined with this was the acceleration of tendencies among the settlers toward consolidation of plots, dispersal from town centers, increased concern for precise titles and boundaries, and definition of proprietary privilege.[29] It is in this context of renewed English land hunger that we must understand the proliferation of new towns in the 1660s and early 1670s in the Connecticut Valley and other former fur-trading areas.

These developments had a similarly direct impact on those native bands that had hitherto retained a measure of autonomy. The Pokanoket Wampanoags, the Narragansetts, the Niantics, the Mohegans, and other allies of one or another colony suddenly found that their patrons—along with other speculators and settlers—desired land above all else. The death of Massasoit of the Pokanoket Wampanoags in 1661 led to the accession of his sons, first Wamsutta and then Metacom, or King Philip, in 1664. The sons' reluctance to continue their father's policy of exclusive loyalty and land sales to Plymouth soon turned the half-century of friendship into a relationship rife with antagonism and tension. In central Massachusetts, between the Boston area and the Connecticut River Valley, lay "Nipmuck country," where a collection of bands had traded furs to all sides. By the late 1660s their lands too were the object of attention by speculators and prospective settlers. In Rhode Island, Roger Williams's retirement as a trader left the Narragansetts and Niantics exposed to powerful speculators, and even the loyal Mohegans of Connecticut felt the pressure. It was in this setting that Puritan missionaries, strengthened by a substantial injection of new funds from England in 1669, launched a new offensive. Most effective were Eliot among the Nipmucks and John Cotton, Jr., among some of the Pokanokets' recent Wampanoag allies. Eliot's success rested mainly on his ability to protect Nipmuck communities from tribute demands and military attacks by Niantics and Mohegans. Cotton went to constituent communities in the old Pokanoket alliance, now geographically fragmented beyond repair, and offered new sources of goods as well as spiritual solace to those who had seen their worlds collapse so suddenly.[30]

Hereafter, the story is a more familiar one because historians have found in war a tangible narrative framework. The economic, political, and cultural pressures on Indian autonomy culminated in the outbreak of King Philip's War in 1675. Essentially, the war was a loose-knit uprising by most of the bands inhabiting a swath of territory extending from both sides of Narragansett Bay northwest through "Nipmuck country" to the Connecticut River Valley. These Indians had continued to participate in a world of indigenous exchange even while growing increasingly tied to the colonial world. Metacom's own complaints to a Rhode Island Quaker peace delegation on the eve of the outbreak suggest that the movement was galvanized around the closely intertwined issues of land sales and autonomy. The loss of land and consequent onset of drunkenness among his people, and the arrogant and perfidious conduct of English political, legal, and religious figures, were the themes he reiterated most often. For Indians who lived closer to large concentrations of settlers and were cut off from this world—the missionized Indians (other than the Nipmucks) and the Pequots and Mohegans in Connecticut—the uprising could have little appeal. For them service on the English side held more promise.[31]

In the war itself the Pokanoket Wampanoags and their allies found themselves caught in a squeeze between the New England settlers and the Mohawks. Having inflicted a series of stunning surprise attacks on English settlements in the fall of 1675, Metacom and his followers sought the aid of a large body of Algonquian Indians from New York and Canada who had gathered at Hoosic, New York, in January 1676. But morale declined as epidemic diseases swept through the gathering. Then, with New York's backing, a well-armed body of Mohawks attacked, driving the fragmented and dispirited New England Indians back to their own region, where winter, additional disease casualties, and a revitalized colonial military effort finally defeated them, ensuring that New England would remain English.[32]

In sum, the middle decades of the seventeenth century in southern New England were simply a logical sequence between the Pequot and King Philip's wars, during which the relentless expansion of the English and retreat of the Indians took a less bellicose form. For the space of a generation, relations between the two groups were characterized by social segregation, to be sure, but also by economic interdependence. The result was an uneasy interface between indigenous interband exchange networks and the profit economies and state policies of the English. Moreover, the interface extended beyond New England to include other Indians, especially the Mohawks.

From the Indians' perspective, such connections were consistent with a deeply held belief in the importance of balance and reciprocity in social relations. They accepted the English and their goods as an enrichment of the Indians' world, not a replacement for it. As Roger Williams observed, the power or "excellency" that the Narragansetts and their neighbors called manitou could be found in human or beast, man or woman, Indian or English.[33] For the Mohawks, the wampum they obtained from New England enhanced their position within the Iroquois Confederacy during its wars with the Indian allies of New France. Life in the Five Nations during the 1640s and 1650s was marked by the escalation of warfare, diplomacy, death, and the adoption of captives into Iroquois families. As exemplified in the story of Deganawidah and Hiawatha, the Iroquois presented wampum "words" to clear the eyes, ears, throats, and minds of potential allies, erstwhile enemies, and the mourning relatives of those lost in epidemics and wars.[34]

The English, on the other hand, considered themselves a people apart. As "civilized" Christians, they assumed sovereignty over the region and its "savage" inhabitants and title to most of the land, with the long-range goal of displacing the natives. Yet, for a time, the English were unable to act fully on their assumptions. Just as the first Plymouth settlers depended on the friendship of Squanto and the Wampanoags, so those who arrived as part of the "Great Migration" of the 1630s depended on their ties with Indians to secure themselves and their society. When larger forces connected to Europe's expansion into North America finally enabled them to break free of their dependence, they relegated the natives to the margins of their society—and of their histories. The result was a rendering of the colonial past that, 350 years later, we are only beginning to question.

CHAPTER 7

The Historical Archaeology of the Mashantucket Pequots, 1637–1900

A Preliminary Analysis

By Kevin A. McBride

The research for this chapter is based in part on a larger effort to reconstruct Pequot cultural history from the late prehistoric period to the present. This effort, known as the Mashantucket Pequot Ethnohistory Project, includes oral history, archival research, and archaeology. Since it was begun in 1983, the project has focused primarily on the documentary history and archaeology of the Pequots from the early seventeenth century to the close of the Pequot War, and on the group of Indians that eventually became known as the Mashantucket Pequots. The principal goals of the documentary research have been to reconstruct the lifeways of the Pequots before the War and to provide a broader historical context for the interpretation of archaeological sites found on the Mashantucket Pequot Reservation in Ledyard, Connecticut. The documentary research has been the major source of pre-War information, but archaelogy conducted on the reservation has provided much information about the reservation between 1666 and 1900.

Much has been written about the Pequot War both as a singular event in colonial American history and as the beginning of a process that eventually resulted in the shattering of Native

American dominance in the region. Often overlooked in these accounts is the wealth of information available on Pequot culture from primary sources produced during the War, between August, 1636, and September, 1637, and from archaeological evidence of that period.

The archaeological data were collected from various surveys of early seventeenth-century sites in the area, including the Mashantucket Pequot Reservation; the Pequot territory in southeastern Connecticut, including Niantic Bay, the Thames and Mystic drainages, and coastal areas; and the site of the Mystic Fort, burned by the English during the Pequot War. The principal residences and occupation sites of the Pequots are believed to have been located between Niantic Bay on the west and the Pawcatuck River on the east. The northern boundary of Pequot settlements is less clear, but probably does not extend much farther north than Pachaug Pond in the present town of Griswold, Connecticut. The Ethnohistory Project also includes areas used by the Pequots for hunting, fishing, and planting. The Pequots appear to have used several islands in Long Island Sound for fishing and planting. Interior areas away from the coast and major drainages would also have been used for hunting.

Archaeological sites dating to the first half of the seventeenth century and located between the Thames and Pawcatuck rivers are considered to have been occupied by Pequots, because documentary sources indicate that only Pequots inhabited that area before the War of 1637. After the War large Indian concentrations were forbidden in the area until 1650, when the Pequots were given a 500-acre tract in Noank. Pequot settlements after 1650 are well documented and generally were confined to specific locales or reservations. Hunting is the only activity mentioned in the post-War documents that would not have been confined to specific tracts.

The Pequot War period is defined for the most part by the associated documents, most of which date from between August, 1636, and the fall of 1637. Determining the precise chronology of archaeological sites is more difficult, since the

Mystic Fort is the only seventeenth-century Pequot site where archaeological information corroborates written information. It is virtually impossible to place any other archaeological site within a time span less than fifty years, although archaeologists can date sites to the late sixteenth and early seventeenth centuries on the basis of aboriginal ceramic styles and European artifacts.

In the spring of 1987 an archaeological survey located the site of Mystic Fort, which was burned by the English in the Pequot War. This area, now referred to as Pequot Hill, is located on the west side of the Mystic River. Several other nearby hilltops were candidates for the fort location, but most of the available evidence pointed to Pequot Hill as the likely site. The evidence consists of eyewitness accounts of the battle and oral tradition, including accounts of farmers picking up Indian and colonial artifacts from plowed fields in the area. In 1875, Horace Clift, a local resident, reported that his father had told him about a circular embankment extending several rods across a field on the summit of Pequot Hill, where charred wood, corroded bullets, and Indian relics were found whenever any plowing was done.[1]

The eyewitness accounts by John Mason, Philip Vincent, John Underhill, and Lion Gardiner suggest that the fort was located two miles south of the place where the English camped the night before the attack.[2] Oral tradition places this spot at Porter's Rocks, approximately two miles north of Pequot Hill. The accounts also indicate that the fort was on the summit of a great hill, one-quarter mile west of the Mystic River, with a small brook on the west side one-quarter mile down the hill. The Vincent source provides us with a description of the fort:

Let me now describe this military fortress, [for which they chose] . . . at least two acres of ground. Here they pitch, close together as they can, young trees and half trees, as thick as a man's thigh or the calf of his leg. Ten or twelve foot high they are above the ground, and within rammed three foot deep with undermining, the earth being cast up for their better shelter against the enemy's dischargements. Betwixt these palisadoes are divers loopholes through which they let fly their winged messengers. The door for the most part is entered sideways, which they stop with boughs or bushes.[3]

The fort area was thickly packed with perhaps as many as sixty or seventy wigwams.[4] The Ethnohistory Project assumed that the destruction of sixty to seventy houses, with all their associated domestic goods, would leave some trace that could be detected archaeologically.

The purpose of the archaeological study at Pequot Hill was twofold: first, to find physical evidence of the fort; and second, to recover material culture (particularly ceramics) associated with the Pequots that might help identify other Pequot sites in the area. The archaeological survey indeed located a late sixteenth- or early seventeenth-century Indian settlement on the summit of Pequot Hill that is believed to be the fort site destroyed in the Pequot War. The most important find at Mystic Fort was a specific type of aboriginal ceramic found only in late sixteenth- and early seventeenth-century sites in eastern Connecticut. This can be used as a reliable date marker for the fort site.[5] The ceramics are most similar to the Niantic–Hackney Pond variety in the Windsor tradition commonly found in sites in eastern coastal Connecticut. These ceramics are easily distinguishable from the Fort Shantok type commonly found associated with Mohegan sites along the Thames River and on eastern Long Island. Fort Shantok ceramics have been dated no earlier than the mid-seventeenth century and have never been found in the Pequot territory between the Thames and Pawcatuck rivers. This implies that the Pequots used a different ceramic style than the Mohegans. Shantok pottery appears to have been produced by the post–European contact, post–Pequot War Mohegan tribe, which included refugee Pequots who were incorporated into the Mohegans after the War.

Documentary sources and archaeological data provide much information on the nature and distribution of Pequot sites. Of the sites considered to be villages, two are fortified villages of the Pequots. In August, 1636, John Endicott

raided and burned two nonfortified villages along the Pequot (Thames) River, of approximately thirty wigwams each, helping precipitate the War. Importantly, the villages burned by Endicott on Block Island one week earlier were also mentioned as having thirty wigwams each.[6] Both the Block Island and Pequot River villages were said to include 200-acre cornfields.[7]

The distribution and placement of these Pequot villages are consistent with reconstructions of settlement patterns during earlier periods in coastal Connecticut. Almost without exception, prehistoric villages and early historic Pequot villages were located in estuarine locations, specifically along the Thames River, Poquetannuck Cove, and the Mystic River. The only early historic-period sites that do not fit that pattern are the two fortified Pequot villages at Fort Hill and Mystic, both of which were located on hilltops some distance from estuaries. No pre–European-contact villages have been found on hilltops at any great distance from a large river or estuary in coastal Connecticut or in the lower Connecticut River Valley, nor are the villages located in what could be labeled defensible locations. This suggests that the existence of the fortified villages is related to European contact, at least in coastal Connecticut.

These fortified villages were larger than the standard Pequot village. For example, Mystic Fort is estimated to have contained seventy wigwams. An additional bit of information also suggests the unique nature of these fortified sites in the region. Adriaen Block, in his account of his 1614 voyage up the Mystic, Thames, and Connecticut rivers, mentioned fortified villages only along the Connecticut River near Hartford. Although that is negative evidence, it is, nevertheless, suggestive and fits well with our current understanding of the archaeological record of the region.[8]

Because the two fortified Pequot villages are different in form, size, and function from any of the other tribal villages, scholars can infer a village hierarchy and, by implication, a political and social hierarchy. The two forts were apparently occupied by the two paramount Pequot sachems: Sassacus, at Weinshauks (Fort Hill); and Mamoho, at Mystic. The two sachems killed at Mystic Fort were referred to as chief sachems of the Pequots. Three unfortified villages in the area are indicated in the documents: the two burned by Endicott on the east and west sides of the Thames River, and Uncas's place of residence at Munhicke (Mohegan). Archaeological surveys have located two other early seventeenth-century villages that were probably Pequot: one on Poquetannuck Cove across from Mohegan, and a second on the Davis farm near Groton Long Point below Fort Hill.[9]

Villages, fortified and unfortified, are the predominant site type mentioned in the documentary sources and identified in the archaeological record, but Mason noted a third type of habitation in his retreat from the Mystic Fort: " . . . we then marched on towards Pequot Harbour; and falling upon several wigwams, burnt them."[10] This community was of a different nature than the thirty-wigwam villages or the fortified villages of seventy wigwams. It may have been a hamlet made up of smaller groups of Pequots such as extended families or lineages. The Pequots appear, then, to have had a settlement pattern comprising two fortified villages (three, if the Western Niantic fort on Niantic Bay is counted) and an undetermined number of secondary villages, mostly located along estuaries and tidal marshes.

Agricultural fields also appear to have been associated with each village, perhaps as many as 200 acres of fields per village. There appears to have been a relationship between villages and cornfields, although not necessarily the reverse. In other words, where there are villages there are cornfields, but cornfields were also placed away from villages, perhaps wherever good soil was found.[11] According to Roger Williams, the Pequots established new cornfields on Long Island, and possibly on Fisher's Island and other islands, in preparation for the War, anticipating destruction of their cornfields by the English:

The Pequots are scarce of provisions and therefore (as usually now especially) they are in some numbers come downe to the Sea Side and 2 islands by name Munnawtawkit and Manittuwond (Shelter & Plum Island?) especially to take Sturgeon and other fish as allso to make new fields of corne in case the English should destroy their fields at home.[12]

Less information is available on Pequot social and political structures; however, a village hierarchy existed, and there is evidence of a social hierarchy as well. There were also different levels of sachems among the Pequots. That these political positions extended into the social realm is shown in one account that states that the Pequots sent their "women of esteeme and children" to Long Island for safekeeping during the war.[13]

At the time of the Pequot War, there were apparently twenty-six Pequot sachems, some of whom may have had more influence than others or were considered more important by both Indians and colonists. The existence of a paramount or chief sachem has been well documented, and some documents infer that the sons of sachems were expected to succeed them. The first chief sachem mentioned in written sources was Tatobem, killed by the Dutch in 1634. He was succeeded by his son Sassacus, who resided in the principal Pequot fort at Weinshauks (Fort Hill). Two other chief sachems lived in Mystic Fort, one of whom was called Mamoho. The larger villages likely contained two sachems; the smaller villages, possibly one, perhaps reflecting one or more lineages.[14] In reporting the events immediately following the Mystic Fort battle of May 26, 1637, Roger Williams described a sachem called Maumanadtuck as "one of their biggest with great troops."[15] This same sachem was also considered, with Sassacus, as one of the Pequots' "two chief sachems" after the Mystic Fort battle.[16] Two of Sassacus's brothers (Sacowausin and Puppompogs) are also mentioned as sachems. At a place called Soudahque along the Shetucket River near the present town of Norwich, Connecticut, five brothers, all sachems, were the sons of the great Pequot sachem's sister.[17]

The division of Pequot society, was likely based on blood relations, but the established hierarchy among the Pequot sachems may not have been.[18] For example, Sassacus's brothers were not referred to as chief or paramount sachems.

Blood ties were undoubtedly important, but other factors may have contributed to the relative importance of Pequot sachems, perhaps including size of lineage or clan. Maumanadtuck may have been one of the principle sachems, because we note that he had a relatively large number of warriors at his command. One sachem, referred to as Momonohuk's son, was considered "a great sachem, as they said greater than Sassacus," perhaps not because of blood or number of relations, but because of meritorious deeds or fighting spirit.[19]

Several interesting events after the War of 1637 suggest that women may have played important political roles in Pequot society. After the War marriages to the widows of principle sachems were much sought after to forge political and social alliances and possibly to acquire land. Roger Williams reported that Uncas "hath Sassacous his sister to wife and one of the wives of Sassacous his father Tattaopame, and that one reason beside his ambition and neerenes that he hath drawne all the scattered Pequots to himself and drawne much wealth from them."[20] Wequash, a disaffected Pequot living in Niantic territory and referred to as a Niantic sachem, attempted to build a power base and expand his influence after the war. Wequash along with Uncus helped lead the colonial attack on Mystic Fort.[21] After the War he married Sassacus's mother, and Roger Williams reported that "he is growne rich and a sachem with the Pequots . . . and hath filled many baskets with beans from Pequot Sachims and 120 Pequots wch he sheltreth now at Niantic."[22]

At the close of the Pequot War, in the early fall of 1637, several bands of Pequots were scattered throughout southern New England. It is difficult to know their precise numbers, but if we assume a total of 3,000 to 4,000 at the beginning of the War and a total of 1,000 to 1,500 casualties during the course of the War, an estimate of 2,000 to 2,500 Pequots remaining at the close of the War is not unreasonable. The post-War Treaty of Hartford, made in September, 1638, between the colonists and their Indian allies, mentions 200 Pequot males to be divided equally between the Mohegans and Narragansetts. That number, however, is well below the estimated 400 to 500 post-War Pequot males that can be calculated from other contemporary sources. Approximately 200 to 300 Pequot warriors (and presumably their families) were probably incorporated into the Mohegan tribe following the War. A second group, nominally under the control of the Narragansetts, was living in southwestern Rhode Island with the Pequot/Niantic sachem named Wequash, and they numbered 120 males. This group, later known as the Eastern or Paucatuck Pequots, was in 1650 provided with the 500-acre reservation on the east side of Long Pond in North Stonington.[23]

A third group of Pequots, although technically under Mohegan domination, did not live at Mohegan. This group, which later became known as the Western, or Mashantucket, Pequots, lived after the War in five villages ranging in size from eight to twenty wigwams, with a total of seventy-three wigwams. One of these villages was located on Niantic Bay, and the remaining four were distributed along the west side of the Thames River. In 1646, when John Winthrop, Jr., settled Pequot Plantation at Nameag (New London), seventy-two males and eight boys were mentioned. According to the documents, there were approximately 350 to 400 individuals in the Mashantucket band of Pequots in the mid-seventeenth century.[24]

Early relations between the Pequots and the settlers at Pequot Plantation were very good. For example, the Pequots sheltered some of the settlers during the first year and hunted for them. The Pequot leader Robin Cassacinamon was a former servant of Winthrop's brother, and this may have been a factor in Winthrop's decision to locate the plantation at Nameag. When, in 1651, with Winthrop's aid, the Connecticut Colony gave the Nameag Pequots approximately five hundred acres at Noank, this was a significant event. The Pequots were not only allowed their own government, but were reestablished in their original territory, in which they had been forbidden to reside after the Pequot War.[25]

Soon after, the Pequots petitioned the Connecticut government for additional land because the land at Noank was worn

out and no firewood was left.[26] The land area that was later to
become the Mashantucket Pequot Reservation was first mentioned in 1658, when the commissioners of the United Colonies decreed that "Cashasinnimon and his companie shall
have a fitt proportion of land allowed them at Wawarramoreke
near the path that leads from the Misticke River to Moheage
about five or six miles from the mouth of the Misticke River."[27]
This description, combined with information from later documentation, places the northern limits of this parcel on the west
bank of Long Pond, the southeastern corner of Mashantucket
in 1666. The Pequots used the land around Long Pond for
planting and orchards shortly after 1658, but it was not until
1665 that the General Court of Connecticut ordered colonists
to lay out "a convenient parcel of land for Robin and his company to plant upon, at or near the head of the Mystic River."[28] It
is this parcel, believed to originally include 3,000 acres, later
reduced to 2,000 acres, that was the core of the Mashantucket
Pequot Reservation. Other documentary evidence strongly
suggests that Pequots were planting and perhaps living in this
area earlier than 1666, but probably not earlier than 1658.

By the end of the seventeenth century the Pequots were in
constant conflict with English settlers over the Pequot lands at
Noank. In an effort to end the dispute, the General Court surveyed Noank and Mashantucket and decided in 1714 that
Mashantucket would be sufficient for the Indians' subsistence
and livelihood. The Pequots were ordered to relinquish their
planting rights to Noank, but would be allowed to fish, fowl,
and gather shellfish there. In 1721 the Pequots formally quit-
claimed their planting rights at Noank in exchange for a survey and clear title to Mashantucket.[29]

Between the initial establishment of the Mashantucket Pequot Reservation in 1666 and the land survey in 1721, the reservation apparently was reduced by as much as 1,000 to
1,500 acres. Consequently, the order for the establishment of
the Mashantucket Reservation on March 20, 1721, described
a 1,000-acre parcel of land around the Cedar Swamp as well
as a 600-acre parcel on Walnut Hill and on hills east of the

Cedar Swamp. The Pequots were also allowed to use land on the west side of Long Pond where they had formerly planted and had their orchards, until the trees died. The agreement resulted in the Pequots retaining only 1,600 to 1,700 acres of the original reservation established in 1666.[30]

Almost immediately the Pequots began to complain to the Connecticut government of encroachment upon these lands by English settlers, particularly in the 600-acre Walnut Hill parcel on the west side of the reservation. This area may not have been occupied by the Pequots, but was used for planting fields and woodlots. English settlers contested the Pequots' right to the land, and in 1732 the Connecticut General Assembly decided to divide the land into 50-acre parcels, each to be shared by colonists and Pequots. The large number of subsequent complaints made by the Pequots, concerning English settlers fencing in and destroying their cornfields, indicates that the arrangement did not work very well. The conflict was finally settled in 1761 when the General Assembly gave the disputed lands to the English, and gave the Pequots clear title to the remaining 989 acres. This 989-acre parcel remained largely intact until 1855, when all but 204 acres was auctioned off by the state of Connecticut.[31]

Throughout the eighteenth century the population on the reservation declined steadily. The mortality rate among Pequot males was high because of their participation in colonial wars, and many Pequot males also moved off the reservation to find work as laborers on nearby farms or as whalers. In 1725 the Pequots on the reservation were listed as 322. In 1732, 66 males above the age of fourteen were mentioned. Most of them were living with the English, but their families probably lived on the reservation. In 1755, Ezra Stiles listed 72 adults above the age of fourteen, 31 of whom were males. In 1762, Stiles mentioned twenty to thirty families on the reservation, living in seven framed houses and seventeen wigwams. In the mid-eighteenth century, between 150 and 230 Indians resided on the reservation.[32]

A significant reduction in the reservation population occurred at the close of the American Revolution, when some Pequots abandoned the reservation and eventually ended up in Oneida, New York, and in Wisconsin as part of the Brother-town Indian movement. Archaeological studies have docu-mented this population movement; many of the sites in one section of the reservation, called Indiantown, were abandoned in the last quarter of the eighteenth century. At the time of the 1856 land sale, only six dwellings appear on a map of the res-ervation, suggesting a total population of no more than fifty.

Just when fixed residency was first established on the Mash-antucket Reservation cannot be clearly determined. During the late seventeenth and early eighteenth centuries the Pe-quots were making seasonal moves to Noank to fish, fowl, and collect shellfish. The agreement in 1714 that allowed the Pe-quots to retain rights to fish, fowl, and clam at Noank is further indication that this subsistence activity continued into the eighteenth century.[33] Traditional shifting agricultural activities are also inferred throughout the eighteenth century. Accord-ing to one source in 1732:

The custom of the Indian is, to set upon a piece and improve it until it is worn out, and then begin upon another: by this means they have cleared about two hundred acres, and two hundred more is partially cleared, and many apple trees belonging to the Indians are standing thereon. The last year the Indians planted fourteen acres.[34]

By the second half of the eighteenth century both the docu-ments and Pequot archaeological sites reflect more European subsistence practices, perhaps as a result of a reduction of the land base. For example, one document indicates that "some of them [Pequots] have made handsome improvements and have [s]ome cattle and seem desirous of improving after the English manner."[35] Archaeological evidence of animal hus-bandry is quite common at many of the later-eighteenth- and nineteenth-century sites on the reservation. Evidence for cattle is rarely found, but the remains of young sheep and pigs are fairly common. Hunted foods, including deer and raccoon, are also common at most Pequot sites, even through the early twentieth century.

Through at least the early part of the eighteenth century, the Pequots were engaged in traditional subsistence practices involving cultivation of maize, hunting, and seasonal movements to coastal areas to procure resources. Orchards, presumably apple, were an important food source as early as the mid-seventeenth century. By the mid-eighteenth century, pigs, sheep, and cattle are mentioned in documents and appear in the archaeological record. By the nineteenth century, overseers' reports indicate that large quantities of foodstuffs were purchased for the inhabitants of the reservation. Clearly, the Pequots grew increasingly dependent on European technology and subsistence practices as time went on.

The Mashantucket Pequot Reservation is a remarkable repository of Pequot material culture, as parts of it have been continuously occupied by Pequots from the prehistoric period to the present, except perhaps for a twenty-year hiatus between 1638 and 1658. The first goal of the archaeological portion of the Mashantucket Pequot Ethnohistory Project is to reconstruct the boundaries of the reservation through time and to locate all Pequot sites on the reservation.

The Ethnohistory Project survey began with a walk over the existing 1,400-acre reservation to locate above-ground structural remains such as stone piles, walls, and foundations. Sites without above-ground remains were located by conducting subsurface testing in areas that were relatively flat, well drained, and within five hundred meters of a stream, spring, or swamp. Even as late as the middle to late eighteenth century, 75 percent of the dwellings on the reservation were wigwams. Such structures are difficult to locate archaeologically unless they are associated with stone walls, wells, or other obvious features. As a result, the earlier occupations on the reservation are likely underrepresented in the site count.

As of 1989 about seventy-five Pequot sites, dating from the late sixteenth to the twentieth century, had been identified. The Ethnohistory Project had also begun more intensive work, through limited excavation, to gather more information on the type, age, and function of the archaeological sites, and more extensive excavations of Pequot sites representative of types and time periods are planned. In the summer of 1987 we began excavation of some sixteenth- and seventeenth-century occupations. So far, however, most of the intensive archaeological research has been conducted in the 1,600-acre reservation established in 1721. Every archaeological site found was mapped and tested intensively enough to estimate roughly its size and age. The project attempted to recover a sufficient sample of diagnostic (that is, datable) artifacts (such as European ceramics) to place each site within a twenty-five- to fifty-year time span. The project has tested enough sites to reconstruct settlement patterns on the reservation in fifty-year increments and to examine changes in house forms and structures through time.

The late prehistoric, seventeenth-, and early eighteenth-century sites located on the Mashantucket Reservation are generally small, limited-activity ones. Sites dating between 1650 and 1750 are fairly evenly distributed. Most of the sites represent short-term occupations, such as hunting camps or sites of other seasonal activities such as planting. This interpretation is generally consistent with the documentary evidence, which indicates that before 1720 there were few, if any, permanent occupations in the area of the reservation. Orchards and planting fields are mentioned on the west side of Long Pond, but few archaeological sites have been found there so far. Small groups apparently lived in the area seasonally to hunt and tend orchards and cornfields; then they returned to Noank.

The earliest sites on the Mashantucket Reservation are relatively small and include few, if any, structural remains. They have a very limited range of artifact classes. By the mid-eighteenth century, however, the sites become more complex. Many of them are characterized by a variety of stone structures and features, and a large number seem to coalesce into what are believed to be distinct communities. This process likely reflects population movement from Noank to Mashantucket and the construction of more permanent facilities. An argu-

ment can be made for at least two distinct Pequot communities at Mashantucket at this time. Early eighteenth-century
records suggest two factions on the reservation: one under the
second Robin Cassacinamon and one under a Pequot sachem
called Daniel. The distribution of archaeological sites tends to
support this, with one community, the largest, located along
the west side of the Great Cedar Swamp and a second, more
scattered group of sites located on the south and west.

The largest of these communities, Indiantown, was abandoned by the first decade of the nineteenth century. The project archaeologists have hypothesized, though it has not been
conclusively demonstrated, that this was the group of Pequots
that began to go west as part of the Brothertown movement at
the close of the American Revolution. By the early nineteenth
century the number of sites had declined dramatically, and by
the late nineteenth century the number had declined further,
presumably as one result of the 1856 land sale and a further
reduction in population.

The changes from seasonal to permanent land uses, the
reductions in the size of the reservation and in its population, and changes in the subsistence base are all reflected to
some degree in the architecture and structure of domestic
sites on the reservation. The use of stone became increasingly common throughout the eighteenth century for walls,
foundations, and gardens, making it relatively easy to assess
the nature and arrangement of Pequot sites in this and later
periods. By the mid-eighteenth century several changes in
site structure and house form can be identified on the reservation, although the basic structure of Pequot sites did not
change from the eighteenth century through the nineteenth
century, suggesting a high degree of continuity in terms of
domestic patterns.

The project has defined many of the Pequot occupations
from the eighteenth century as farmsteads because they contain several features found in contemporary Euro-American
sites. These self-contained units included dwellings (a combination of both framed structures and wigwams), outbuild-

ings (sweat lodges and animal pens), fields and gardens, wells, storage facilities, stone walls, middens, and cemeteries. These sites are broadly similar to contemporaneous Euro-American farmsteads, but there are some differences, most obviously in size and scale and in occupation/activity areas. Many of the Pequot farmsteads contained multiple dwellings, and probably they included more than one family. A few of these farmsteads coalesced into villages or identifiable communities. According to one visitor in the 1780s:

> We got to a part of the west that which they called Indiantown, a small village that is very scattered and the miserable Indians that still keep themselves here, the number of families which would amount to a total of fifty or sixty they are moderately well dressed, and you have your corn plants in the Indian style with neither circles nor any divisions.[36]

This community was abandoned during the Brothertown Indian movement after 1783, which correlates with both the documentary and archaeological evidence.

Pequot farmsteads are usually defined archaeologically by a generally discontinuous pattern of low fieldstone walls, within which several structures can usually be identified. Fields are identified by patterns of small stone piles, usually confined to an area that does not exceed one to two acres. These areas likely served as gardens, where from three-quarters to one and one-half acres may have been cultivated per family. Documentary evidence indicates that in 1732 the population of the reservation was estimated at approximately 250 individuals, yet only fourteen acres are mentioned as under cultivation.[37] Orchards are frequently mentioned, as are pigs. Archaeological evidence confirms that pigs, sheep, and a variety of wild animals were consumed by reservation residents. The archaeological and documentary evidence suggests a combination of traditionally grown and hunted foods as well as some European-introduced crops, animals, and technologies.

Within a typical farmstead, one and possibly two outbuildings or structures can be identified. These usually consist of circular enclosures ranging in size from ten to fifteen feet in diameter. These outbuildings were made by using one or more glacial erratics as walls, and then forming the enclosure by using smaller fieldstones. The function of these structures is unclear, but some of them may have served as animal pens, storage facilities, or possibly sweathouses. More formal storage facilities such as root cellars have been identified, although they are not common. There is some indication that these structures served more than one farmstead.

Some documentary information is available on the floor plan, supporting structure, covering, and interior arrangements of Pequot wigwams and houses. The best-known description is by Ezra Stiles, who described and depicted in drawings several mid–eighteenth-century Pequot/Niantic wigwams in Niantic.[38] Such dwellings were probably the most common house form or type on the reservation in the early to mid-eighteenth century. Nonetheless, except for one or two exceptions, very little is known about the interior arrangements or contents of these structures.

Archaeological evidence indicates a somewhat different house form in the mid-eighteenth century, perhaps intermediate between wigwams and Euro-American frame houses. These dwellings are identified on the basis of the concentrations of domestic debris such as bones, charcoal, and ceramics. They were built into south-facing hillsides with a fieldstone retaining wall constructed against the hillside. A low stone wall two to three feet wide was then built in a U or D shape from the back of the retaining wall. It is not known whether a sapling frame and mats were used in these structures, or if they supported some kind of more formal frame structure with shingles.

Pequot house forms changed throughout the later eighteenth and nineteenth centuries as stone foundations were used and frame houses became more common. By the early nineteenth century, increasing numbers of Pequot dwellings began to resemble European-style frame house. Of the twenty-three Pequot dwellings mentioned by Ezra Stiles in 1762,

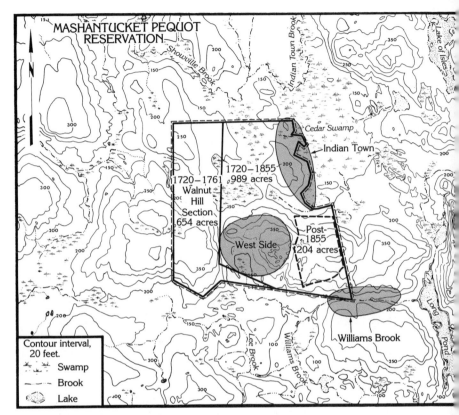

Mashantucket Pequot Reservation, 1720–1983. The boundary of the reservation was first surveyed and mapped in 1721. The Walnut Hill Section was "shared" by Pequots and white settlers until 1761, when it was formally given to whites. East of Walnut Hill, the remaining 989 acres of the reservation was used and occupied by Pequots until 1855, when all but 204 acres was auctioned off by the state of Connecticut. The last 204 acres were all that remained of the reservation until the land settlement of 1983.

sixteen were wigwams and seven were described as frame houses.[39] In the mid-nineteenth century all of the Pequot dwellings were frame houses, of a relatively standard size and form. According to an account in 1848, "The houses on the reservation are seven in number, one story in height, and varying from one to four rooms."[40] Another document adds to our understanding of Indian dwellings in that period: "The overseer of said Indians be directed to build three dwelling houses on the reservation land for Indians, of the following dimensions: 22 feet long, 14 feet wide and 1 story high, with suitable partitions."[41] Although they were rare, there are some suggestions that house forms existed other than the standard small, frame houses and wigwams, indicating some status differences. According to one local historian: "One of the leaders in this remnant of the Pequots at 'Indian Town' was Mark Daniels. He lived at the northerly end of the reservation. . . . He occupied the most pretentious of the dwellings and was very friendly with the English residents."[42] This house is still standing, just off the modern-day Mashantucket Pequot Reservation, and measures roughly forty feet by twenty feet.

The significance of these changes in site structure and house form is not clear, but they may reflect the increased permanence of habitations on the reservation as more traditional seasonal pursuits, such as fishing and fowling in coastal areas, declined. The continued reductions and restrictions of the population on the reservation may also have been a factor. Some ethnohistorians believe that the architectural shift from wigwams to frame houses during the eighteenth and nineteenth centuries represented a weakening of Indian cultural patterns; however, although house form changed, the function of the home as the place of residence of one to four nuclear families may not have. The limited archaeological work done on these sites also suggests that the dwellings served primarily as sleeping places, with most of the domestic activities occurring outside of the dwelling. It does not seem reasonable to assume a deterioration of Native American cultural patterns solely because architectural elements became more similar to those of nearby Euro-American sites. On the Mashantucket Pequot Reservation changes in house form reflected the availability of certain kinds of technologies, but did not necessarily reflect changes in social and domestic patterns or site structure.

CHAPTER 8

The Emergence of the Mashantucket Pequot Tribe, 1637–1975

By Jack Campisi

Two themes run through Pequot history: a tenacious persistence to maintain the tribal identity and an unswerving struggle to hold on to tribal land. It is important to know that these themes are interconnected.

The identity of the Pequot tribe was often a function of the identification of the land at Mashantucket as tribal. Yet it would be an error to believe that the only thing that held the Mashantucket Pequots together was their small land base of ridges, ravines, and swamps. Rather, it was their identification with their tragic past, their close social ties with other tribal members, their shared beliefs and traditions, the land that constituted their tribal estate, which had been handed down from generation to generation, and finally, their claim to other lands that had been unjustly and illegally taken by whites. Typical was the response of a Pequot woman who, when asked in the 1970s about the nearby Mohegans, replied that the Pequots had not had much contact "ever since what they did to us." As she explained, what the Mohegans had done was to join the English in the massacre and enslavement of the tribe in 1637.[1]

But first, a caveat is in order. We cannot claim to have a

clear and complete picture of reservation life or of the tribe's beliefs, interests, or aspirations during most of its history. Our data are distorted by the interests of non-Indians, namely the periodic desires of outsiders to own the tribe's land. The tribe defended its interests as best it could and, in the process, left a record of its visibility. It is this record on which we must rely for an understanding of Pequot tribal persistence.

At the close of the Pequot War, the tribe faced annihilation, a majority of the tribe having been killed and the remainder enslaved. In disposing of the few survivors, the colonies sent some Pequots to the Narragansetts, the Mohegans, and the Eastern Niantics. In addition, a few were sold into slavery and shipped to Bermuda, or given to local English settlers to work on their farms.[2]

These arrangements did not last, partly because the English quickly realized that they had unwittingly strengthened their potential foes, and partly because the enslaved tribal members were unwilling to accept their condition. By the 1650s the two groups of Pequots under the control of the Narragansett sachem Miantonomo and Uncas, sachem of the Mohegans, had achieved independence from their captors. Having freed themselves, the Pequots again presented a problem to the English: what was the colony of Connecticut going to do with them? Its answer was to establish four Indian towns supervised by two Pequot "governors." Under this arrangement Robin Cassacinamon, who headed the Western, or Mashantucket, Pequots, as they later were called, controlled Nameag and Nawpauge, while Caushawashett, also known as Wequash Cook and Harmon Garrett, leader of the Eastern Pequots, controlled Pauquatuck and Weeapauge.[3]

The land problems of the two Pequot tribes remained unresolved, while a growing border dispute between Massachusetts and Connecticut added to the difficulty. In 1661 settlers in Rhode Island, desiring the land on which the Indians had settled, drove the Eastern Pequots across the Pawcatuck River into the town of Stonington, Connecticut. These Pequots, for their part, settled on land belonging to other settlers. Massa-

chusetts further exacerbated the conflict by granting the Pequots acreage in Stonington. The Connecticut Colony refused
to honor Massachusetts's generous grant, but it did agree to
give the Eastern Pequots a smaller tract of land in the area.
Despite strenuous efforts by Connecticut, the Eastern Pequots
remained where they were. Finally, in 1685 the Connecticut
Colony purchased 280 acres for the tribe's use near Lantern
Hill, on Long Lake, the site of the present-day Paucatuck Pequot reservation. Thus part of the settlement problem was
resolved.[4]

The other part remained, however, as the Western Pequots
were experiencing similar problems. Their leader, Cassacinamon, had requested that the Connecticut Colony set aside
land at the headwater of the Mystic River for their use. Instead,
they were granted a tract of two thousand acres in the town of
Ledyard. The land grant, called Mashantucket, was confirmed
by the colony in the mid 1660s; however, Cassacinamon stead-
fastly refused to accept it and remained with most of his followers at Noank, where he died in 1692.[5]

After Cassacinamon's death, the General Court appointed a
tribal member named Daniel as governor. He died shortly after
his appointment and was replaced as governor in 1694 by
Scattup. James Avery and James Morgan were named as ad-
visors. In 1698 the Connecticut General Court relinquished its
direct control over the tribes by placing them under the authority of the colonial governor.[6] Thus, by the end of the seventeenth century, the Pequots were divided into two separate,
recognized tribes, each with a similar form of government that
was significantly different from that which had existed at the
beginning of the century. They had gone from a collection of
villages, each with their own political organization, through a
stage when they were subjected to the authority of other Indian tribes, to two semiautonomous tribes with relatively strong
centralized authority, yet dependent upon the Connecticut
Colony for advice and protection. Their economic system persisted, with subsistence agriculture augmented by hunting,
fishing, and shellfishing. At the very least, the Pequots survived

from the end of the seventeenth century onward as two separate social and political entities.[7]

At the turn of the eighteenth century, securing title to the
land at Mashantucket remained a principal issue and concern
for the Western, Mashantucket Pequots. Until Cassacinamon's
death the tribe had used the land at Noank while minimally
occupying the land at Mashantucket. In 1712 the town of
Groton passed a law allotting the land at Noank. The Pequot
leader Robin Cassacinamon (the second) filed a complaint
with the Connecticut General Assembly (also known as the
General Court). The Mashantucket Pequots, as they were more
commonly called, were joined in their complaint by the Society for the Propagation of the Gospel in New England, whose
agent, Samuel Sewall, petitioned on behalf of the tribe.

At first the General Assembly took the side of the Mashantucket Pequots. It ordered the town of Groton to return the
land or make restitution to the Indians, and appointed a committee to resolve the complaint. The committee reported that
the Pequots had abandoned their lands at Noank some forty
years before to occupy the land at Mashantucket. On the basis
of that report, the General Court concluded that the tribe had
abandoned the Noank land, while retaining fishing and hunting rights, and that they had sufficient land at Mashantucket
for their needs. The General Assembly went on to assure the
Mashantucket Pequots that "if they should be at any time molested and disturbed in their planting or improvement on the
said Mashantucket lands, upon application made to this Court,
shall be heard and relieved by this Court."[8]

The Mashantucket Pequots soon had an opportunity to test
the Connecticut Colony's resolve. In 1722 the colony reinforced its prohibition against the unauthorized purchase of Indian land by providing for forfeiture and fine. The act followed
a complaint made the previous year by Cassacinamon through
the tribe's overseer, James Avery, to the General Assembly, al-
leging that the heirs of John Winthrop, Jr., had taken five hundred acres of land at Mashantucket. The General Assembly
appointed a committee to investigate the complaints. After a

desultory investigation, the committee reported that the claims of Cassacinamon were exaggerated, the result of pressure from James Avery.[9]

In spite of the adverse report, Avery continued to file petitions. He claimed that he had witnessed the destruction of Pequot crops and the illegal seizure of land. According to Avery, the committee appointed by the General Assembly had never interviewed him or Cassacinamon. To further complicate matters, Scattup, who represented the majority of the tribe, petitioned to have Avery removed and James Morgan appointed in his place. After hearing a number of committee reports, and after the collection of conflicting petitions, the General Assembly voted to grant Avery the power to prosecute to recover the land for the use of the Indians. In May, 1723, Avery reported that twenty-eight lots, containing twenty acres each, had been taken from the Mashantucket Pequots. The General Assembly ordered Avery to take steps to recover the land, but in 1728 it nullified its 1723 action by accepting a committee finding that only one encroachment had occurred, thereby making it impossible to recover the bulk of the land. As to Winthrop's claim to five hundred acres, the Mashantucket Pequots took steps to resolve this by offering the tract in question to the town of Groton in exchange for six hundred acres elsewhere. The town then took on the responsibility of negotiating with the Winthrop heirs.[10]

The tribe's land problems were far from over. In the original grant to the Pequots, the town of Groton had reserved "herbage" (grazing) rights on the Mashantucket lands; however, the settlers went beyond that restricted use. A petition from "the sachem and sundry others of the Pequot Indians" complained "that the inhabitants of the town of Groton are continually cutting down and carrying away their timber and firewood . . . and make pretence to lay out to themselves, and fence and improve, certain valuable parts thereof."[11] The General Assembly appointed a committee, which reviewed the salient facts and found that the Mashantucket Pequots had partially or fully cleared some four hundred acres, had planted crops on fourteen acres the previous year, and had sizeable orchards on the remainder. They reported the number of males fourteen years and older to be sixty-six, and gave the tribe's population as about three hundred. They outlined briefly the arguments of the two sides: the settlers claimed that as long as title to the land remained with the Indians, they would be unable to fence and use it for grazing their cattle. In turn, the overseers argued that granting the settlers title would result in the loss of the tribe's rights to the land. The committee offered the following solution, which was accepted by the General Assembly:

We are of opinion that the one half of said lands is fully sufficient for the Indians to dwell on and cut firewood, and that if the one half of said lands on the west side was laid out in fifty acre lots, or thereabouts, as the land will suitably accommodate, and the English allowed to fence the same, so as to secure themselves and the corn of the Indians growing on such lots, and their apple trees, and that the proprietors were allowed to clear said lots, only allowing ten acres in every fifty acre lot, and so pro rata for greater or lessor lots, a forest for firewood for the Indians, and the Indians allowed to plant in one or more of said lots as it may be needful for them, and be also allowed to remove their planting to other lots once in three years if they desire it, and the other half of the lands remain unsurveyed and unfenced as it doth now, for the Indians to live on, plant, and get firewood, and be a greater benefit to the proprietors.[12]

The compromise was a sham; it resolved nothing and could have pleased no one. Under the provisions of the 1732 act, half of the reservation was divided into fifty-acre lots to be leased to the English farmers. The settlers neither gained the clear title they desired nor the sole use of the land. They were permitted to fence the land, but this was more to protect Indian interests than their own. The Mashantucket Pequots lost effective control over half their land, even though they maintained right of use; with the colonists having a right of occupation, it was doubtful that the tribe would have the freedom of access assured by the General Assembly without continual appeals to that body.

The fears expressed by the Mashantucket Pequots and their

overseers concerning the joint use of half of the Mashantucket Reservation were soon realized. In 1747, Joseph Wyouke (Wyock) and the rest of the tribe, along with its overseers, John Richards and Daniel Coit, complained to the General Assembly that the inhabitants of Groton "have cut up and destroyed the Indians' corn there planted, so that the Indians are prevented from using said land."[13] The General Assembly dutifully appointed another committee to investigate. In 1750 the tribe, under the leadership of Wyouke, repeated its complaint, and again the General Assembly appointed a commission to inquire into the matter.[14] The following year the tribe renewed its complaints, asking for a new committee because the previous one "had not been able to attend said services, though repeated applications had been made to them for that purpose."[15] The General Assembly acquiesced and appointed two of its members, who reported back that the allegations were true. The General Assembly then charged the overseers with the responsibility "to take the best and most effectual care that said Indians be not molested in their improvements of said land" and ordered the proprietors of Groton to appear before the General Assembly to give reasons why the 1732 act should not be repealed.[16] In October, 1732, the General Assembly repealed the 1732 statute and empowered the overseers to prosecute suits against the proprietors to protect the property and rights of the Mashantucket Pequots.[17]

Six years later the tribe, through its overseers, entered court to recover some eighty-three acres of land that the tribe alleged had been illegally taken in 1725 by William Williams, Jr., of Groton. The complaint was made by thirty-four men of the tribe. The tribe lost the jury trial, but almost immediately appealed to the legislature to order a new trial, which was ordered in 1759.[18]

While the appeal was pending, a more serious threat arose to the land base. Several proprietors from Groton petitioned the General Assembly to grant them title to that portion of the Mashantucket Reservation that had been the subject of the 1732 act. In 1761 the General Assembly, acting on its committee report, passed a resolution reducing the size of the reservation to 989 acres and liquidating any Pequot claims, pending or future.[19]

Why had the Pequots, who had so tenaciously defended their property in the past, so passively accepted the loss of nearly half their reservation? One possible reason may have been their participation in the French and Indian War. One writer has insisted that many of the tribe's men served in the battles of Louisburg (1758), Ticonderoga (1759), and Crown Point (1759) and that "so many of them were killed in battle and died of disease, that the women and children at home were well nigh reduced to starvation."[20] According to historian John De Forest, the tribe numbered 176 in 1762 and had between twenty and thirty families.[21] With many of the Pequot men gone, it was an easy matter to legislate a land cession.

Twelve years passed before the General Assembly moved to set the boundary of a reduced reservation. Finally, in 1773, Daniel Quotcheath and other members of the tribe petitioned the General Assembly to have the lines drawn at tribal expense. The General Assembly complied and appointed a surveyor. Still, no lines were drawn. The following year the tribe repeated its request, this time through its overseers, Edward Mott and Elisha Fitch. The General Assembly appointed another committee to complete the work.[22]

The Revolutionary War interrupted efforts to adjust the boundaries, although it did not prevent further encroachments on reservation land. With that war's end the tribe once more appealed to have the boundaries determined. In 1785 the Connecticut General Assembly, "upon the Memorial of Joseph Charles Scordawb, Immanuel Simons, Joseph Sonsomon, Peter Churchs, Joshua George, Daniel Quatcheebek, the Reads of the Ancient Tribe of Indians called the Masunteket Tribe," directed that a survey be carried out because "said tribe are interrupted in their Possessions etc. by the People round about destroying their Timber and Crowding in upon their said Lands."[23] At long last, and after thirty years of frustration, the surveyors drew the lines around the reservation. As a final irony, the tribe, now possessed of their land, was forced to petition the General Assembly for permission to sell some to pay for the survey. This tribal request was made by Joseph Charles and Manuel Simonds, Indian leaders on behalf of the tribe.[24]

In 1800 the Mashantucket Pequots were faced with more than just the threat to their land base. Like other New England tribes, they had served with the colonial forces and had suffered serious losses in man power. In addition, some had joined the Brothertown Indians and moved to the Oneida Indian country in New York.[25] Of those who remained in Connecticut, a large number had moved off the reservation land and were indentured in white households or had moved onto white-owned farms, where they lived in virtual servitude. Timothy Dwight, in a noted account of the period, could as well have been describing the Pequots at Mashantucket when he wrote of those at North Stonington: "Here some of them live in wigwams; and others, in houses resembling poor cottages, at the best small, ragged, and unhealthy. Others still live on the farms of the white inhabitants in houses built purposely for them, and pay their rent by daily labor."[26]

The result was a marked reduction in the reservation population. A census taken in 1774 identified 151 tribal members in residence at Mashantucket. By the early 1800s this number had fallen to between thirty and forty, with an undetermined number living on farms and in private homes away from the reserved land.[27]

Throughout the first half of the nineteenth century the Mashantucket Pequots continued their opposition to what they considered incursions on their land. In 1800 their overseers, Samuel Mott and Isaac Avery, on behalf of the tribe, petitioned the legislature over a land dispute with the proprietors of the town of Groton. This dispute involved the land that the tribe had been forced to sell in 1793, but for which they had not been paid. Because the proprietors refused to accept the appraisal, the legislature directed the overseers not to sign the deeds until the tribe was paid, leaving the land in tribal control.[28]

While the proprietors and other residents of the town were reluctant to purchase one particular piece of property, that did not stop them from buying other portions of the Mashantucket Reservation. The overseers sold four parcels totaling slightly more than sixty-two acres in 1800 and 1801 for the peculiar sum of $394.44 and 22 shillings. Some or all of the following members of the tribe subscribed to these deeds: Josiah Charles Scordaub, Benjamin George, James Sunsimon, James Boney, Benjamin Charles, and Joseph Quocheets—"all of Groton in the county of New London and the State of Connecticut and all of us belonging to the Pequot or Mashantucket Tribe of Indians."[29]

Not all of the members of the tribe viewed with favor the actions of their overseers in selling the land. In 1804 they complained to the legislature that their overseers had sold and leased land without proper accounting, and they asked the legislature to remove the overseers and replace them with individuals who would "assist us in council and oversee our affairs."[30]

The petition demonstrates another characteristic of the Mashantucket Pequots, namely, their willingness to challenge the actions of their overseers when they felt it in their best interest. They saw the overseer as their agent, not the state's, which accounts for their frequent petitions requesting a change when the overseer was not responsive to their desires or had failed to account properly for tribal funds. Not only did they ask for the removal of overseers, but also they usually made recommendations regarding a replacement. It is clear that they did not see themselves as passive recipients of a service from the state. The tribe paid the overseers and logically felt that therefore they should be accountable. Despite summary dismissal of overseers by the legislature on a number of occasions, the tribe continued to recommend individuals, pay their salary, and petition for their removal.[31]

From the data available it is possible to outline the political organization of Mashantucket Pequots during the first half of the nineteenth century. For at least the first two decades, the

Pequots chose two men to act as councillors who performed a number of duties for the tribe, including petitioning for redress and communicating tribal needs and views to the overseers and the General Assembly. But the councillors were only spokesmen, and it is doubtful that they were vested with any power of decision making. The available evidence indicates that tribal members maintained a council house, met frequently on tribal business, and took an active part in their community affairs.[32]

An analysis of the names on the petitions, as well as the census lists provided by the overseers, indicates that the political leadership throughout the nineteenth century was vested in a limited number of core families who maintained an active role in the political and social life of the Mashantucket Pequot community: Fagin (Faggin), Skesuchs, Niles, Babcock, Dick, Simmons, Watson, Lawrence, and George. William Morgan, overseer for the tribe for many years, grouped the core families into seven extended families headed by Betsey Wheeler, Hannah Miller (Fagin), Anna Wait, Ezra Niles, Rhoda Cottrell, Esther Dick, Susan Simmons, and Amasa Lawrence.[33] By comparing tables 2 and 3, one can see that the principal families were represented in the political process throughout the period.

The census list points up another important aspect of Mashantucket Pequot sociopolitical life. By midcentury the women of the tribe had taken over the major political roles in the community. For example, the census of 1858 shows that one man and eight women lived on the reservation, while another three women lived in nearby Griswold.[34] Similarly, the vast majority of signers of the various petitions to the state were women.

The de facto control of tribal affairs by a few elderly women is best explained by the economic conditions in that part of Connecticut during the first half of the nineteenth century. Many men were forced to seek employment on neighboring farms, a condition that separated them from their families for weeks or months at a time. In most cases, the women remained on the reservation, where they tended a few crops,

Table 2. Signers of Mashantucket Pequot Petitions, 1839–1859

NAME	1839	1848	1849	1855	1857	1859
Hannah Miller Fagin	X	X	X	X	X	X
Betsy Wheeler	X	X	X		X	X
Esther Dick	X					
George Cottrell		X	X		X	X
Nancy Fagins		X	X	X	X	
Samuel Fagins		X	X		X	
Mary Ann Sears		X	X		X	
Caroline Wheeler		X	X	X		X
Rhoda Cottrell			X		X	X
John Babcock			X			X
Henry Fagins			X			X
Peter George				X		
Amasa Lawrence				X		
Joseph Fagins						X
Jane Wheeler						X
Anna Wait						X
John Tobey						X
Hannah Aaron						X
John Skesuchs						X
Peter Babcock						X
Ed Sears						X
Esther Dick						X
Lyman Dick						X
Charity Dick						X

made baskets, picked berries for sale, and raised their families. The men returned when there was no work, but the separations prevented their active participation in the political process. As Mystic developed into a fishing, whaling, and shipping port, many of the young men were drawn to the sea, which often meant long periods of absence from the community. The women had to carry out the political responsibilities. Unfortunately, while women acted as chiefs, the values of the surrounding white communities did not allow them to be accorded the title of chief or the status of leadership.

The tribe had three sources of income: the lease of land, the sale of firewood, and interest from its bank account. Under the system adopted by the state of Connecticut, the tribe did not have direct access to these funds, which were under the control of the overseers. The overseer's role was a fiduciary one: he collected the money due the tribe, brought suits on its behalf, and paid out the income derived for the benefit of the tribal members. For these services the tribe paid the overseer's salary and expenses.

The title of overseer was not honorary, nor were the duties

Table 3. Census of the Mashantucket Pequot tribe for the year 1858
listed by family

1.
Hannah Miller, aged about 61, on reservation with her children
Joseph Fagins, aged about 37, gone to parts unknown
Henry Fagins, aged about 35, in California
Nancy Fagins, aged about 31, on reservation
2.
Betsy Wheeler, about 71, on reservation
Caroline Wheeler, aged about 43, on reservation
Jane Wheeler, aged about 16, on reservation
3.
Anna Wait, aged 33, last heard from in N.Y.
John Tobey, aged about 28, last heard from in N.Y.
Hannah Aaron, aged about 39, on reservation
John Skesuchs, aged about 22, at sea
4.
Mary Sears, aged about 62, on reservation
Peter Babcock, aged about 28, on reservation
Martha A. Sears, aged about 21, residing in New Haven
Edward Sears, aged about 15, on reservation
5.
Rhoda Cottrell, aged about 68, near reservation
6.
Amasa Lawrence, aged about 66, on reservation
Lyman Dick, aged about 36, at sea
Esther Dick, aged about 27, on reservation
7.
Luke Simons, aged 57, residing in Griswold
Sallie Simons, aged about 47, residing in Griswold
Celia Watson, aged about 64, residing in Griswold

superficial. In 1835, George Ayer wrote the county court to explain that he had been persuaded to take the position against his better judgment, that he had a family dependent on him, "that time with him ought to be money," and that upon taking over his responsibilities, he found the affairs of the tribe in a state of chaos requiring him to spend considerable time and effort to rectify the conditions. Ayer then detailed his activities. He prosecuted cases against individuals who had illegally removed firewood, and had assisted one Peter George who had raised money to build a house and then improvidently squandered the funds. He also reported spending considerable time laying out a road through the reservation and seeing to it that the property was properly fenced. When the county court proposed to reduce the amount he had charged for his services, Ayer reminded the court of the money that he had recovered for the tribe. As he prosaically observed, "his time would have been more advantageously spent in attending to his domestic affairs than in receiving the full amount charged—that he faithfully discharged the duties of his office without fear or favor—that there were sacrifices of time and property in addition to the services charged by having more or less of the tribe almost daily at his house."[35]

Some overseers showed very little interest in tribal affairs. The overseers' accounts for the period from 1813 through 1819 indicate that the overseers spent between one-half and three days a year on Pequot affairs and that they were paid at the rate of seventy-five cents a day. This neglect of tribal matters was the principal cause of the tribe's efforts to have overseers removed. William Williams and Ebenezer Morgan ended their tenures as overseers in 1819 at the request of the tribe and were replaced by Enos Morgan and Stephen Billings. In 1836, Elisha Crary resigned and, after three years of waiting for the legislature to replace him, the tribe finally petitioned in 1839 to have Erastus Williams appointed to fill the vacancy. In fairness, it should be pointed out that part of the problem of finding competent overseers was the nature of the position;

most found it an onerous task with little reward and considerable heartache.[36]

But if there were pitfalls, there were also opportunities for profit and for abuse. With land to lease, rents to collect, and accounts to pay, the tribe inevitably leveled charges of impropriety and dishonesty against their overseers. In 1848 the tribal members petitioned the county court to investigate the activities of its overseer, William Morgan: " . . . the said tribe are desirious of having exhibited and made known to them the particular and full amount of their present overseer embracing every item charged for disbursements in repairs and support of the tribe—and, every article of timber, wood, rent, etc., which ought to be credited, as receipts."[37] This was followed by a request for Morgan's removal and replacement by Luke Gallup. In 1849 the Pequots repeated their request for Morgan's removal, characterizing him as a person "whom we do not respect nor consider a suitable person to manage our affairs."[38]

But the tribe had more to worry about than the petty abuses of the overseers. There was the General Assembly, which in 1854 and 1855 passed two laws that materially affected the tribe. The first, "An Act For The Preservation Of Indians, And The Preservation Of Their Property," provided for the appointment of overseers by the county court, limited their term to one year, required their bonding, prohibited suits against Indians, prohibited the sale of alcohol to Indians, and voided all conveyances of Indian land. In addition, it prevented the acquisition of Indian land by adverse possession, but it did permit the transfer of land when "such sale or exchange would be beneficial to the owner of such estate, and not injurious to the interests of the tribe." Unfortunately, while the 1854 act placed the overseers under greater scrutiny, and more tightly protected the interests of the tribe, it also gave greater control to the local governments, which were more susceptible to local political pressure. Significantly, many of the protections had been previously embodied in law, but with little effect.[39]

The Act of 1855 radically changed the conditions of Mashantucket Pequot life. The legislation provided for the sale of
the majority of the reservation without tribal consent. Under
the act the county court could appoint a committee of three
"judicious and disinterested persons, to sell and convey the
lands reserved by the state for the use of the Pequot Indians, in
Ledyard."[40] The court immediately appointed Isaac Gallup,
William Morgan, and John Gary, who divided up the land, reserving some 180 acres for the Pequots and selling the rest,
more than 600 acres, at public auction on January 1, 1856.
The total sale price was $8,091.17, which was deposited to the
tribe's account. All of the expenses incurred during the sales
were paid by the tribe. The Mashantucket Pequots protested
the legislative action and the resulting sales, but without success.[41] Thus, on the one hand, the legislature took action to
protect the land and property of the Indians of the state, and
then it acted to deprive the tribe of the land base the acts
sought to protect.

The tribe continued to have problems with the overseers. In
1855 they brought charges against Amos L. Latham, who they
claimed had been appointed without their knowledge or approval, and who had sold wood from the reservation for "small
and ruinous prices." They sought monetary damages, as well
as his replacement by Joshua Main. Neither the court nor the
legislature took action.[42]

The tribe asserted its autonomy in other ways. In 1856,
Celia Watson petitioned the Superior Court, charging that the
overseer had denied her the benefits due her as a tribal member. After reviewing the issue, the court found in her favor, determining that she was a member by virtue of her mother
having been a member, and thus she was entitled to a "just
proportion of the monies" and an allotment of land. Three
years later Jabez Niles petitioned for recognition of his tribal
membership. After a review of the facts, the court ruled that,
as the son of Prince and Anne Niles, he was entitled to membership. These cases indicate that the state courts recognized

descent from either parent as a basis for membership. They further show the willingness of tribal members to press their claims and the court's acceptance of the tribe's existence.[43]

The monies received from the sale of the lands at Mashantucket served as a basis for the funding of the tribe's welfare activities throughout the remainder of the nineteenth century and the first half of the twentieth century. Through the overseer, the tribe paid for food, medical care, housing, and funerals for its members. Women continued to earn a little money from the sale of splint baskets. Many of the men joined the whaling fleets, returning on infrequent occasions with "several hundred dollars in their pockets," which they spent "all in a few weeks in lavish generosity or gross dissipation," much to the consternation of their more parsimonious white neighbors.[44]

The first four decades of the twentieth century saw little change in the Mashantucket Pequot community. The major cottage industry, basket making, declined after 1900 because of deaths of the principal practitioners.[45] This coincided with a decline in the on-reservation population as housing on the reservation deteriorated, while the lack of funds prevented the construction of new units. Although fewer members lived on tribal land, tribal membership remained relatively constant until the Great Depression. Speck estimated that there were twenty-five members in 1907. In 1933, Judge Allys Brown of the Superior Court confirmed a tribal membership list of twenty-six, while a state commission in 1935 reported the population as forty-two, with nine living on the reservation and the remainder in the neighboring communities. This modest increase can be attributed to the effects of the depression, which caused some to return.[46]

The number of people returning to share in the tribal resources, the low yield that the capital funds provided, and the lack of jobs, placed enormous pressure on the tribe's resources. To complicate the problem, the local towns refused assistance. Tribal capital dropped from a balance of $4,701.76 in 1935 to $2,788.57 in 1940. As the principal declined, the

major income source of the tribe—interest—declined, resulting in a greater draw on the remaining principal. Fewer individuals could receive assistance, forcing others to leave.[47]

The increase in the numbers claiming tribal rights raised
the problem of eligibility and led the State Park and Forest
commissioner in 1936 to promulgate the following rules regarding tribal membership:

(a) Children of resident members will be members by birth.
(b) Children of nonresident members will be eligible for membership upon proof of parentage.
(c) All other admissions to a tribe will require written application,
accompanied by reasonable proof of descent and presence of Indian blood. Such applications should be endorsed by the recognized
Leader of the Tribe, if any, or in lieu thereof the endorsement of two
resident members. In doubtful cases the Commission will hold a
public hearing with due notice to the interested parties before granting or refusing the application.[48]

The commissioner's report is particularly important because, among other things, it establishes tribal continuity
through the first two decades of the century. Using the overseers' reports and contemporary findings, the commissioner
determined a means for establishing membership that relies
upon the support of the adult on-reservation members, who,
at the time of the report were two women: Elizabeth George
Plouffe and Martha Langevin Ellal. There is a strong implication in the commissioner's findings of a continuous tribal
operation centered on and around the reservation lands.

To deal with the economic conditions and to gain greater
control over the tribes within its borders, the state of Connecticut attempted to transfer the two tribes, the Eastern (Paucatuck) Pequots and the Western (Mashantucket) Pequots, to
the authority of the State Park and Forest Commission and
then to the control of the commissioner of welfare. While
these acts did away with the office of overseer, they did little to
improve the living conditions of the tribal members.[49]

Beginning sometime in the mid-1920s, Atwood I. Williams,
a Pequot who at times had resided on both Pequot reserva-

tions, began acting as spokesman for the two tribes. In 1933 he received tacit recognition by participating in court and overseer deliberations regarding the tribes. The judge reported:

So far as the matters that appear on the short calendar in relation to the Ledyard Tribe of Indians and the Eastern Tribe of Indians, I want to state for the record that as a result of the conference I have had with the overseer, Mr. Raymond, and Mr. Atwood Williams who I am informed has been recognized as the sachem, as evidenced by a paper executed by a majority of the members of the two tribes, I propose to enter certain orders which will be prepared by the overseer in pursuance to the discussion which has been had in chambers. . . .[50]

The first of these orders listed the names of the other members of the two tribes and stipulated that notice would be sent to Williams "as sachem of the tribes, or to his successor, to see whether or not there is any objection."[51] As single leader for the two tribes Williams lasted less than two years, after which time John George became the recognized spokesman for the Mashantucket Pequots, while Williams continued as the leader of the Eastern Pequots.[52]

While John George was designated the Mashantucket chief, the actual tribal leader was Elizabeth Plouffe, née George, who, with her half-sister, Martha Langevin Ellal, lived on the reservation until their deaths in the 1970s. The report of the State Park and Forest Commission for 1936 includes the following description of the tribe's resident population:

Pequot Indians

These tribes, put in charge of this Commission by act of the 1935 Assembly, are located on two separate reservations, one in the Town of Ledyard and the other in North Stonington. The resident members of Indian blood are listed below, with such data as is now available about their land and dwellings. Each tribe has some tribal funds, a statement of which appears in the Treasurer's report.
Ledyard Reservation:
   178 acres of land
     3 houses (insurance $600.)
     9 resident Indians
41 years   Mrs. Eliza Plouffe

15 years	Donald Clady
13 years	Eva B. Clady
8 years	Theresa V. Plouffe
6 years	Loretta E. Plouffe
35 years	Mrs. Martha Ellal
30 years	Mrs. Alice Guevremont
12 years	Regina Guevremont
8 years	Joseph Guevremont[53]

The same report showed that the Mashantucket tribe had a fund balance of $4,216.36 and had expended $485.40 in the first six months of 1936 on medical services and household supplies, building maintenance, and overseers' salaries.[54]

Conditions worsened on the Mashantucket Reservation during the 1940s. The housing deteriorated to such a point that one of the two remaining families was forced to leave. Elizabeth Plouffe, as acknowledged tribal leader, complained bitterly to the state about its neglect of tribal interests, prompting a visit by Hartford officials. They concluded that it would cost between $600 and $800 to repair the house in which Plouffe lived. They recommended that, instead of repairing the existing building, a new house be constructed at a cost of $1,800, and they suggested that tribal funds be used for this purpose. Since there was some question as to the legality of such an action, the officials requested an opinion from the state's attorney general about whether it was within the state's responsibility to provide shelter and whether the state's agent to the tribe could draw upon the principal in the tribe's bank account to pay for the necessary repairs. The attorney general responded:

We advise that it is your duty to keep the property belonging to the Indians in good repair only to the extent of income available, and inasmuch as you have found the income inadequate for such purposes, you should bring the matter to the attention of the Legislature for its consideration.

We advise that you have no authority to draw on the principal of the tribal funds, either to repair or replace existing shelters.[55]

The effect of the attorney general's opinion was to create an impasse, the result of which was the continued deterioration of the only house on the reservation and an increasing level of conflict between tribal members and state officials. A memo from the Office of the Commissioner of Welfare, dated November 26, 1941, indicates that Plouffe again complained about her deplorable housing as well as inadequate medical care. On this occasion she was told to get estimates for the medical expenses, but the housing problem remained unresolved.[56]

The lack of adequate housing, more than any other factor, forced Plouffe's children to move off the reservation. But they did not move far, and they were prompt to return when she summoned. At this time the Mashantucket tribal organization centered around Plouffe and her sister, but other members of her family as well as members of other families, were consulted regularly.

Between 1940 and 1960 the number living on the Mashantucket Reservation declined. According to tribal members, the state's agent prevented tribal members from moving back to the reservation once they had left, using as a pretext the argument that some did not possess the necessary blood quantum. While this is difficult to document, it is in keeping with the agent's general attitude toward the Mashantucket Pequots, which is most accurately described as racist and hostile. The agent's notebook for the period is filled with derogatory comments concerning the Pequots' presumed racial origins, their supposed lack of morality, and their alleged tendencies toward criminal behavior. None of the statements recorded by the agent bore a shred of truth.[57]

For the two and one-half decades following World War II, the two leaders, Plouffe and Ellal, protested the state's treatment of the tribe and tried to secure minimal services from the government, protection of the Pequots' unique status, and assurances of the maintenance of their land base. As in the 1930s, the town of Ledyard refused to provide services, leading the two women to seek them from the state. When the state ignored their pleas, they took steps on their own to protect their rights. Trespassers were driven off the Mashantucket Reservation at gunpoint. The women resisted every effort of officials to enforce the state laws on the reservation. On one occasion, they traveled to Hartford with other members of the tribe to protest the efforts of the state to collect dog license fees. Rather than pay the fees, they disposed of the dogs, pets of long standing. Toward the end of their lives, their frustrations in dealing with state and local officials turned to extreme belligerency, and they treated the officials as trespassers when they ventured on reservation land. Nevertheless, they were never successful in making the state, county, or town provide them with the services extended to others. They died without achieving the improvements in housing they had so vigorously pursued. Defiantly independent, they received no public assistance and earned their livelihood by picking berries, making baskets, and the like. Their accomplishments were to preserve the Mashantucket Pequot tribe's land base, the meager financial resources of the tribe, and the tribe's identity.[58]

Amos George became the Mashantucket tribal leader after the deaths of Plouffe and Ellal. The major problem of housing continued to plague the tribe and prevent utilization of the land. To solve this problem required outside assistance, which in turn dictated the establishment of a more formal tribal structure. During the early 1970s tribal members held a series of meetings to determine tribal membership and write a tribal charter. By 1974 these meetings had produced a Mashantucket tribal constitution, ready for approval by the membership.[59]

Richard Hayward was elected president at the annual meeting of 1975 to replace Amos George. While the change in leadership marked a significant change in tribal activity and direction, it was not occasioned by any dissatisfaction with the job done by George, who continued to serve on the board of directors. For the next two years, the tribe concerned itself with defining more precisely its membership and setting rules for the use of its nearly two hundred acres of reservation. The tribe allocated house lots of two acres each to members, retaining title to the land and reserving the right to alter the lot size, if necessary, and to determine the location of wells and roads.[60]

The Mashantucket tribe set two major goals for itself: the development of adequate housing on the reservation and economic self-sufficiency. In a sense, these were two aspects of the same goal. If the tribal members were to be encouraged to live on their land, then it was necessary to create jobs. In order to do that, the tribe had to develop an income, and since it had few saleable resources in sufficient quantities to meet the financial demands, the tribe authorized the chairman to seek grants from state, federal, and private sources. Hayward reported the first of a series of successful small grant applications in December, 1975.[61] The following year the tribe received its first federal revenue-sharing check for the munificent sum of $127.[62]

At this time Mashantucket tribal administration was scattered throughout the homes of the leaders. To consolidate its activities, the tribe used some of its funds to purchase a trailer to use as a tribal office. To encourage Indian awareness and to provide income opportunities for members, the Board of Directors initiated a crafts project supported by a small grant, and began selling maple syrup and firewood. This was followed by the construction of a hydroponic greenhouse. By the mid-1970s the tribe had established a pattern for economic development—a mixture of self-financing and external funding—and had established an efficient on-reservation administration to carry out the many projects it had initiated. The annual meeting in 1976 reflected the increased tribal activity. The tribal accounts showed, besides some $200 held by the state of Connecticut, profits from the sale of wood, income from a bicentennial grant, private donations, and income from the sale of crafts. In addition, there were expenditures for capital goods and reports on revenue sharing, the Comprehensive Employment Training Act program, the projected clearing of some five acres for a community garden, the need for more house-lot assignments, and a proposal to expand the maple-sugar business.[63]

Land had always been at the core of Mashantucket Pequot identity. Tribal members, who had grown up on the small reservation, had learned the importance of maintaining their land base. They had watched as the senior women of the tribe had kept outsiders and state officials off their land. And they had heard the stories of how much of reservation lands had been taken illegally in the nineteenth century. The lessons were well learned. After Hayward took over as tribal chairman, he and others conducted more extensive research on the issue. They were convinced that their land had been stolen.[64]

In the early 1970s, Thomas N. Tureen, working for the Native American Rights Fund (NARF), instituted a legal action against the state of Maine for the recovery of land taken from the Penobscot and Passamaquoddy tribes. Following the legal theory in that case, that no taking of Indian land by a state was legal without federal approval in accord with the Indian Trade and Intercourse acts, Tureen began visiting other tribes in New England to see if similar instances of state land takings had occurred. He arrived in Mashantucket in the fall of 1974, and based upon the evidence provided by the tribe, he was convinced that they had a case. He recommended that NARF take the case, which it did. After further research conducted by NARF, the tribe filed suit in 1976 for the return of the land lost in 1855.[65]

The Mashantucket Pequots had nearly come full circle. The remaining segment of their emergence would have to wait another ten years, until their recognition by Congress and their purchase of their lost land. That final part of the struggle is the subject of chapter 10 in this volume.

CHAPTER 9

The Mystic Voice

Pequot Folklore from the Seventeenth Century to the Present

By William S. Simmons

Pequod, you will no doubt remember, was the name of a celebrated tribe of Massachusetts Indians, now extinct as the ancient Medes.
—Herman Melville, *Moby-Dick or the Whale.*

Herman Melville's passage invites two comments. First, he is correct that Pequot (or Pequod) is a well-known American Indian tribal name. The second is that very little is accurately known about the Pequots. Melville illustrates this latter point through two ethnographic errors. The Pequots live in Connecticut, not Massachusetts, and they are not extinct. Pequot sachems once ruled the country from the Pawcatuck to the Connecticut rivers in southeastern Connecticut. English forces overran their stronghold at Mystic in 1637, thus ending Pequot rule over their old domain. Colonial authorities resettled many Pequot survivors on two reservations, Mashantucket and Lantern Hill. The Pequots continue to live on those reservations and in nearby towns such as Old Mystic, Ledyard, Groton, North Stonington, and New London.

Existing overviews of northeastern Indian folklore have made little or no use of Pequot materials because sources have not been available. For this chapter I have combined ethnohistoric

141

research in manuscript and published sources with new field-work among the contemporary Pequots of the Mashantucket (Western Pequot) Reservation in Ledyard and the Lantern Hill (also known as the Paucatuck or Eastern Pequot) Reservation in North Stonington. This material consists mainly of legends and *memorates* (firsthand accounts of experience), in addition to weather, plant, animal, dream, luck, and other lore. I am particularly interested in the legends and memorates. For simplicity, I refer to both genres henceforward as legend.

Legend conveys one generation's interpretations to the next. Through legend, people select some experiences and not others for retelling. They depict these experiences in terms of motifs and symbols that are available to them at that time. These may come from ancestral tradition or from external sources to which one has been exposed. Legends float through a twilight between what may really have happened and what people believe to have happened. Although they are a collective phenomenon, no two individuals tell them in the same way. Names, places, and events are pressed into stories that have a life of their own through legends. For example, the early Pequots had legends of a giant culture hero who waded far out to sea to hunt whales and large fish. When the first European ship appeared on their horizon, they accounted for it as the return of their culture hero. Legends open our eyes to the insider's point of view.

Compared to the written sources available for the Indian groups in Massachusetts Bay, Plymouth Colony, Martha's Vineyard, and Rhode Island, early writings on the Pequots are not extensive. The several accounts of the Pequot War describe military and diplomatic events, but give little attention to Pequot society, language, and culture. However, a few seventeenth-century observers, such as Roger Williams, Edward Winslow, Thomas Mayhew, Jr., and William Wood, have provided enough material to enable us to reconstruct a great deal about the world-view and folklore of the Narragansetts, Wampanoags, and Massachusetts—tribes who lived near the Pequots.

Throughout this area powwows, or shamans, were the prin-

cipal religious practitioners. They were usually men who controlled guardian spirits that took the form of snakes, birds, and
other creatures, as well as of inanimate objects. Shamans
were believed to be able to direct these spirits to send injury
or illness to their enemies, to heal their friends, change the
weather, improve hunting, read the future, and the like. Shamans
claimed extraordinary abilities such as swimming great dis-
tances under water and being impervious to arrow and musket
shot. In their many ritual feasts the shamans often collected
valuables from the participants as offerings to particular gods.
They held such feasts at times of harvest, midwinter, illness,
warfare, mourning, naming children, and other important occasions. Persons, creatures, events, or inventions that were out
of the ordinary could be considered a manitou, or spirit. English ships, guns, and windmills, for example, were thought to
be spirits, as was the great and powerful Pequot sachem Sassacus. Their religious universe was populated by many spirits
that presided over various phenomena such as corn, colors,
directions, seasons, the heavenly bodies, fire, men, women,
children, the house, and so forth. The shamans were particularly familiar with a spirit of the dead, known as Cheepi. The
creator, Cautantowwit or Kytan, sent the first corn and beans
and ruled an afterworld in the southwest. The crow, believed to
have carried the first corn and beans to earth, was one of
many sacred animals. They had legends of a giant culture
hero who shaped the modern landscape and of Little People
who lived furtively in the surrounding woods. Their indigenous
world was saturated with mythical figures and meanings. The
weather, landscape, illness, health, and natural phenomena
such as earthquakes and comets all had special significance.
Through their myths and legends they communicated this
knowledge from one generation to the next.

A few passages in early Dutch and English sources can be
attributed to Pequot speakers. These ethnohistoric fragments
fit squarely into the southern New England pattern. They mention the culture hero, the giving away of property at shamanis-
tic rituals, guardian spirits, healing and witchcraft, great physi-

cal feats by shamans, and the godlike qualities of certain prominent people. As the English gained the upper hand in war, the Indian survivors attributed their success to the greater power of English gods.

The Wampanoag, Narragansett, and Long Island Indians had legends of a culture hero known as Wetucks or Maushop.[1] According to the Wampanoags of Gay Head on Martha's Vineyard, where these traditions are best preserved, he was a giant human who waded into the sea to catch whales, which he roasted over an immense fire. He had a wife, named Squant, whom he turned into stone and who can be seen today as Sakonnet Rock off the Rhode Island coast. When the English came he transformed his children into killer whales that still swim in the sea. Like European giants, Maushop was said to have built huge stoneworks that can be seen in the water off the Gay Head cliffs at low tide.

The Pequots knew of Wetucks or Maushop. When the first European ship sailed into their waters, they believed that this strange visitor was in fact Wetucks returning from the sea. Many North American Indian groups had legends of their first sightings of Europeans. In Massachusetts Bay they described ships as floating islands. The Wampanoags of the Taunton River believed that they had seen a giant bird. According to this legend, recorded by Ezra Stiles in 1760, the Pequots interpreted this unprecedented event as the return of their culture hero:

Uncle Eldad adds about the Giant that he remembers hearing his Father conversing about it with the Dutchmen, & that the Tradition among the Indians was that the Giant "was peaceable & would not hurt the little Indians," and that the little Indians would give him meat to eat & he would receive it kindly; tho they said they always was afraid of him. They however weren't afraid of him when they approached him with a piece of meat or food which he would take without hurting them. He would knock the Bears off the Trees with his fist or a Club. . . . When the Indians first saw Vessels passing in the Sound off against Paucatuck, they said at first it was Weetucks a coming again.[2]

An early Dutch text presents a shaman's eye view of the property-offering ritual, wherein a guardian spirit in the form of a snake and another spirit take possession of the valuables: "They have a hole in a hill in which they place a kettle full of all sorts of articles . . . as a part of their treasures. Then a snake comes in, then they all depart, and the Manittou, that is the Devil, comes in the night and takes the kettle away, according to the statement of the . . . devil-hunter, who presides over the ceremony."[3] Roger Williams also reported a statement by a Pequot shaman in a letter that he wrote to John Winthrop just before the Pequot War: "The Pequots hear of your preparations etc., and comfort themselves in this, that a witch amongst them will sink the pinnaces, by diving under water and making holes . . . as also they shall now enrich themselves with store of guns."[4]

In 1637 a group of Pequot men ridiculed a company of English soldiers, "saying Englishmans God was all one Flye, and that English man was all one Sqawe, and themselves all one Moor-hawks."[5] About that same time Pequot warriors jeered the soldiers at Saybrook Fort saying, "come out and fight if you dare: you dare not fight, you are all one like women, we have one amongst us that if he could kill but one of you more, he would be equall with God, and as the English man's God is, so would hee be."[6] Following the English victory over the palisaded Pequot village at Mystic, a group of Indians allied with the Pequots called out to John Mason's men *that they would not Fight with ENGLISH MEN, for they were SPIRITS.*"[7] This changed view of the English was reflected in the words of Wequash, a Pequot or Niantic who helped the English in this war and who then worried about his own salvation. He told Williams, "me so big naughty Heart, me heart all one stone!"[8] Wequash also confided to the English that before the war, "he had low apprehensions of our God, having conceived him to be . . . but a *Musketto* God, or a God like unto a flye; and as meane thoughts of the English that served this God, that they were silly weake men; yet from that time he was convinced and perswaded that our God was a most dreadfull God; and that one

English man by the help of his God was able to slay and put to flight an hundred *Indians*." [9]

His contemporaries believed that Wequash had been poisoned (a common idiom for sorcery) as punishment for his Christian conversion. When they urged him to seek the help of an Indian shaman, he is reported to have said, "*If Jesus Christ say that Wequash shall live, then Wequash must live; if Jesus Christ say, that Wequash shall dye, then Wequash is willing to dye, and will not lengthen out his life by any such meanes.*" [10] A Stonington Pequot sachem told the Reverend James Noyes in 1693 that although he recognized the greater healing power of English prayer over Indian shamanism, he did not believe that he could convert: "one very witty and wise *Sachem* . . . told me he would be a christian, but he was afraid his heart would not be right, without which, profession would be in vain, and he was afraid *wine* and *women* would be his ruine." [11]

The last text above suggests that by the late seventeenth century some Pequots were still attached to their own traditions even though they did not deny the power of Christianity. The following text probably refers to this same time period, the late seventeenth century, and in it we see a strongly persistent belief in the shaman's ability to cause magical injury. This particular shaman had an intertribal reputation for his powers:

. . . sometime after the English lived at Stonington, there came an Indian (of that place) to Mr. Stanton (who had the Indian tongue) and told Mr. Stanton, there was an Indian (of that place) that had a quarril with him, and had sent for a greate powaw from Long Island, who had undertaken to revenge the quarril; and thereupon shewed a greate feare; whereupon Mr. Stanton sent for the powaw, and desired him to desist, telling him that Indian was his pertecaler friende, but the powaw refused without so greate a rewarde might be given, that the Indian could not be able to give, and the Indian powaw grew still more high and positive in his language, until he told Mr. Stanton he could immediately tare his house in pieces, and himself flye out at the top of the chimney; and grew at length to be so daring that he raised the old gentlemans Temper, so that he started out of his greate chayre and layed hold of the powaw, and by main strength

took him, and with a halter tyed his hands, and raised him up to a
hook in the Joyse, and whipped him untill he promised to desist and
go home, which he did and the poore fearefull Indian had no harm
from the powaw; there were many Indians without the house, who
came as neare as they dare, and saw the discipline, and expected the
house to be tore in pieces (as they said), who, when they saw the
matter so concluded went away much Surprised.[12]

Experience Mayhew of the missionary Mayhew family of
Martha's Vineyard visited the Stonington and Groton (now
Ledyard) Pequots in 1713 and 1714. After lecturing a Stonington Pequot audience about the proof for the existence of one
god that made the world, a Pequot objected that "they tho't
the mention of that unnecessary, because they said they knew
that as well as I."[13] Mayhew returned the following year to
Stonington, where he preached again. On this occasion he recorded the following exchange with an elderly shaman who argued a point similar to that raised by the sachem with Reverend
James Noyes in 1693—that Indians cannot become Christians. Of course the sachem and the shaman represented the
traditional order and had an interest in preserving it.

Hereupon an old Indian stood up who is Counted a Pawau among
the Indians, and speaking in broken English I perceived that he de-
sined to discourage the Indians as much as he could, I told him I
would not discourse with him unless he would speak in Indian that
all the Indians might understand what he said and also my answer
to him.
He then spake in Indian and said if the Indians present should
make any good promises at that time, yet they could not keep them
but would as soon as I was gone, be drunk and be as bad as ever.
I told him that was more than he knew, and that it may be some of
that people would now be reformed as many Indians had been, and
tho they had not power in themselves to forsake their Sins, yet the
great God whose Truth I had been speaking of was able to help
them, & I was not out of hopes but that he might help some of them.
The English said he would pretend to teach the Indians to be
Christians, if they will teach any, let them teach their own servants,
that live with them.
Yea, said I, let them do so, English people may observe this and

do it; but this is not all that is required of us we must also teach others if they do not refuse to hear and learn of us, and you should not only learn to know and Serve God yourself, but being an old man, should Encourage others to do so too.

If I should said he, the young people will grin at me and hate me for it.

What do you say to this, said I, to the young people present is this true that this old man saith of you.

He never tryed (said they) and if he had, we should not have been offended at him for it.

I own, said the old man, that there is a God, and I pray to him in my way, having by the English learned something of *him*.

Tis Well said I if you know something of *God* but if you worship God only in your own way, and not in *his* which is Sett down in his word, your worship will be in Vain, you and others should therefore learn what is said in the Scripture that you may know how to Worship God. What say you; would it not be well if the Indians knew how to worship God aright and did accordingly: yea said he I do not deny that, but the Indians Cannot do it, you affirm said I, that which you know not.[14]

By the mid-1740s, most Pequots had converted to Christianity in the seismic enthusiasm of the Great Awakening. Unfortunately, little has been recorded about the events and testimonies of their conversion. Between 1757 and 1774 the Reverend Joseph Fish of North Stonington worked on behalf of the educational and religious interests of the Stonington Pequot community. His diaries and letters during this period include expense accounts, lists of Indian names, and sermons, but provide little cultural information and no folklore.[15] When Fish died in North Stonington in 1781, an aged Pequot woman, named Esther, insisted on seeing the minister one more time and asked, "Oh, Mr. Fish, are you going to leave me in this wicked world?."[16]

In the years following the Pequots' conversion, Christian motifs entered their folklore just as European cultures and Christian teaching were changing their identity as a people. Several became clergymen to Indian congregations. Ruth

Pomham, a Pequot woman who died in 1833 at 101 years of age, remembered when she and the other Pequots hated the Christian religion. She had converted, however, and near the end of her life described herself in the following terms: "I am a withered shrub: I have stood a hundred years:—all my leaves are fallen, but water from the river of God still keeps my root alive." [17] She once told a minister: "Last night I had such views of heaven that I thought I heard the music of the angelic host, and saw the Savior face to face. I could not believe but I was there, till I called to my child and she answered me." [18] Sally George, a Pequot woman born in Groton in 1779, also attested to intense religious experiences that included Christian symbolism:

. . . and one night when I was in bed mourning, like the dove for her absent mate, I fell into a doze. I thought I saw the world on fire—it resembled a large bed of coals, red, and glowing with heat—I shall never forget the impression it made on my mind. . . . I was greatly in fear of dropping into hell . . . I cried earnestly for mercy—then I was carried to another place, where perfect happiness seemed to pervade every part. [19]

Near the end of her life Sally George was very sick and confined to her bed. William Apes, a Pequot author and minister, reported a remarkable circumstance involving George that seemed to be an act of Providence. She desired to visit a neighboring village about eight miles away. With the strength of the Lord she arose from bed, visited her friends in the nearby village, bade them farewell, and returned home to die. [20] Another aged Pequot woman, Eunice Mahwee, who was born in 1759, expressed sadness in her later years for the changes that had affected her people: "She spoke sadly of the decay of her people, and almost contemptuously of those whose blood was mixed with other than that of the Indian race." [21]

Among the Eva L. Butler papers at the Indian and Colonial Research Center in Old Mystic is a text, entitled "Curse of Cuppacommock," which Butler found in an old scrapbook owned by Anne Holmes Brockington. The clipping recounts a legend of the Pine, or Mast, swamp in Ledyard and the red- or bloody-heart rhododendrons that grow there. Polly Stoddard, who lived in Ledyard, wrote this legend as she heard it from Stonington Pequots, probably in the latter part of the nineteenth century. In 1903, Charles M. Skinner also published a slightly edited version of this text in his *American Myths and Legends.*[22]

The Pequot legend of the Cuppacommock Swamp and the bloody-heart rhododendrons bears a strong resemblance to a Yankee legend collected by a Works Progress Administration fieldworker in this same area in 1936. This Yankee legend of "Micah Rood and Peck's Hollow" concerns a peddler who came to Micah Rood's farm with many desirable items for sale. The farmer lured the peddler under the cover of an apple tree, where he plunged a dagger into his heart and stole his goods. The next spring the white blossoms of the tree were stained red and for many years thereafter the apples from this tree contained a red globule like a drop of blood. This phe-nomenon, coupled with his guilt, caused Micah Rood to pine away until he died a pauper in 1727.[23] The early twentieth-century Narragansetts also told a legend of red-hearted spruce trees that "grow where a drop of Narragansett blood was shed."[24] Clearly this version of the ineradicable bloodstain motif was present in both Indian and Yankee folklore in this vicinity in the nineteenth and twentieth centuries and proba-bly earlier. Through this symbol the Pequots and Narragan-setts remembered the devastating events of colonial warfare in the seventeenth century. Nature can be a chronicle of past events to those who know the legends and how to read the symbols. By 1986, when I began research, this story had been forgotten; however, many people, both white and Indian, will attest that red-heart rhododendrons continue to grow in the lovely swamp:

Among the papers of Miss Polly Stoddard of the Mast Swamp country, a venerable, precise spinster who died recently, was found a manuscript relating the tradition of the famous bloody hearted rho-dodendrons of that locality. This superb flower is profusely abundant and covers many square miles of the historic and extensive swamp in Eastern Connecticut, which since the white man's time and up to and including the last war furnished the masts for most of the sea-going vessels built in Connecticut.

The Mast Swamp Rhododendron is a tall, scraggy laurel with leathery tropical foliage and which differs from the ordinary rhodo-dendron in that its magnificent pink and purple blossoms have a dark crimson heart which seems to drip with blood so rich is its col-oring instead of being centered with the original splashes of gold usually seen. The Mast Swamp flower is accordingly widely sought after during its season of blossoming which is in the early part of summer. The treacherous morasses of the swamp are at that time visited by hundreds of daring rhododendron hunters. The swamp while in the heights of its floral glory is commonly called "Ledyard's Flower Garden" for the rugged township in which it lies.

Miss Stoddard's manuscript was written as a result of many con-versations held by herself on its subject with remnants of the Pequot tribe of Indians on the Indian Town Reservation in North Stoning-ton—over 60 years ago. The tradition of the bloody hearted laurels was one of the very few that came down with the last of Pequots to anything like the present time. Miss Stoddard's paper is entitled the "Curse of Cuppacommock" and it shows that Mast Swamp was first known to the white men invading this territory early in the 17th cen-tury as a place of refuge for the Pequot Indians. The Indians called the place Chomowauke or the Owl's Nest, from the great number of owls which took shelter in the dark recesses and also Cuppacom-mock or the "Hiding Place" from its remoteness and inaccessibility.

Until the white man came the Pequot who was fortunate enough to reach the shelter of Cuppacommock always succeeded in eluding his pursuers in its mazes and very likely managed to slay his would-be destroyers. The curse of Cuppacommock was the direct result of the destruction of the Mystic fort of the Pequots by Major Mason in the early colonial days—A ragged remnant of this aboriginal tribe under the leadership of Puttaquapouk after being pursued for some time took refuge within Cuppacommock's borders entering the swamp by means of a serpentine path which was then unknown to the whites but which is still in existence. There late in June 1637 just as the Rhododendrons were sending forth their glorious clusters of flowers the Pequots were surrounded by 120 soldiers from the Mas-sachusetts colony under Captain Stoughton and guided by Yotash, a

Narragansett chieftain, and his band. The miserable and enfeebled fugitives were told they need expect no quarter and that they would be exterminated sooner or later whether they surrendered or not. With the true Indian spirit they held out however until their women and children were nearly dead from starvation. They then cried for mercy. More than 100 prisoners were taken. Of these nearly 80 women and children were placed in bondage under the whites and the men, 30 in number, were bound and placed on a sloop commanded by one Gallop and carried down the Thames River to the mouth of New London harbor where they were made to walk a plank overboard one after another and left to drown.

Miss Stoddard's story says that the life of Puttaquapouk had been temporarily spared by Stoughton on his promise to aid the whites in unearthing some of the other enemies of the invading Englishmen but when the Pequot learned of the fate of his little band of warriors he refused to act further with the whites and was himself shot. The shooting took place in Cuppacommock, where Puttaquapouk, held as a prisoner, was lying on his back bound with withes under the great boughs of blossoms of the rhododendrons. Before he was slain, the tradition says, he gave utterance to a curse upon Cuppacommock for compelling him to surrender because of starvation and upon the whitemen for so blood-thirstily taking the lives of the warriors of his band. He declared that the golden hearts of Cuppacommock rhododendrons would turn to blood as a perpetual reproach to the invading Englishmen for the mercilessness of Gallop and Stoughton and ever since that time the Cuppacommock laurels, until then flecked with yellow, have blossomed with hearts of blood.

The Pequots as a nation were quickly subdued and their few descendents have long ago passed away but the Cuppacommock laurels by their red-hearted blossoms every succeeding year keep alive the memory of the curse.

It is supposed that some property of the soil of Cuppacommock give these flowers their peculiar coloring, for the Indians of the Indian reservation to the last one always declared that when the root of the laurel was transplanted to another soil, its blossoms would speedily revert to the golden hearted beauty of former days." [25]

In the fall of 1903 the anthropologist Frank G. Speck visited the Mashantucket and Lantern Hill reservations with a Mohegan named Skeesucks. He interviewed several persons includ-

ing Cissie Lawrence and Martha (Hoxie) George of Mashantucket and Leonard Ned of the Lantern Hill community. Of
Martha George he noted "how much the people seemed to
fear her very name."[26] Leonard Ned he described as "a man
over eighty years of age who still wears his hair long."[27] Speck
learned very little on this one-day visit and apparently did not
return, despite his long-term research interest in southern
New England.[28]

In 1936 and 1937 fieldworkers for the Works Progress Administration gathered data in the Stonington, North Stonington, Ledyard, Mystic, and Groton areas. They collected much
Yankee folklore, but paid no attention to Indians. A search of
the WPA files at the Connecticut State Library produced only
two Indian-related legends, which seem to be Yankee legends
about Pequots rather than legends that originated among the
Pequots themselves:

There is a cave in the ledges of Ledyard called the "Juda hole." It
is said that an old Indian squaw named Juda lived in this cave; her
reputation was such that anything reported missing in the village
was attributed to her thieving.[29]

There is a region in Groton called Candle Wood Hill where rattlesnakes are occasionally killed, much more so in former generations
than during the present. The following legend is told about this region. An Indian, one of the few survivors of the Pequot tribe, agreed
to rid this district of the rattlesnakes which were highly bothersome
to the inhabitants. The Indian first captured one of these harmful
creatures alive. While an assistant held the snake by means of a
forked stick, the Indian cut a hole through the skin on the back of the
snake and into it slipped a strong cord which he tied firmly around
the body of the animal. To the cord the Indian attached a well-filled
powder horn, its muzzle closed with a punk-wood stopple reaching
well down into the powder. He then set fire to the outer end of the
stopple and let the snake go. The creature disappeared into his hole
with the powder, and upon a signal the neighborhood assembled
with rocks, clubs and guns. In due time there was an explosion with
rocks and stones thrown about with the snakes with them. Others
who attempted to escape were dispatched by the men and boys who

were waiting. From then on the district was not often annoyed by rattlesnakes.[30]

Eva L. Butler (1897–1969) of Ledyard was a seasoned authority on Pequot ethnohistory and ethnography. In 1939 she recorded the following "Notes from Pequot Indians 1939 Chiefly Martha Langevin." Martha Langevin, a daughter of Martha (Hoxie) George, was a resident of the Mashantucket community. These notes indicate that a fair amount of plant, animal, weather, dream, and medical lore was current among twentieth-century Pequots and that Speck may have given up too easily. These notes constitute Butler's main ethnographic contribution to our knowledge of Pequot folklore:

> Heat fresh cow manure, put it on a cloth and use as a poultice to draw out poison after stepping on a nail, or put on face for neuralgia.
> When dogwood is in blossom it's time to go fishing for shad.
> Plant beans in June in the last quarter of the moon.
> When a cricket comes in the house leave it stay in. Don't put it outside 'cause it's good luck. My mother always used to say that.
> If you pick up toads you'll get warts.
> A dog howling is the sign of death. That's what my mother always said.
> If you kill the first black snake that you see in the spring you are conquering your enemy. I thought that was funny. But I ain't got the courage to kill them.
> If a wild bird flies into the house it is a sign of a death or something like that.
> In the morning mother would come to the foot of the stairs and say, "Rise and shine" and we'd have to tumble out of bed. She'd say if you sing before breakfast you will cry before night.
> If you accidentally put your clothing on wrong side out and wear it wrong side out all day you will have good luck. But she couldn't do it when she was going to work.
> If you wish on the new moon over your left shoulder your wish will be granted.
> If you can hang a powder horn on the points of the new moon it is a wet moon.
> Clip your hair when the moon is old to make it grow fast and strong.

Never let the rats get hold of your hair or it will make you crazy. She always made us clean our combs and put it in the fire.

Never cut the finger nails of a baby.

Burn up a child's tooth.

My mother said it would cause a fight when the fire sputters and cracks so she always threw salt on it to stop the fight.

My mother says to dream of muddy water is bad luck.

Mable she is awfully superstitious of dreaming of colored people being bad luck.

My father found a well by a branch of an apple tree. He dug and found water.

When we were kids we use to catch those grandfather long legs and hold them up and say Tell me where huckleberries are or I'll kill you. And then they would point their legs. Of course I'd never kill them and we always knew where the huckleberries were anyway.

When the snow is falling my mother always used to say a woman is shaking her feather bed.

It's a good idea to bury the bones of the red snake.

My mother says take a pack of cards and go down to the four corners of the road at 12 o'clock at night and the devil will come to you. I was tempted to do it for I wanted to see if it was true.

Adam and Eve grows in swampy places, Adam, the male's, white and Eve's blue.

Popple, the old name for poplar trees is still used.

I've heard if you catch a black snake and start at the head bite clear down to the tail that it would cure toothache but who'd want to do that foolishness.

My grandmother said that it was good to wrap an eel skin or a snake skin around the knees like garters to cure rheumatism.

When we had hiccoughs Mother took a dipper and put in our hands the wrong side and we drank out of it that way.

Angleworm oil rubbed on you will make you limber.

My mother used to bind salt pork on our throats when they were sore.

SPECKLED ALDER: Cook little twigs and rub on sprains and for headache.

AILANTHUS: Steeped and put with alcohol for rubbing, young twigs.

BEESWAX: Good to chew.

RUNNING BLACKBERRY (Rubus hispidus): Cook roots and drink for dysentery.

BONESET (Eupatorium perfoliatum): Make a tea of it for colds and fever.

BURDOCK (Artium minus): Eat like rhubarb.

DANDELION: Cook for a physic.

DOGWOOD: Boxwood.

SLIPPERY ELM: Chew the bark for a cold. It's also good for pregnant women.

EVERLASTING (Anaphalis margaritacea): Indian posy you cook and drink for colds.

FLAG: Sweet flag, Calamus or Flagroot (Acorus calamus Linnaeus): Sweet flag is good to chew but it bites your tongue.

HARDHACK (Spiraea tomentosa Linnaeus): Hardhack leaves steeped are good for dysentery.

HOPS: Hop blossoms are cooked and you drink it and it puts you in a deep dope-like sleep.

INDIAN CORN (Veratrum viride, Lin.) (White hellebore): My mother always called it Indian corn.

JACK-IN-THE-PULPIT (Arisaema triphyllum): Good for asthma.

JEWEL WEED: "Touch-and-drop-off." Good to rub on poison ivy.

MALLOW: CHEESES (Malva rotundifolia, Lin.): We eat the cheeses.

MAYWEED (Anthemis cotula): Steep and drink for fever.

MOTHERWORT (Leonurus cardiaca): Make a tea for women to drink.

MULLEIN (Verbascum thapsus): Smoke leaves for asthma.

NIGHT SHADE (Solanum nigrum, Lin.): Good for red snake bite. Used it on the dog and he got better. Cooked the whole plant and drank it.

OAK: WHITE OAK (Quercus alba): Cook and steep and drink for dysentery as a last emergency. It's too powerful, much more powerful than hardhack. Used just once.

ONION: Cut up onions and cook slowly a long time. The syrup is good for colds.

PENNYROYAL (Hedeoma pulegioides) (Trichostema dichotomum, Lin.?): Make into a tea for stomachache.

PIGWEED: Good as a green like spinach.

PINE: You can chew the pitch from pine for chewing gum and the bark cooked with wild cherry bark is good for colds.

PIPSISSEWA (Chimaphila umbellata): Steep and drink for kidneys.

PLANTAIN (Plantago major): Very cooling for fever, lay on forehead.

SASSAFRAS: Bark good to chew, make a tea of it for medicine.

SENNA; bush: Leaves dried for physic.

SKOKE (Phytolacca americana): Eat like greens, berries make good dye. Poke.

SPEARMINT (Mentha spicata): Steep and make a tea for worms.

SPICEWOOD (Benzoin): Spicebush twigs are good to chew, you cook them and make a tea for worms.

SPRUCE: Spruce gum's good to chew. Spruce sap's good for lung trouble. Walter was gassed in war. I told him to chew the little blisters on the tree.

SUMACH (Rhus hirta): Berries used to make a tea.

SWEET FERN (Myrica asplenifolia): Mother steeped sweet fern and put it on her hair to darken it. Also good for poison ivy too. Sweet fern has red flowers. We used to eat the seeds.

TANSY (Tanacetum vulgare): Eur., good for the stomach.

THISTLE (Circium arvense): A drink made of this is good for the lungs.

TOBACCO: Used to smoke Indian tobacco going to school.

WHITE PINE (Pinus strobus): Used to get from pine tree in front of house, colds tea.

WILD CHERRY (Prunus serotina): Drink made from the bark. Good for colds.

WILD INDIGO (Baptisia tinctoria, Lin.): Steep root and bathe cuts. We used plants for umbrella, picking berries.

WILD MUSTARD (Brassica nigra): Bandage on skin for toothache, but if you use your father's pipe it makes you too dopey to feel the pain. Horace Main pulled 2.

WINTERGREEN (Gaultheria procumbens): Leaves good to chew, also make a tea.

WITCH-HAZEL: Good to chew and rub on bruises.

YARROW (Achillea millefolium, Lin.): Used for medicine.

The place where "Grandmother Betsey's" garden used to be is overrun with wild ginger, bloodroot, tansy, star of Bethlehem, live for ever, horse raddish, elderberry, wild geranium.

Tree toads always chirp before a thunderstorm.

Red sky after sunset means we're going to have a frost.

June 14, 1939. You should always plant pole beans when the moon is waning. I nearly planted yesterday but my sister stopped me in time.

Always soak corn, beans and peas before you plant them. Plant pumpkins and squash with your corn.

Don't bury near water—bodies get watersoaked after petrified.
Leave me alone, by God I've anchored.[31]

Butler also recorded a brief item of Mashantucket place-lore
regarding Rachel's Rock and what appears to be a ghost story
about an Indian grave that she quoted from "an early account." The ghost story is reminiscent of Wampanoag legends about ghosts that frighten people who meddle with their
possessions.[32]

Rachel's Rock, where lived Indian Rachel, said to have been the
last Pequot Indian to have a traditional bark-covered dome-shaped
wigwam, is still known and pointed out.[33]

In the grave where another body was laid years after were buried
a gun with seven pounds of powder and seven pounds of shot for
the use of the hunter when he should arrive at the happy hunting
grounds. A white man is said to have coveted these then precious
articles and hired a man to rob the grave, but his courage failed before the time came for the attempt to be made, and the Indian is
supposed to still retain the gun and ammunition.[34]

In 1986 and 1987, I interviewed seven persons on the topic
of Pequot folklore. These included Helen Le Gault of the Paucatuck Pequot reservation; and Loretta Libby and her sister
Theresa Hayward, Theresa's son, Richard Hayward, and Alice
Brend, all of the Mashantucket community. In all I collected
about forty legends in addition to other shorter texts about
dreams, medicinal practices, sayings, and so forth. The majority of these concern ghosts and the dead, the Devil, and
witchcraft.

Legends about ghosts and the dead are the most numerous. The most distinctive of these concerns the ghost of a
whistling boy. There are no other whistling ghosts in Yankee or Indian folklore in this region, and the motif of a slave
being killed and buried with his master is also unique. The
seventeenth-century content of this legend (Mamoho was a late
seventeenth-century leader), and the fact that many people on
the Mashantucket Reservation know the story, suggest that it

may have been told here for many years. It is as distinctively
Pequot as the John Onion story is distinctively Narragansett.[35]

There was a chief named Mamoho in the 1700s. He befriended a
colored boy who was a mute. No one knows where he came from.
Chief Mamoho and the sachems were going out. This boy befriended the chief. He knew how to whistle. Whenever the old chief
would go he took the colored boy with him. Wherever they went the
whistling colored boy went. The chief got old and died. The kid was
still a kid. They took him up on a hill and buried him.

When they went up there to bury the chief they killed the little
whistling colored boy and buried him at the chief's feet so that they
could go to the happy hunting ground together. Every year they can
hear the colored boy walking through the woods. They can hear him
whistling.[36]

There was a chief; my grandmother said that this chief was an Indian chief of the Pequot tribe or he claimed to be anyway. He had a
little Black boy working for him, helping him. I guess he was kind of
a slave. The chief, whoever he was, was old. She said that he would
wait on him and give him things and take care of him and do things
for him. And he stayed with him. So when the chief died they killed
the boy and buried him with him. I know where they buried him,
where the grave is, where my mother said it was. This little boy did a
lot of whistling. And once in a while you'd hear him whistling. In fact,
I'd heard him whistling myself a couple of times. My mother said,
"Well listen, there's the whistling boy again."[37]

The Indian chief, we don't know his name—the story was told by
Aunt Martha [Martha Langevin, Martha Hoxie's daughter]. These
were the seven graves that we came across. His companion was a
little Black whistling colored boy. When we were kids she would tell
us she could hear them, either the chief chanting in the woods or the
little boy whistling. They were buried together in the same grave. We
just came across nine graves up there. Kevin opened up one of
them. It was really eerie that night when they dug it up.[38]

The next three accounts describe visions of the departed
that appear to their survivors as images in the sky. Visions in
the sky are an old Indian motif in southern New England. In
1700 a group of Connecticut Indian soldiers reported seeing

the figures of an Indian and an Englishman fighting in the sky and understood it to be an omen.[39] I recorded a similar sighting by Laura Mars, a Narragansett women, in 1983.[40]

There is a story about Martha Hoxie and the sky. My sister Eva in Florida saw that. It was right after her death. They were outside playing outside the homestead and they came running in and said, "Come see, Grandma's in the sky." My sister in Florida, she swears. By the time Mom got out it had faded away. I don't think she saw the image of her mother. Mom and her mother had a thing that whichever one went first, she would come back to tell her something. If anyone could have come back she would have. She was a strong person.[41]

There is a story that Martha Hoxie appeared as a face in the clouds.[42]

When I was working in the woods on the CETA program I was sitting on a stump and when John went down the path he came back and said, "Loretta, I just saw your mother looking down at you sitting on the stump." And the next day we saw an owl feather and one of his friends had passed away.[43]

Throughout the Indian communities of New England death may be linked with strange sights and sounds, as in the last example above. The next text below concerns unfamiliar animal cries in the woods after Elizabeth George passed away. In the second below Alice Brend recalls a vision of her sister at the very time that her sister almost died some miles away. In the third text below, Richard Hayward associates crows with death in a manner reminiscent of the seventeenth-century Algonquians of this area, who considered the crow to be a messenger from the afterworld.

I know that after my mother passed away that we heard some terrible animal noises that I've never heard before. Even Martha that used to live with my mother heard it. I never heard sounds like that ever. We know the different animals [that live here] and we never heard anything like that. John Stevens from Passamaquoddy had heard the same story. They call it the cry of death. It was our mother's spirit. It would be screeching over here and then over there. We even heard it after the funeral. We never heard anything like that before or since.[44]

I know what happened, about my brother. I saw my brother and it wasn't him. I saw my sister and it wasn't her. My sister Martha was working at the state hospital as a nurse. She just got her cap and her white uniform and was supposed to come over that day. It was on a Thursday. I came home from school. I got up the road and I heard our phonograph playing "Moonlight and Roses." I'd never forget that. It was playing and then I looked up. The door was open and I saw my sister come out with the uniform with the cap on and go around to the other door and go in. I kept on running into the house, and I said, "Where is she?" to my mother. "Where is who?" I said, "My sister." I used to call her Nan. "Where is Nan" Where did she go? Is she hiding?" And so I went running all over the house looking for her. . . . "She's not here. I tell you she's not here. Don't you believe me" I tell you she's not here." And I said, "Well, I saw her. And I saw her come out of the kitchen door, out through and go around the house and went in the other door." "She's not here. No one was here. She didn't come today." Then my mother got a message. A man came up with his horse and wagon and told my mother to get to the Baptist hospital as fast as she could, that my sister was dying. She went up there. My sister had appendicitis. She got better and was well enough to come out.[45]

I often hear the sound of crows cawing. Now, when someone dies on the reservation crows come right down on the street. I don't like it when the crows come. I don't know what it is. They go right to the windows.[46]

Cyrus George of the Mashantucket community came home one night from Mystic, dead in his horse-drawn wagon. Although some suggest that there had been foul play, others claim that there were no signs of injury and that he died a natural death. The horse carried him home out of timeworn habit. For many years after this incident, people reported hearing the sound of that horse and wagon coming home in the evening:

Cyrus George was riding his wagon to Horace Main's house. Someone at Mystic or Groton shot him and the horse took the

wagon with him to the house. And when he came home he was
dead. After that we could hear the sound of the wagon wheels on
Indian Town Road.[47]

A man died. Sounds of the wagon carrying his corpse were heard
here long afterwards.[48]

In the following Lantern Hill Pequot legend, an old Indian
couple who had long since passed away continue to protect
their grapes from children and others who would steal the
fruit. In both Indian and English legends of this vicinity, ghosts
are known to protect buried treasure. Indian ghosts also are
known to be protective of their personal property. This is the
first legend—Indian, English, or Afro-American—that I have
encountered in this region where ghosts protect crops.[49]

And the old folks that lived up on the hill from there, they had a
grapevine. And when the grapes were ripe she [Helen's mother] said,
"Don't pick those grapes. . . ." There was an old couple that lived up
on the hill in the back and they were very, you know, these kind that
they go out only just when they have to and kind of hermits like.
They stay in there. They were little old small people and acted peculiar and didn't like children and so forth. And they had this grapevine
and that was a story that went with that grapevine. So every time I
used to go by the old Pitcher house I used to think of that grapevine
because it went right up in the back of the old Pitcher house. And we
lived right down a little ways from there. And [we] crossed the brook
to get up in there. So I remember I used to tell a youngster that was
always teasing me and I didn't like him at all and I told him that if he
came down there I'd push him into that grapevine. And then he
would get poisoned. And he used to laugh and make fun of me all
the time. But I believed I could push him in there and make him poisoned if he had those grapes. . . . This was after they had died though.
They couldn't pick 'em, no. They had already died, yes, why they
came and got the grapes after they had died . . . they were Indian
people. . . . Carpenter was the last name of the old gentleman. I
don't know what the old lady's name was.[50]

Haunted houses, barns, and natural landmarks are common in nearby Indian and Yankee folklore. So, too, are the

ghosts of persons who died violent or tragic deaths. Ghostly lights, while an indigenous motif in Yankee and Afro-American lore, are also an old Indian element that can be documented as early as the seventeenth century. Such lights are mentioned by twentieth-century Narragansett, Mohegan, and Wampanoag sources. The ghostly Indian figures that pass over Long Pond on the Lantern Hill Reservation are warm reminders of Indian identity and heritage.

My grandparents were gone when I was a little girl. . . . I remember my grandmother when I was about five years old. She lived right next door to us but she didn't live there very long 'cause she was a very old lady when I was small. But I can remember my mother telling about stories that they used to tell her 'bout this old house where they lived which was right next door to us but it eventually fell down. But she said they had stories of the attic up there in that home. I've been up those stairs myself many times. And she said that they would believe in noises that they heard. And most of 'em would have a name. They would have a name of an old person who had lived there in years gone by. And that they were unhappy about something. And that they were making themselves known to the people who lived there. They were really unhappy. And I remember 'em having a pantry in the back part that run into the side of the hill there. And I can remember them telling me about stories about that pantry and the bedroom that was in the back there. At night in that pantry whoever slept in that room didn't sleep very much because of the noises and the disturbances that came out of that pantry. And it was built over a brook. And to us kids we were told to be careful and so we were. We listened to Grandmother. 'Course she didn't live very long after I was big enough to remember what she said and did. But they had an old barn up on that hill in there where we lived too. And Grandmother used to say, "Don't go near the bottom part of that barn because it's haunted." And my mother used to say to her, "Well, tell them what haunted means." She'd tell us. And Grandmother would explain to her that someone died there. One time they said a man hung himself in that basement. And she said, "Well, if he hung himself in there, which he did, he is very unhappy wherever he is and that's why he keeps coming back and making these noises and appearing." For people used to say they saw things when they went by there. I remember we used to go up there to go over into a field in the back. And we'd always be shy of that building because she had told us that it was haunted.[51]

That's an old story . . . they still talk about it. Some people come in here . . . they've been here before and they ask where the lantern was on Lantern Hill. . . . The lantern that came on every night and . . . people stayed there and waited for that lantern to appear and it never did. In the years gone by I mean they tried to prove it but people talk about it even on the sea—seeing that light off there. It's quite a story. And there was an Indian maiden that committed suicide up there too. In that same place—in that area where they had the lantern that used to come on every night. . . . Another story that went with a bottle of whiskey that the warrior ended his life over too. In that same area where the lantern appeared.[52]

We lived right next to a place called the Pitcher house and that was haunted they said. . . . It was a three-story and the first two parts of it were open, and there was a peak in the top and that's where a light used to come. Every night a light would be there. People would come from all around to see that light, but it wouldn't do it every night. It was only certain times. The children learned to say the Pitcher house was haunted. So we all believed it was haunted. And it was so near our house that when we went from our house down the lane way to go down to the main street [of North Stonington] we wouldn't go that way. We'd cut 'cross on the little swamp . . . because we didn't want to go by the Pitcher house. And we didn't want to see that light from so close. So I remember that when they sent me to the store I used to go always across. . . . I wouldn't go around that way because I believed it was haunted. But there were many houses that were haunted in the town where I lived that they would say—the old-timers would say—were haunted.[53]

On this lake many years ago a canoe with a light and a warrior and his bride . . . every night came down this lake and went through the bridge that separates the two lakes and went over the other side and around and came back here. And it could be followed. . . . This had been seen by people even within my day. . . . They told me of the feeling they had when this happened. Even the other day not too long ago now there was a person telling my neighbor about how . . . she had been at one of the cottages visiting and this woman that owned the cottage said, "Well if you are around here tonight at ha'

past eleven, between ha' past eleven and twelve o'clock, you will see
our visitor that we have nights." And so the woman said that she
didn't believe in stories. . . . She said that she actually did see it and
she took me to the window where she said she saw it. Later, when
my friend bought that house, I asked her if she ever saw the canoe
that comes down the lake. And they said how beautiful it was. . . .
This is really a legend that . . . the old-timers, some of 'em even live
now that were acquainted with that story. They really believed it because their close friends had seen it. . . . I remember a cousin of
mine came here to stay a while and he and his wife had a canoe and
they dressed in their regalia. They had some beautiful clothes. And
they used to go up and down this lake with that canoe and go to the
other side and come out through. . . . I know that same lady who just
died in March. She had moved to Maine and died. She told me that
she used to watch some of this. It was such a pleasure to watch. And
it was so beautiful she said with their regalia bright and their canoe
that was white. . . . They would go so gracefully down there and
back again. . . . As long as she had a cottage here she used to enjoy
that, she said. So there is a legend about that canoe and the occupants. . . . I think it [the legend] still lives here too. Because once in a
while you can hear someone bring it back and go over it . . . what
their friends have told them. They enjoy it. . . . They didn't mention
that they knew anything or why it appeared like it did. But it was just
an old story that these people had learned to live with, and believed
in it and didn't want to forget it. . . . But when my cousin came and
went down through they just brought it all back.[54]

On Shewville Road in Pequot country is a dark overgrown
area known as the "dark hall" because of its eeriness. This location is reminiscent of Black Brook at Gay Head on Martha's
Vineyard, which is also known for strange presences.[55] The
ghostly cow that appears to Martha Hoxie in the following story
is very similar to the ghostly horse and oxen that Gay Head
Wampanoags have seen over the years. The ghostly cow motif is also widespread in English and American folklore.[56]

My mother told me a story about when she drove the horse to
Mystic and came back late at night. There's a place we call the "dark
hall" on the road to Shewville on Shewville Road. She came through
the "dark hall" and saw a great big cow come out and walk in so

close that the horse was rearing. This cow passed by and she said, "Whose cow is that?" She could see that the bag was ready to be milked, and it was late at night around eleven o'clock, something like that. She said, "I wonder whose cow is that?" She inquired all around but nobody ever knew. That was the "dark hall" on Shewville Road.[57]

Two nineteenth-century authors refer to Pequot migration legends. De Forest, for example, wrote that the Pequots originally lived on the banks of the Hudson River and that "all the traditions of the Indians on the history of the Pequots agreed in asserting that they migrated from the north shortly before the arrival of the English."[58] Brinton wrote that the Pequots were descended from a branch of the Shawnee tribe that settled in Pennsylvania and New England: "According to ancient Mohegan tradition, the New England *Pequods* were members of this band. These moved eastwardly from the Hudson river, and extended their conquests over the greater part of the area of Connecticut."[59] Brinton attributed this legend to the early nineteenth-century manuscript papers of the Reverend John Heckewelder. Three twentieth-century Mohegans, Fidelia Fielding, Emma Baker, and Lemuel Fielding, also remember legends regarding Mohegan migration from the northwest to the southeast or from west to east.[60] Emma Baker, an aged Mohegan woman, told Speck that, "when a child of seven years, my great-great-aunt used to take my sister, brother, cousin, and myself on the hill near where the church now stands, point to the northwest, and tell us that was the way that her folks came, and that we must never forget it, away to the hills of Taughannick, and after that for several years she used to impress upon our minds that it was something that we must not forget."[61]

Helen Le Gault of the Lantern Hill Reservation believes that west and northwest are favorable directions. Good weather and good omens come from there, whereas evil and unnatural sounds (such as groaning and whistling) come from the east and southeast. These associations are strongly reminiscent of the nineteenth- and early twentieth-century migration legends previously noted. In this account, as in the legends of

the whistling boy, whistling is a ghostly, unnatural phenomenon. These associations are distinctively Pequot and do not
occur in other folklore traditions in this area.[62]

Of course there was always whistling. Yeah, the whistling through
the forest. . . . Sometimes it would come from east most always
from the east and the south. The part from the west you'd never hear
because that was a good clear direction . . . good weather and everything from the west the northwest good omen, but when it comes
from the east and southeast it was evil. So the whistling would come
from that direction. And I suppose that would make it sound more,
you know, like unnatural things. They used to tell about the whistling
tunes and the groaning sounds with the whistle and when it came
with a groaning sound it was a bad omen. But when it came with a
sound clear without the groaning . . . the gods were happy. And it
would make you think . . . and make the kids think. Most of the
grown people didn't pay any attention but the kids did.[63]

Anglo-American and Afro-American motifs about the Devil
entered Indian folklore early in the colonial period. Legends
about the Devil from other Indian communities, such as Narragansett and Gay Head, for example, closely resemble those
told by their non-Indian neighbors. Pequot Devil legends are
clearly part of this wider southern New England cultural sphere.
The Devil in these legends serves as a kind of social con-
science who would discourage drinkers and gamblers from
their activities. Place legends about the Devil's footprint also
are known throughout the Indian and white communities of
this region.[64] Near the Mohegan church in Uncasville, for example, is a large hooflike impression in a stone that is known
as the Devil's Footprint. One such footprint also exists on the
Mashantucket Reservation.

My mother told me about the Devil. My father had been drinking.
He used to walk, carrying the groceries; he didn't have a horse. After
he got off the trolley, a man walked up to him facing him, and said,
"Hello, Napoleon [Napoleon was French-Canadian]. Come on back
to Norwich and let's have a drink." My father said, "Oh no, I've had
enough, I'm going home." So he continued walking, and got as far
as Sandy Hill when this man came again, a tall man, and said to him,

"I was heading back to Norwich. Let's go have a drink." He said, "No, I saw you way back at the trolley tracks." He said to my mother, "This man has been meeting me every once and a while and asking me to go back for drinks up in Norwich. I think he's the Devil." So my mother said, "What man? I don't see no man!" Then my mother saw the attic door open and close. That's the only thing I know about the Devil. That's what my father saw. For a long time after that he said, "That man just kept meeting me on the way." And my mother said that you never saw anybody as sober as he was when he walked in that door. He was sober, he was scared, he was afraid. He never saw him after that. But he would never go up in that attic. That's where the Devil is.[65]

Down by Slippery Hill my dad was coming back late at night and he heard something and saw a thing that had the body of a donkey and the head of the Devil. When he got to the house he was all upset.[66]

There was a story of the Devil in the shape of a mule. My grandfather was talking to him and the disappeared. He was part Mohawk and part French Canadian.[67]

And I can remember when Grandmother Durfee used to come to our home in the center of North Stonington and tell us the stories about the card games that they used to have on the reservation there. And they would play just about so long and then be interrupted. And so she said, her nephew said one night he would like to know what the interruption is to their card games that he was annoyed by. And she said . . . "Let's set a trap for 'em." And he agreed with her that was good. So when it was time for that noise to come and the interruption, she told him to be on the outside of the house so he could see what came to that door and the windows . . . that annoyed them and made such a noise. . . . And then they would hear what sounded like hooves that would go by in the distance as they ran away. And I remember sitting there with my eyes as big as saucers listening to that story and I've never forgotten it. And she said that after that interruption that . . . her nephew saw tracks outside of the window. And she said they tracked it as far as they could before it disappeared on the road. . . . They never saw what it was, no, but she said, "Well, I know what it was, it was Satan, it was the Devil. We were playing cards and we shouldn't be." Because they had a little pile of pennies that they used to play with and they thought that that was gambling.[68]

The four corners where the Devil will meet you is at Long Pond, on the road to Lantern Hill. They go there to make league with the Devil.[69]

I know where there is one up there on the reservation. I don't know if they probably bulldozed it up by this time, but there was a man's shoeprint there . . . some of them used to say that was the Devil [as he] comes through and he stepped on it. . . . This footprint is up on the reservation there. I know where it was but they bulldozed through there and everything else. Maybe it's not there.[70]

They say there is a foot of the Devil back there in a rock.[71]

The Algonquian people of northern New England have many traditions of Little People who live in the woods and around lakes and rivers. Such beliefs surely existed among the southern New England groups, but have largely disappeared. The best-preserved legends of Little People in this area were those collected by Frank Speck from Fidelia Fielding at Mohegan early in this century. Other vestiges also survived in the folklore of twentieth-century Wampanoags at Gay Head and Mashpee.[72] Helen Le Gault narrated the following account of Wooden People, which is unprecedented in southern New England folklore; it may be an Eastern Pequot survival from earlier Algonquian belief. The fairy mentioned below by Alice Brend could represent a fusion of English and Pequot tradition.

They call them Wooden People. And they used to make 'em out of wood. The two of 'em to look like 'em. These are the Wooden People. And they used to come out of the woods. And they used to tell us kids about 'em but we never saw any. We only saw those that they made. I remember . . . old man Jackson used to make the Wooden People and put 'em on a—like he had an old cellar door over there and he used to put 'em, tack 'em on that cellar door over there . . . to let the children know those Wooden People were in the woods and to keep away from 'em. They'd always warn the children about these people that were . . . not living people but imaginary people. . . . I don't remember that they had a name, just Wooden People. . . . And then he said to the children, "Now this is what they look like." And maybe they did to him. They perhaps looked just like he made them on there. . . . He was always tellin' about what, he'd put food out for them. . . . They were always hungry. I don't know why. . . . That's what he used to tell us. . . . Mr. Jackson . . . would . . . have cereal left over and he'd put the cereal out in the pan. I thought he was puttin' 'em out for the dog. And I said to him, "What are you doing that for?" And he said, "For the Wooden People. . . ." He did look forward to seeing them. . . . Wherever he was, he'd look and say all the time . . . at springs . . . boiling springs had delicious water. And I'd say, "Where are they coming?" And he'd say, "To the spring to drink. . . ." We got our water there for years. . . . They were just wood, just like a gingerbread man . . . on the square side, I remember. They had like this cutout in wood and the arms out like this and their legs were straight and there they'd be just nailed to this little cellar door . . . an old cellar door that wasn't being used.[73]

My grandmother used to say there was a fairy that used to dance across the street from her house. She said that sometimes she'd get ready at night to go to bed and she'd look out the bedroom window, and she'd see this little fairy dancing over there. That's the only thing she said about Little People.[74]

People on the Eastern and Western Pequot reservations know many witchcraft legends. They are most similar to stories recorded among the Wampanoags and Mohegans, but also are reminiscent of Yankee and Afro-American accounts. They explain misfortunes by attributing them to the ill will of someone nearby. The most unusual one concerns a buzzing noise behind someone's mirror that proved to be an evil spirit sent by a person from another community. The witchcraft stories among Indians, whites, and Afro-Americans are an old and indigenous aspect of folklore in the Northeast.

The following texts cover a range of topics including historical lore, supernatural lore, animal and medical lore, and conventional wisdom. Some are traditions passed on from earlier generations. Others originated as firsthand experiences, memorates of the person who narrated the story.

A woman was visited by three angels. She reformed from drinking after that.[75]

Thunder is an old man falling down the stairs.[76]

I saw a hill throbbing as a heartbeat.[77]

A treasure is buried in the swamp. Gold, all kinds of treasure. I heard this from my grandmother.[78]

My grandmother said that all of New London was a cornfield and that in 1824 the last person living in a wigwam at Mashantucket was Ann Wampey.[79]

The first black man to come here was killed.[80]

There are many stories about the oaks near where the mixed-race children are buried.[81]

Mat [Martha Langevin] went out with a shotgun after snakes. A snake killed every chicken, broke every egg. She killed all snakes, wouldn't use the eggs if snakes had been around, if they got into the chicken coop. She walked around where a snake passed for fear it would leave poison on the ground. Copperheads give off a scent like cucumbers. If you're in the woods and smell cucumbers, that's what it is. Mat shot copperheads till there was nothing left but shredded wheat. She wouldn't do that with any other snakes.[82]

There was a woman on the reservation with a hoop dress. Another woman would hide under it and no one would threaten her.[83]

My mother knew everything, and of course taught me quite a bit, about different herbs and what's good for you and what's not. We used to cook greens, and we used to get different things out of the swamps and the woods, picking different things. Then she'd cook them up and we'd have them for greens on the table. She knew how to get the stuff for colds, and showed me where it was to get it. And then for rattlesnake bite, our dog got bit by a rattlesnake and my mother went and got these vines. I knew what they are to see them, but I don't know the name of them. These vines had orange berries on them. I went with my mother to get them. The only thing with which we tried to save the dog from that rattlesnake bite is this kind of vine my father told me about. She said her father knew about the vine. So we went way up in the highlands and we found some up there. My mother got a bunch of it and took it down and steeped it and cooled it. My father held the dog and poured the bottle down its throat. He drank it all. My mother said it's really poison stuff, for us never to drink it because she didn't know what it would do to a person. But she said it was a cure for snakebite.[84]

Tobin Spring was right off the road about one-tenth of a mile down the hill. My mother always put her ash sticks in there. She made baskets and put her ash sticks in the spring. I used to help her make baskets. I know how to make baskets, but nobody wants to learn; they don't want to do it. Of course, now that I'm older I don't bother about it either. But I used to make them with my mother and I would sell them for fifty cents a basket. And now—I don't know if you talked to Red Wing [Mary Congdon, Narragansett, also known as Princess Red Wing]—I don't know if she's still living [she died in 1986]. She told me if I made a basket she'd give me $100 for it. But I wouldn't do it myself—but if I knew somebody would do it I would show them how to do it, how to soak it, how to cut it, strip it, and how to polish them, and how to use different berries to stain them different colors. Not different colors—I only know about red because that's about the only thing we used. My mother used to make the blue, but she used ink. The reason I said I'd try to make a basket is because I saw a tree appear. It was a black ash tree and so I asked the fellow who lived over on the Indian reservation, "Would you cut a tree down for me and split it and everything? If you could pound it out for me, I would make a basket." But he had a heart condition and I saw how sick he was, so I never bothered him with it. But I got a little piece of it and I pounded it out myself. It was only this long, this stick that I had. And so I made three little baskets with it. I gave them to my daughter. She puts little flowers in them. I made these little baskets about four or five years ago. Just for the fun of it. I wasn't doing anything and I thought I would just do that. I pounded it out myself, and I stripped it with a jack knife and shaped it out, and used a little sandpaper to make it shiny and smooth. And I gauged it and put it together and made the handle and everything. I just made the three little baskets. Nobody was interested in making any of the Indian baskets, so I never pushed it.[85]

Balsam buds, mixed with alcohol and rubbed on, is good for arthritis.[86]

White oak will bind you up. If you have dysentery, steep the bark of it.[87]

Skok [perhaps a survival of the Pequot word for snake] is an edible green like Swiss chard. I recently made a kettleful.[88]

Mother said that a red sky after sunset meant a hot day not a frost.[89]

Mother said that if you dream of muddy water it means bad luck.[90]

In the following passage, Alice Brend recalls the only Pequot word that she now remembers, *katunk,* the word for cane. During my second interview with her, I heard a slightly different pronunciation—*kwitunk.* She heard this word and others from her grandmother. This is surely the Pequot equivalent of *quett-hunk,* "a stick to poke the fire with," recorded by Thomas Commuck, a Brothertown (Wisconsin) Narragansett in 1859. Commuck, who was then fifty-two years old, included this word on a list of six that he had learned from his grandmother, and said that these were "all I know of the language of my tribe."[91] Alice Brend said:

I only know one word in Pequot. I used to know more—my grand-mother told me different words before—but I always remembered "cane." She used to say, "*Katunk, katunk.* Get my *katunk* for me." And that was her cane.[92]

We have heard many Pequot voices from four consecutive centuries. As the Pequots interacted in new ways with the wider society, they appropriated aspects of that experience into their own identities. Folklore is sensitive to the impressions left by such interactions. Pequot legends and other narratives draw upon the motifs of several cultural traditions for their symbolic content. One tradition is Indian—stories heard from Pequot parents and grandparents, but also from close Indian neighbors such as the Narragansetts and Mohegans. Yankee, French-Canadian, and Afro-American motifs also influenced Pequot folklore. Indian and non-Indian sources merge over time as the Pequots adapted much of what they borrowed to fit their particular experiences.

The evidence of radical symbolic changes appears as early

as 1637, when Wequash and others revised their ideas about the power and importance of the English God following the Mystic fight. In eighteenth-, nineteenth-, and twentieth-century accounts, we see the strong imprint of Christian symbolism on individual and group identity. Individuals like Ruth Pomham and Sally George spoke of the importance of their Christian conversion. Angels and the Devil upheld community values by frightening drinkers and gamblers. Pequot Devil and ghost stories are often similar to the Devil and ghost stories of non-Indian Americans.

Beneath these convergences with the wider culture, a degree of separateness is also apparent in Pequot folklore, some of which can be traced to indigenous Indian origins. Old Indian motifs that span the seventeenth to twentieth centuries are the figures that appear in the sky and the belief in misfortune caused by witchcraft. The Wooden People and the fairy described above may be the last evidence of Pequot belief in Little People. Contemporary ideas about favorable winds and omens from the north and northwest are reminiscent of earlier legends regarding ancestral migration from those directions. The ghost of the whistling boy appears to be indigenous to the Mashantucket Pequot community. Ghosts remind the living of ancestral misfortunes, protect Indian property, and give a kind of Indian signature to the many landmarks of Pequot country such as Lantern Hill and Long Pond. The nineteenth-century legend of the bloody-heart rhododendrons conveys an Indian account of seventeenth-century events while drawing upon a motif that was shared by both Indians and Yankees (the ineradicable bloodstain) to do so. It would be rewarding to investigate the ways in which Indian folklore in southern New England may have influenced the legends and other traditions of their non-Indian neighbors.

Melville named the doomed ship *Pequod* because he assumed that the people for whom he named it had been destroyed. He chose the wrong symbol: the real Pequots survived the battering. Legend, which links meaning with events and the past with the present, is a chronicle of their journey.

Through their legends, we have heard some impressions of Pequot experience as they told it and as they continue to tell it. They have constituted a small universe that is both submerged in and yet separate from the wider society. Is there an Indian voice still to be heard among the contemporary people who identify with the ancient tribal name? According to legend there is. The remaining roots of their Indian identity are no longer shrouded by folklore; they are revealed by it.[93]

Contemporary Federal and State Policies and Southern New England Indians

Changing federal and state policies have significantly affected the American Indians of southern New England over the past two decades. Perhaps the greatest change has been their fervent quest for federal acknowledgment. In the first chapter of Part Four, Jack Campisi describes this Byzantine process of "status clarification." Recently, three Indian communities in southern New England—the Narragansetts, the Mashantucket Pequots, and the Gay Head Wampanoags—have been federally acknowledged. Washington officials have finally recognized that a government-to-government relationship between these Indian communities and the United States exists and has always existed. Campisi discusses the history of the process as well as the problems American Indians face in meeting the criteria for federal acknowledgment. He shows that New England Indians' lack of such acknowledgment is caused largely by whims of history, reinforced by racial discrimination, and impeded by bureaucracy and politics.

Robert Bee offers the reader another perspective on how Indian policies are made in state capitals, in this case, Hartford. Showing the direct relevance to other states, Bee describes how Indian affairs in Connecticut have evolved from over-

seers' administration of the Indians' dwindling estates to pater-
nalistic social-welfare management, to the establishment of
the Connecticut Indian Affairs Council in the early 1970s. Bee
then examines the work of this council in theory and in practice. The late Governor Ella Grasso's administration focused
on Indian betterment for the first time in the state's history, and
under her leadership the council went beyond public displays
and was given respect and recognition. Bee concludes that
Hartford policy makers continue to support Indian-sponsored
legislation, but he notes that the state has not consistently supported Indian interests when the issues include land claims or
tax revenues. Nevertheless, he insists that Connecticut's policy
makers are without doubt more progressive than many officials in other states.

CHAPTER 10

The New England Tribes and Their Quest for Justice

By Jack Campisi

In the 1970s and 1980s, five northeastern tribes reestablished a government-to-government relationship with the United States as a result of congressional legislation: the Gay Head Wampanoag, the Houlton Band of Maliseet, the Mashantucket Pequot, the Passamaquoddy, and the Penobscot; a sixth community, the Narragansett, has been recognized by the petition route through the Bureau of Indian Affairs' Office of Federal Acknowledgment. These victories have been hard fought battles in the face of hostile administrations. In addition, other tribes are at various stages in the Byzantine process, struggling to overcome more than a century of official neglect, racial prejudice, and bureaucratic stupidity and myopia. That any have made it through this gauntlet is a testament to their fortitude.

Federal recognition has always been serendipitous. One can crisscross the entire terrain that is Indian law and Indian-white relations with a divining fork and never hit a coherent policy. Tribes that opposed the United States, negotiated with the United States, sold land to the United States, signed treaties with the United States, or received appropriations from the United States were deemed federally recognized. Others, such

179

as most along the eastern seaboard, had long been passed by when the United States came into being. They remained isolated Indian communities, often independent and self-sufficient until the states within whose borders they resided decided to assert some control. Those tribes that have benefited from and suffered under the federal relationship should understand that their acknowledged status was an accident of history that has spared them the social vivisection to which their eastern brethren have been subjected.

How does an Indian tribe go about achieving recognition of its relationship with the federal government? There are at present three ways to accomplish this: (1) a tribe may take action in court to force the United States to recognize its trust responsibilities; (2) it may apply to Congress; or (3) it may follow a process established by the Department of the Interior. All three have their peculiar limitations and risks.

Eastern tribes had an immediate impetus to secure federal recognition when they realized in the early 1970s that they could file lawsuits for land lost because of state or local actions during the nineteenth century. In recent years the tribes have applied the provisions of the Indian Trade and Intercourse acts (1790–1834), which prohibited states and private citizens from purchasing Indian land without federal approval.[1]

Since the New England tribes' lands were lost in the nineteenth century, one might well ask why it took more than one hundred years for the tribes to seek redress. The answer lies in the not-so-benign neglect exhibited by federal officials and the sanctimonious paternalism of their state counterparts. That paternalism was self-serving. It insulated the states from court action by the tribes. In general, the tribes along the eastern seaboard were gradually incorporated within the states' governmental systems, although the tribes maintained high levels of autonomy over their internal affairs. In some cases—Mashpee, Gay Head, and Narragansett—the states completed the process of destroying the land base by converting the reservations into towns. In other instances, such as in Connecticut, the state appointed overseers who disposed of the tribe's land. In all instances, the tribes were powerless to seek redress.[2]

For the nineteenth and most of the twentieth century, the accepted legal theory was that the tribes in the seaboard states were outside the protections of the Indian Trade and Intercourse acts. This concept was articulated in a New York state court decision in 1891 and is called the Thirteen Original States Doctrine:

The original states, before and after the adoption of the Federal Constitution, assumed the right of entering into treaties with the Indian tribes for the extinguishment and acquisition of their title to lands within their respective jurisdictions. They exercised the power, which had before been vested in the crown, to treat with the Indians, and this they did independently of the government of the United States. This was notably true of the state of New York.[3]

The doctrine stayed in force until 1958, when it was challenged in a United States Supreme Court decision involving the Tuscarora Indians.[4] The doctrine was finally demolished in 1974 when the Supreme Court ruled in the Oneida case that the principle "that Indian title is a matter of federal law and can be extinguished only with federal consent apply in all of the States, including the original 13."[5] With this bar removed, it appeared that the road was clear for restitution.

But another problem quickly arose. Without exception, the eastern tribes were federally unrecognized. Thus, when they sought assistance from the Justice Department to bring an action on their behalf, a fundamental question arose: Was there a federal trust relationship?

This question was addressed in two cases, but with markedly different results. In 1972 the Passamaquoddy and Penobscot tribes sued the United States to force it to bring an action on their behalf. After a careful review, United States District Court Judge Edward Gignoux ruled that "the Nonintercourse Act is to be construed as its plain meaning dictates and applies to the Passamaquoddy Indian Tribe."[6]

It seemed then that a tribe need only bring a court action for the loss of land, since the Indian Trade and Intercourse acts applied to all bona fide tribes, whether or not there was an explicitly stated recognition of a federal trust relationship. In 1978 the Mashpee Wampanoag Tribal Council, following the precedents set in Oneida and Passamaquoddy, filed suit to recover some eleven thousand acres lost through state action in 1870. The defendants, the Town of Mashpee and the New Seabury Corporation, promptly raised as a defense the question of standing. They argued that the Mashpees were not a tribe within the meaning of the Indian Trade and Intercourse acts. United States District Court Judge Walter Skinner set the trial on this threshold issue for October, 1977.

The Mashpee trial lasted forty days, and a parade of historians, anthropologists, and sociologists, as well as a dozen or more tribal members, took the witness stand. When it was over, Judge Skinner presented to the jury his definition of a tribe, one that was fashioned from a 1901 United States Supreme Court decision. That definition held that a tribe was "a body of Indians of the same or similar race, united in a community under one leadership or government, and inhabiting a particular, though sometimes ill-defined, territory."[7] While this definition is fairly straightforward, and was in fact recommended by the plaintiff in the Mashpee case, Judge Skinner managed to modify each of its parts in ways that seriously compromised the tribe's chances. For example, on the question of whether the Mashpees were Indians, Judge Skinner directed the jurors to determine if intermarriage with nonmembers had changed "the character of the group from an Indian group to a mixed group, so mixed that it could not be fairly considered, all other things being equal, as an Indian Tribe."[8] Using this definition, he required the jury to find that a tribe existed on each of six dates, beginning in 1790. If they failed to find for the tribe on any of these dates, the jury was instructed to find against the tribe on the issue of standing. Needless to say, the tribe lost.[9]

The courtroom and jury box are not the proper forums to

determine tribal status. For our purposes, it is important to understand the impact of the decision. Tribes could not assume that their status under federal law would go unchallenged by defendants, nor could they expect any assistance from the United States in redressing their grievances. The risks of litigation rose sharply after the Mashpee decision. Yet, there was little choice. Many had already brought actions before the decision, and could not pull out of them without endangering their right to sue later. We might have expected the defendants to press to dismiss the cases, but this did not happen for several reasons. First, the cases came before different judges and there was no reason to assume that other courts would adopt Judge Skinner's strained logic. Second, the defendants and the issues were significantly different so that parallels with Mashpee case were difficult to draw. Third, in some instances, defendants saw decided economic advantages to settlements that included the funds to buy the land in question.

Three land claims—by the Gay Head Wampanoags, the Mashantucket Pequots, and the Narragansetts—have been settled since that of the Mashpees, each building upon and affected by the ones that preceded it. The first was the Narragansetts, which was scheduled for trial in the spring of 1978. During that winter the tribe, the state of Rhode Island, and the defendants worked out a compromise whereby the tribe received some 1,800 acres of land, 900 of which was a state-owned cedar swamp, and an appropriation of $3.5 million to buy the remainder.[10] However, the settlement contained a requirement that the tribe receive acknowledgment of its government-to-government relationship from the Department of the Interior. This was to be achieved by submitting evidence as required by a newly initiated procedure called "Procedures for Establishing that an American Indian Group Exists as an Indian Tribe."[11]

The process of acknowledgment, as established by the Department of the Interior, contains seven criteria, all of which must be satisfied in order for a tribe to be recognized. Briefly, the group must show that it has been identified as "American

Indian" throughout its history; that it constitutes a separate, identifiable Indian community with a leadership that has maintained influence over its members throughout the tribe's history; that its members can trace descent to some known tribe or tribes; that they are not members of other tribes; and that they have never been terminated by Congress.[12]

The difficulties inherent in meeting these criteria are enormous, since all of the New England groups have been subject to state laws for over one hundred years, have had their forms of government and governmental officials imposed upon them, and have lost most, if not all, of their land and much of their ability to direct their own affairs. It was equally devastating that, when these groups were described in academic literature, they were frequently the subjects of salvage anthropology and *Last of the Mohicans* history, as though they were quaint curios on the New England landscape. To make things worse for these groups, once a petition was submitted to the Department of the Interior, its progress was impeded by a bureaucratic mill that made continental drift look like a speedy process!

The Mashantucket Pequots chose a different approach. They prepared a petition and simultaneously negotiated a settlement. Both processes were completed in 1982, at which time they chose to seek recognition through legislation. In December, 1982, Congress passed the "Mashantucket Pequot Indian Claims Settlement Act," which provided a fund of $900,000 to buy back the tribal land, extinguished all tribal claims to other land, extended federal recognition, and allowed the tribe to place in trust any of its land.

The way seemed clear for a relatively painless settlement. Then President Ronald Reagan decided to veto the act. In his veto message of April 11, 1983, the President raised four objections. While the claim was against private citizens, the federal government was paying the largest share of the settlement: the settlement did not comply with his formula for evaluating claims. "That formula," he wrote, "would take the value received by the Tribe for the land transfer, subtract it from the actual value of the land at the time of the transfer, and calculate a simple interest rate of 5% per annum for recognized title and at 2% per annum for aboriginal title for the period between the date of transfer and the effective date of the settlement." The state's contribution did not equal half of the value as determined by the formula. Finally, Reagan agreed to reconsider the bill if the state could show some additional contribution and if the tribe would submit a petition of recognition to the Department of the Interior through the Federal Acknowledgment Project (now called BAR—the Branch of Acknowledgment and Research).[13]

The tribe and the congressional delegation reacted swiftly to the veto. The Mashantucket Pequot effort to override the presidential veto was led by the tribal chairman, Richard ("Skip") Hayward; Suzanne Harjo, then an attorney for the Native American Rights Fund; Sandra Cadwalader, from the Indian Rights Association; and Thomas N. Tureen, counsel for the tribe; they were ably assisted by Connecticut Senator Lowell Weicker and Congressman Sam Gedjenson. A small cadre of "foot soldiers," which also included James Wherry and Jack Campisi, divided into two teams, visited nearly every senator, and at the end of a week, had enough commitments to force the White House to compromise. Under the agreement, the state would put up more money and the tribe would submit a petition, which would be given the most perfunctory review and approved. During the summer of 1983 the Congress passed the reintroduced legislation and, on October 18, 1983, the president signed it.[14]

The two sticking points—the state contribution and the use of the acknowledgment process—may seem like trivial matters, but the first, at least, had some far-reaching effects. The administration's insistence that the state pay half of the settlement had little to do with the Pequot case; rather, it was a means to establish a formula that could then be used in the settlement of the much-larger Cayuga and Oneida claims. The formula, which was derived from the Indian Claims Commission, was also a just way to reduce the federal govern-

ment's liability. The Pequot bill was held hostage for this reason. The acknowledgment issue was an attempt to assert
administrative authority in an area traditionally understood as
the sole domain of Congress, namely, the recognition or termination of the government-to-government relationship.[15]

The Gay Head Wampanoag was the next major case. The
Gay Head Wampanoag Tribal Council had brought suit for the
recovery of most of the town of Gay Head on Martha's Vineyard at about the same time as the Mashpee and Narragansett
cases were pending. After the Mashpee decision, the attorneys
for the Wampanoag tribe shifted their strategy to one of negotiation. But the negotiations were hampered by a more recalcitrant defendant and by a split within the tribe. Once the terms
of the settlement were agreed to, the opposing faction within
the tribe increased its activities to prevent any legislation.[16]

The Gay Head Wampanoag Tribal Council prepared a petition for federal acknowledgment, which it submitted in an
incomplete form when it thought settlement legislation was
imminent; however, the Branch of Acknowledgment and Research had no intention of approving the petition without an
exhausting review. The first efforts at a legislative settlement
failed because the administration refused support until the
BAR had made a finding, and because those in the tribe opposed to the settlement expressed their views at the congressional hearings. At that point, Henry Sockbeson, from the
Native American Rights Fund, became the tribe's attorney.

In the process of federal acknowledgment, after a group has
submitted a petition it is given a cursory review. The tribe then
is usually sent what is called "A Letter of Obvious Deficiencies
and Significant Omissions," generally referred to as an "OD"
letter. In 1984 the tribe received this letter, which, among other
things, raised two issues, namely, that there was insufficient
evidence of community and leadership. In fact, the petition
contained no sections relating to these two crucial criteria. At
the same time, there was another effort to secure settlement
legislation, and consequently, the law firm pressed for some
research to satisfy the criteria. The problem was that these cri-

teria are the two most difficult to prove, the most time-consuming, not to mention expensive, aspects of the petition. Adding to the problem was the split within the tribe, which intensified, polarizing the tribe and making thorough research a virtual impossibility.

After the tribe filed its answers to the OD letter, the petition went on active status. At that point two events occurred which significantly influenced the course of events. First, staff changes at the BAR placed individuals with little experience in the process in charge of evaluating the tribe's petition. Secondly, at this critical juncture in the review process, John A. Shapard, Jr., the able chief of the BAR, was assigned to temporary service elsewhere in the Bureau of Indian Affairs. In addition, the BAR was undergoing some subtle changes. It was under attack from petitioners for the length of time it was taking to review petitions, criticized for arbitrariness in some of its decisions, burdened by threats of legal actions from unsuccessful petitioners, and facing an increasingly hostile Congress. The BAR adopted a bunker mentality; its paramount need was to preserve itself and protect its members. Consequently, as the acknowledgment process developed, the definition of what constituted sufficient evidence to sustain a favorable finding increased. Given the cost of researching and writing a petition, tribes looked to the previous findings as a guide by which to measure sufficiency. The BAR, in response to the attacks on its findings, demanded more and more data in order to protect itself from legal action should its determinations be considered "close calls." All of these factors were to affect the Gay Head petition.

The result was a preliminary finding that the Gay Head Wampanoag Tribe did not meet two of the seven criteria: they had not demonstrated that they were a community of Indians or that they had maintained political influence over their members. The finding was announced at congressional hearings at the end of June, 1986, and was to produce an immediate response.

The eminent historian Francis Jennings, who lives on Mar-

tha's Vineyard and is well-acquainted with the tribe, characterized these preliminary findings as racist and excoriated the
BAR researchers for their lack of understanding and compe-
tence. He wrote to the BAR:

The writers of this report have not surveyed the evidence with judicial
detachment. Instead they have produced—or copied?—a prose-
cutor's brief in which facts favorable to the tribe are omitted and the
facts included are twisted about to look somehow bad. I have been
coming to Martha's Vineyard as a "summer person" for more than
forty years, and have lived here as a permanent resident for five
years. During all that time, I have never heard the Gay Head Indians
mentioned as other than a tribe until those hired guns, the lawyers,
appeared on the scene. That they can make white appear black
should surprise nobody; it is their lucrative livelihood. But that a government agency proposes to adopt such malevolent distortions and
falsehoods is shameful. Interior's proper function is to do justice.
The Gay Head Indians are a tribe in social fact, regardless of legal
fictions, and should be recognized for what they are.[17]

Others joined Jennings in their criticism of these preliminary
findings. Anthropologist Gloria Levitas, whose doctoral disser-
tation dealt extensively with the tribe, challenged the BAR's conclusions, which it had allegedly based in part on her disserta-
tion. William Simmons, the noted anthropologist-folklorist of
New England Indians, challenged the finding that the Gay
Head Wampanoags had no continuity or sense of community.[18] Ironically, Simmons, a nationally known expert, had recently published a major study of the New England tribes,
which the BAR researchers had failed to consider when making its determination. In it, he wrote:

The Gay Head Wampanoag community on Martha's Vineyard, where
one finds the largest and most continuously recorded body of folklore, also possesses the most robust and explicit survivals. Situated
on a remote peninsula on an offshore island, Gay Head is the most
bounded of the four enclaves under discussion. In comparison with
Mashpee, Mohegan, and Narragansett, the Gay Headers enjoyed the
greatest continuity of effective local autonomy, beginning with the
Mayhew administration in the seventeenth century and extending to

today's Indian control of town selectmen. Gay Head was also the
most tightly integrated community, with communal production patterns and Indian churches and ministry. The numerous culture hero
legends of Maushop and Ol' Squant, which thrive only here, are
clearly derived from pre-European narrative tradition. Beliefs and
legends regarding the mischievous aboriginal spirit Cheepi are more
developed here than elsewhere. Beginning as a spirit of the departed
and a shaman's helper, Cheepi persisted as an agent in folk medicine, a component in ghost beliefs, and an Indian equivalent to the
European devil.[19]

The three statements taken together seriously undercut the
bases of the BAR's finding.

Under the Department of the Interior rules, the tribe had
180 days in which to reply to the finding. The Native American
Rights Fund directed that more research be done to substantiate the tribe's position on the two critical issues of community
and leadership. While this was being accomplished, the researchers conducted a detailed analysis of the finding. So
complex was the research problem that NARF received an additional thirty days to complete the tribe's response. On December 1, 1986, the tribe filed its response to the preliminary
finding. It consisted of a sharply worded critique of the finding,
a comparison with other findings, and a section responding to
the two contested areas of leadership and community.

Now it was time for the BAR to retaliate. Some in BAR
viewed these critiques as personal attacks on one of its staff
members. Gradually, however, the entire staff reviewed all of
the evidence and, with the new material submitted in the response, made a final finding in favor of the tribe. It is to BAR's
credit that its staffers were open-minded enough to reverse
their position.

But the battle was not over. The tribe still had to negotiate a
final settlement with the Department of the Interior. On April 9,
1986, prior to the preliminary finding, the Senate Select Committee on Indian Affairs held hearings on the proposed legislation to settle the land claim. Hazel Elbert, deputy to the assistant secretary of Indian Affairs, appeared as a witness for the

department. After reading her prepared text, she was questioned by the committee's staff attorney, Pete Taylor:

MR. TAYLOR: Among the criteria, the three criteria, that were spelled out in the earlier letter of Assistant Secretary [Ross] Swimmer, and your testimony here today, we have the matter of the State Contribution.

This bill, as it was introduced, provided for an appropriation, or authorized an appropriation, of $3 million. It is our understanding at this point that the State is preparing to take the necessary legislative action to appropriate $1.5 million to go toward the settlement. That is 50 percent of the cash, in addition to the lands that will be transferred.

In light of that proposal by the State to contribute $1.5 million in cash, would this meet the criteria that you have set out for State contribution?

MS. ELBERT: Yes, sir; that would satisfy our concerns about the third criteria.

MR. TAYLOR: Your statement, Ms. Elbert, also indicates that you acknowledge the role of Congress in resolving certain of these legal issues and indicates that the only other issue that would remain unresolved, other than the State contribution, is the question of tribal existence.

If that existence is, in fact, acknowledged through your FAP [Federal Acknowledgment Process] process, would the Department of the Interior support this legislation?

MS. ELBERT: If the tribe. . . .

MR. TAYLOR: In other words, the third issue there was the question of, I guess, meritoriousness of the claim, but it seems in the testimony that you are acknowledging the function of Congress to take a hand in the resolution of that issue.

MS. ELBERT: Yes; if our process acknowledges them as a tribe, then, of course, that satisfies criteria [sic] No. 1, and if the State comes across with the $1.5 million, that takes care of No. 3. I think No. 2 depends on No. 1; if there is an existence of a tribe, that takes care of criteria [sic] No. 3.

MR. TAYLOR: I have one other question I will ask you, and I think it may be redundant, but I am not sure.

Will the Bureau of Indian Affairs' lack of participation in the negotiation of the settlement in any way affect the BIA's position on the terms of the settlement, or will the Department insist on reopening

negotiations with the goal of a new settlement, in which the administration is a new participant?
Ms. ELBERT: Are you asking if we would change our criteria for settlement of claims? I though[t] those were pretty well laid out.
MR. TAYLOR: No, but if, in fact, the State contribution is met, the acknowledgment of the tribe is met, do you have any other problems
with this legislation?
Ms. ELBERT: I am not aware of any other problems.
MR. TAYLOR: So it would appear, upon the meeting of those three or
two criteria—however we look at it—that that would remove any further Interior Department problems.
MR. ELBERT: Any concern on the part of the Department; yes.[20]

It was very clear from Elbert's testimony that the tribe had
only to satisfy two criteria to gain the administration's support
for the settlement legislation: a 50 percent contribution for the
state and acknowledgment from the BAR that the Gay Head
Wampanoags constituted a tribe. But a year later, after the
tribe had achieved those goals, the administration suddenly
found new issues to raise. Timothy Vollman, associate solici-
tor for Indian Affairs, questioned the merit of the claim despite
Elbert's previous statement that this was essentially a congressional matter. Vollman demanded proof that the land in
question—essentially the town of Gay Head—had been the
property of the Gay Head Indian tribe, despite the evidence
that the state of Massachusetts had taken the land from the
tribe in 1870. In response, Henry Sockbeson of the Native
American Rights Fund and I furnished documentary evidence
that not only had the state taken land from the tribe, but so
had the federal government by accepting an offer from the
tribe to establish a lighthouse. Furthermore, in researching the
documents it became apparent that the tribe had more than
an aboriginal claim to the land. The case could be made that
the tribe still had actual title. This, of course, delayed the legislation for a couple of months.

In June, 1987, Sockbeson and I had a meeting with Vollman to review the material we had submitted. During the
course of that meeting, he raised a new issue. Based on the

Pequot formula, was there justification for a federal contribution of $1.5 million? He insisted that we demonstrate land val-
ues at the time of the taking, around the date of 1870, that
would support the federal share. Sockbeson was furious and
obliquely threatened to call off the deal and take legal action
against the property owners. Nevertheless, Vollman was not
impressed.

Sockbeson then arranged a meeting with Elbert and members of her staff, including Vollman. He explained the difficulties in arriving at comparable values because of the lack of
an adequate number of sales and the variability in prices paid,
and because few sales were recorded immediately after the
town's formation. As the discussion continued, it was clear
that the BIA was raising a new set of objections. Sockbeson
drew Elbert's attention to her previous testimony, in which she
had told the Senate subcommittee that, if the tribe met the criteria outlined by her and Assistant Secretary Swimmer, the BIA
would have no further objection. Her response was: "That's
what I said at the time, but I didn't say I wouldn't change my
mind." Sockbeson was enraged at what appeared to be at
best duplicitous behavior, but he controlled his anger. Subsequently, he received a commitment that he could use values
from the neighboring town of Chilmark to substantiate the
claim. And that, in fact, was the basis of the settlement.

Because of the dilatory practices of the BIA, over a year
passed before the settlement legislation was accepted by Congress. On August 21, 1987, President Reagan signed the bill
into law. Ironically, because of the delay the appraised value of
the property in question had risen by $1.5 million, half of
which had to be paid by the federal government!

These cases, even the ones that do not go to trial, cost a lot
of money—between $250,000 and $500,000 each. They require an enormous amount of research, negotiation, compromise, and patience. Those tribes that are in the process now
should understand that these determinations are not easy or
painless. Tribal leaders who have to make difficult decisions
about whether to pursue litigation or seek settlement do not

have a free rein. They are under legal and political pressures from the outside, in addition to those pressures which emanate from within the group. As the Pequot and Gay Head cases demonstrate, the fate of the tribe may be determined by issues unrelated to their claims.

In the 1980s the acknowledgment process of the Department of the Interior has most certainly been embedded in the settlement process. The early promise of a speedy, fair, impartial process, free of political manipulation, has faded, replaced by a cumbersome and increasingly rigid bureaucracy, which shows little consistency in its application of the rules. Even more disturbing is the callousness of the BIA toward these nonrecognized tribes. As the Mashantucket Pequot and Gay Head cases demonstrate, tribes seeking recognition of their existence and just treatment of their claims can expect little assistance from the BIA. Because of this, the nonrecognized tribes along the eastern seaboard face an increasingly difficult task of achieving recognition of their claims and status.

CHAPTER 11

Connecticut's Indian Policy

From Testy Arrogance to Benign Bemusement

By Robert L. Bee

When asked to write on the subject of Connecticut's Indian policy, my first reaction was to ask "*What* Indian policy?" My second thought was to ask why, "even if there *is* a state Indian policy, it should have any effect on the Mashantucket Pequots? They have been doing their own thing for years. Others who have tried to keep up with what is happening between the Indian tribes and the state may well have the same reactions. Are they justified? A brief synopsis of the Indians' relationship to the state will establish the context of the events of the past two decades.[1]

The creators of the federal Constitution made it clear that the federal government—not the states—should control relations with Indian tribes.[2] To underscore its apparent concern about state meddling, the fledgling Congress in 1790 passed the first of the Indian Trade and Intercourse acts demanding that any land cessions or other commercial agreements between Indians and the states be approved by Congress itself. The message to the states seems obvious enough.

But Connecticut ignored it. So did the Congress, for that matter—at first, perhaps, because it feared a major confrontation with the states, which might have threatened the still-

194

fragile union. Then later attention shifted to the major "Indian problem" festering along the western frontier.

Connecticut simply continued the practice of appointing white overseers to handle Indian land and other Indian issues, a practice begun while it was an English colony. After the European diseases and warfare in the seventeenth and eighteenth centuries had done their damage, the state's Indian population was small. As far as the whites were concerned, it would be only a short time before those small groups would disappear into the ranks of the state's more impoverished laborers. Until then there was Indian land to be overseen—leased, encroached upon, traded, and finally diminished to tiny parcels. The tiniest was the Paugusset domain of one-quarter of an acre in Trumbull. The Mohegans—who of all the Connecticut tribes had remained most staunchly allied with whites—ended up with no reservation land at all. Meanwhile, the Indian people scattered away from the reservation areas and into the cities, or out of the state entirely.

Because the Indians were few and scattered, it was easy for whites to nibble away at the reservations. The tribes' lack of political clout made them victims not only of sinister intent, but also of state ignorance and indifference.

In 1935 the authority over the remaining Indian reservations was transferred to the state's Park and Forest Commission. Implicit here was the notion that surviving Indian people and Indian cultures were less important than the land. More explicitly, the land was a state resource.[3]

In 1941 the state Welfare Department assumed responsibility for Indian affairs. The implicit message this time was that people mattered more than land, which was at best a slight improvement over the earlier message. (As Indian groups have argued for years, both the land base and the cultural heritage are vital for preservation of Indian identity.) The "people concerns" of welfare involved economic need, not the preservation of Indian ethnic identity. Although surely a few Indian families needed the aid that welfare customarily dispensed, what most Indians needed and wanted was help in preserving their ethnic identity. Welfare could not supply this. The switch in state administrative departments implied a switch in stereo-types regarding Connecticut's "Indian Problem": the land problem was now an economic-dependency problem.

Indian people who can remember are still angry about the arrogant attitude manifested by state welfare officials. Welfare's handling of Indian land—which was still regarded as a state resource—was a predictable example of stifling bureaucratic control. The Welfare Department was governed by chapter 824 of the state statutes, which required that Indians petition the welfare commissioner for approval to hold gatherings on reservations or even to spend the night on reservation land.[4] Indians needed the commissioner's approval to build a home on the reservation—which was to be granted only after all de-sign specifications had been carefully reviewed. The commis-sioner chose the building site and had to approve any sub-sequent repairs or remodeling of the dwelling. The home reverted to state ownership after the original owner died or abandoned it. It could not be passed on to heirs. Tribal mem-bers were forbidden to conduct any type of business on the reservation. The state occasionally appropriated some money for the Welfare Department's administration of Indian affairs, but tribes had no say in decisions about how the money was to be spent.[5]

With no ready access to their reservations, the Connecti-cut tribes—the Mohegans, the Mashantucket Pequots, the Paucatuck Pequots, the Schaghticokes, and the Paugussets—remained scattered throughout the state, angry and frustrated but for the most part politically fragmented. Not only was there little unity among the five tribes; in some cases there was long-standing factionalism within them.

Members of the Schaghticoke Tribe, led by Irving Harris, are credited with launching the drive for major policy reform in the late 1960s.[6] The Schaghticokes wanted greater access to their reservation, hoping to use it for activities that would strengthen the tribe's social and cultural cohesion. It was a need that had already motivated collective action by tribes in other states. But the Schaghticokes got nowhere with the welfare bureaucrats.

Harris and others then circumvented the agencies by going to the legislature itself. There they found some interest in policy overhaul, but not for the Schaghticokes alone: it would have to apply to all the Connecticut tribes.

Between 1970 and 1973 representatives from the Connecticut tribes met together and, despite opposition and active obstruction from the Welfare Department,[7] produced two bills for policy reform. Both called for the creation of a state Indian affairs commission that would have sole responsibility for administering Indian policy. The first bill was approved by the legislature in 1971, only to be vetoed by Governor Thomas Meskill. He claimed the cost of creating the separate commission—$25,000—was unwarranted.[8]

The second bill became part of a compromise package that the Indians viewed with ambivalence. The compromise called for the creation of the present state Indian Affairs Council—not an autonomous commission. The new council was to serve as a liaison between the tribes and the Department of Environmental Protection (DEP), which would take over the administration of Indian affairs from the Welfare Department. The Indians generally liked the idea of the council, but were not pleased that administrative authority would go to yet another state agency. To them it seemed merely another shift in twisted administrative stereotypes—from that of destitute welfare recipients back to what they had been before: parts of the environment along with the parks and forests.

But the compromise looked like their best alternative. The legislature that had passed the 1971 bill had become more ambivalent by 1973 and was by then balking at the idea of an autonomous Indian commission. They felt that the population of the five tribes—between 2,000 and 2,500—did not justify a separate body.[9] Once again their relatively small numbers had been a factor in a policy decision. The compromise bill nevertheless passed by such an overwhelming majority that Governor Meskill had little choice but to sign it. Public Act 73-660, as it was now known, became law on October 1, 1973.

The campaign to pass the measure and the act itself had a remarkable impact on the state's policy process. An important part of the impact was social and psychological: the effort had brought the scattered tribes together for a common purpose. By working on a common goal, they developed a more broadly based sense of cultural identity, whereas earlier they had had an individual sense of Indian identity, or at most a tribal one. Now there was consciousness of a more inclusive Indian constituency. In political terms, this shift in perspective meant that some important issues, which were once considered strictly individual or merely tribal, would now be supported by all five tribes. And the council structure ensured that the tribes could maintain their contact with each other.

The shift of Indian affairs to DEP also brought a dramatic attitudinal change. Gone was the recalcitrant arrogance; now there was something like benign bemusement among state officials. The difference may have been due partly to the different group personalities of Welfare and DEP. But it was most fundamentally due to the new regulations that Public Act 73-660 promulgated.

The new regulations declared that the Indian Affairs Council would advise the commissioner of environmental protection on the administration of Indian affairs, but the commissioner's decisions were the binding ones. It would be made up of representatives of each of the state's five tribes and three non-Indians appointed by the governor. The members would receive travel expenses but no salary for their services.[10]

In addition to its role as advisor, the council would be responsible for drawing up new programs for the reservations, for recommending changes in regulations pertaining to Indians, and for determining "the qualifications of individuals entitled to be designated as Indians for the purpose of administration [of the statute,] . . . and shall decide who is eligible to live on reservation lands, subject to . . . [statutory] provisions. . . ."[11] This set of responsibilities proved to be a constant source of conflict and frustration.

The reservations henceforth would be assigned to the use of each tribe and "shall be maintained for the exclusive benefit of Indians who may reside on such lands." They would be preserved as "Indian historical areas" under the protection of the Department of Environmental Protection. Tribal members would be free to hunt or fish on reservations without a license. Homes could be passed on to heirs who were members of the tribe. Tribal funds would still be controlled by the commissioner of environmental protection, but with advice from the Indian Affairs Council.[12]

In sum, although the new council was still well short of the autonomous Indian administrative body that the tribes wanted, other provisions of the new law granted them the access to and much of the control of the land that was so crucial to their ethnic identity and cohesion. It was a major policy breakthrough.

The formal policy structure now operates like this: tribes or individuals take issues to the Indian Affairs Council. The council either resolves them or passes them along to the DEP commissioner's office. If new legislation is needed, DEP staff and the council collaborate on a draft proposal and pass the draft to the governor's Office of Policy and Management. There it is screened carefully before being forwarded to the legislature. Because the proposal comes from DEP, it is typically given to the environment committee in both houses for study and hearings. Assuming both houses vote in favor of it, it comes to the governor for signature and returns to DEP for implementation.

There is no Indian budgetary process. DEP has no annual budget for the separate reservations. The Indian Affairs Council's budget goes almost entirely to reimburse members for their travel expenses to council meetings.

So much for the ideal, formal structure. How has it worked in day-to-day administrative reality?

It became immediately apparent that the Indian council had a communication problem. Structures do not interact, people do. And as is the case with so many of the Connecticut citizens councils, the Indian Council members had other responsibilities that kept them inaccessible during working hours. There was no person designated to funnel information back and forth between the council and the department, or to handle telephones and mail between the council's monthly meetings. DEP therefore created the position of Indian affairs coordinator.

At first the coordinator was regarded as a "go-fer." That changed very quickly as the calls and letters demanded immediate responses and the administrative and legal implications of the council's activities became increasingly complex. The coordinator now operates not only as a communications link between the council and the department but also as a mediator between DEP and Indian individuals seeking help or complaining about DEP services; as a scout for the council and the tribes, keeping a constant lookout for federal monies or programs that might be tapped for tribal programs; as a repository of information about the tribes for the general public; and sadly but inevitably, as a convenient whipping-person when the Indians are unhappy or the governor's office feels the heat of an Indian controversy.

The job requires keen political sensitivity. The coordinator officially works for DEP, not for the council. The salary comes from a variety of DEP funding sources and includes no money earmarked for council or tribal use. But occasionally frustrated Indians forget this and wonder aloud why the coordinator is being paid from "Indian money" or does not vigorously support their petitions against DEP. Yet the coordinator must do everything possible to represent the council's wishes. Otherwise he or she will have no credibility with the council, and its collaboration with DEP would break down. The position carries no decision-making authority of its own, and so the coordinator lacks political clout. Thus, when conflict between the council or tribal member and the state cannot be easily resolved, the coordinator has little choice but to hunker down and let the principals fight it out face to face. The present co-ordinator and his predecessor are both Native Americans, but—significantly—not from Connecticut tribes.

The creation of the Indian affairs coordinator position did not entirely eliminate the communication problems. Another important, persistent difficulty has been arranging in-depth, face-to-face discussions between the council members and DEP officials.

Communications problems occasionally have created delays and confusion, but the Indian Affairs Council's most vexing issue has been tribal membership and the rights it entails. This problem's various dimensions have dominated council proceedings from the outset. Before the council's creation the decisions about who is and who is not a tribal member were handled somewhat chaotically by each of the tribes. In some tribes, particularly the Mohegans and the Paucatuck Pequots, conflict had been simmering for years between in groups and those who felt that they had been unfairly left out. The new council immediately came under a barrage of claims by individuals and groups emotionally loaded with years of pent-up frustration.

The council's first reaction was well considered: it established an orderly procedure for submitting and handling all claims. But then the ideal, formal policy structure once again clashed with political reality. In fact, some council members were being asked to reverse hard and controversial decisions that they and their constituents had made earlier—decisions that in their minds were nonnegotiable and irreversible. This was something they could not do.

Also, the council was having second thoughts about its ultimate legal right to decide tribal membership. The issue of tribal sovereignty had become crucial to tribes elsewhere in the country by then, and the U.S. Supreme Court's *Martinez v. Santa Clara Pueblo* decision in 1978 seemed to uphold tribes' rights to determine their own membership.[13]

Instead of staying with its formal procedures and moving ahead with decisions about tribal membership, the council adopted a confusing operating principle: it would continue to receive petitions for tribal membership, but only in unusual cases would the council as a body decide a membership issue. It would instead simply forward the petitions on to the tribe for action.

What are *unusual* cases? Apparently unusual cases are those that provide enough overwhelming genealogical evidence and/or apply enough political pressure to motivate the council to take collective action. A recent example is the case of an individual who petitioned the council for admission to the Paucatuck Pequot Tribe. The petition was turned down in the mid–1970s. Years later the petition was presented again, with additional genealogical evidence. After lengthy consideration the council this time decided the individual should be entitled to tribal membership. Yet, as it was making this decision about the Paucatuck Pequots, it was telling another group petitioning for membership in the Mohegan Tribe that their petition would have to be decided by the tribe. Both cases were long-smoldering membership issues for the respective tribes, which had already rejected the petitions in earlier actions.[14]

Does the Indian Affairs Council "determine the qualifications of individuals entitled to be designated as Indians" or not? In principle, no—they want the tribes to do it. But in fact, yes—sometimes.

What action is open to those whose petitions are rejected, or to the tribes who wish to block admission of new members? They can take their case to the state superior court. This court ruled in the mid–1970s that the Indian Affairs Council is a state agency, and that as such, its decisions can be appealed through the courts. In the Paucatuck Pequot case just mentioned, tribal members filed a grievance in superior court protesting the Indian Affairs Council's decision. The court determined that the tribal members were not aggrieved by the council's action, and thereby upheld the council's finding.[15]

The appeals procedure merely increases the confusion by apparently contradicting the Supreme Court's *Martinez* decision. It takes ultimate decision-making power away from both the council and the tribes and puts it in the hands of the courts, thereby diluting the importance of Indian input. Yet for those with valid criteria for membership there is currently no other available option.

Consequently, the council seemed stuck on a treadmill. It continued to be bombarded with petitions for tribal member- ship and distracted by the time and conflict involved in acting on them. Its operating procedure seemed tailor-made for per- petuating both the bombardment and the conflict.

The second most-vexing issue for the council was legal ju- risdiction on the reservations. This problem emerged once the reservations were made more accessible to tribal members. Here, too, confusion reigns.

The issue involves the extent to which Indian residents on reservations are governed by the same laws as are those living off-reservation and the non-Indians in the state. For example, do the state police have jurisdiction on reservations? Can tribal members on reservations operate businesses that do not con- form to state statutes, and do not charge state taxes on their goods? Must tribal members on reservations pay town auto- mobile and property taxes? The issue is less involved for the Mashantucket Pequot now that they are federally recognized, but it continues to simmer among the other four tribes.

The chief state attorney's opinion is that state police do have jurisdiction on reservations and other state laws do apply except as noted in chapter 824 of the state statutes. That cer- tainly seems clear enough. Yet both Indian reservation resi- dents and state troopers seem confused when an incident on reservation land is reported. Sometimes the police respond; sometimes they claim they have no jurisdiction. When tribal members come to the Indian Affairs Council with jurisdictional complaints, the council simply refers them to law-enforcement officials because it has no statutory authority to act in such cases. Once again, a good deal of council time is consumed in the process.

In fact, then, for much of its existence the council has been kept busy looking into complaints and settling squabbles rather than launching ambitious overhauls of Connecticut regulations or developing major new programs. This is probably inevitable, given that there is no other administrative structure for dealing with such complaints and squabbles. And surely it takes time to fine-tune the adjustment between the ideal and the real—between policy formulation and policy implementation.[16] But in the mid–1980s the council has had difficulty in gathering a quorum for its meetings, which may well be a sign of burnout from trying to settle too many squabbles and frustration at failing to free itself for a major role in policy reformulation.

Having described the general structure of the state's Indian-policy process and the discontinuity between the ideal and real in the Indian Affairs Council's role, I will shift to the topic of Indian leverage in the policy process. I will show how it has operated in some actual cases and then draw some general conclusions about how it might best be wielded.

To the extent that who you know in state politics is crucial, Indians should understandably be eager to win the governor over to their side. From Thomas Meskill to William O'Neill, then, what has been the governor's Indian policy role?

Thomas Meskill was generally unpopular with Indians even though the major policy overhaul came during his administration. He merely did what he had to do politically. In contrast, his successor, Ella Grasso, was dearly loved. The two governors came from different ranges of the political spectrum. Grasso was a liberal Democrat. Indians recall her keen memory of names and issues, and her personal interest in Indian problems. She gave tribal leaders and the Indian Affairs Council the public recognition that remains so important to them, often inviting them into her office for signing ceremonies on items that focused on Indian affairs.

Her action went beyond public displays. A special portion of chapter 824 of Connecticut's statutes dealing with Indian housing authorities was needed by the Mashantucket Pequots. Those close to the process recall that Grasso was involved and was "very helpful." And in 1977 she intervened directly to make it possible for the Connecticut tribes to receive revenue-sharing funds as state-recognized municipalities. In doing so, she took a minor risk because she circumvented the conventional but time-consuming process of building a firm legislative base for her action beforehand.

This was recalled as an "incredibly important" action—not so much for the money involved (only about $100 per tribe per quarter while revenue sharing was an active policy), but for the legitimating effect it had on the tribes as entities. By recognizing them as municipalities, it created a basis they could then use to apply for funds from other sources.

Grasso's successor as governor, William O'Neill, has been generally supportive but personally more removed from Indian issues. The Mashantucket Pequot land-claims settlement came early in his administration and certainly required his support. But his personal staff seemed most anxious to disassociate him from any involvement in a more recently factional conflict among the Schaghticokes that was heavily played up in the newspapers. His staff in DEP did take positive action in the conflict, however, and the result could have important implications for the state's future Indian policy.

This limited survey of governors' involvement in Indian policy suggests that Ella Grasso may indeed have been a special case. While personal contacts with a chief executive can always be crucial—Grasso's action was taken only after she had been contacted by Indian representatives—the tendency is for governors to let the agencies handle things without themselves committing personal political capital to Indian issues. This makes political sense, given the small number of Indian votes relative to those of other minority groups. Also, to come out too strongly for Indian rights in the abstract could alienate non-Indian voters whose interests could conceivably be pitted against the Indians' in land disputes or tax and jurisdictional issues. Thus governors tend to stand pat rather than innovate policy, and wait for issues to develop, rather than react to them. And, at the same time, they maintain a generally supportive posture in Indian issues so long as doing so does not cost the state or non-Indians much of anything.

This last factor is important, because it introduces a less-benign component of the state's Indian policy. So far we have been talking of policy as rather narrowly confined to relations among the tribes, the Indian Affairs Council, and DEP. Perhaps this is best termed "administrative" policy. When the policy concept is expanded to include land claims and tax revenues, the state of Connecticut has not been consistently supportive of Indian interests. For example, even after the Mashantucket Pequot claims settlement in 1983, state authorities insisted on their right to regulate the tribe's bingo operation until a federal court decision stopped them. And despite section 47-65 of the state's regulations and the repeated requests of the Indian Affairs Council, the state still has not surveyed the boundaries of all the state reservations. One recent guesstimate set the cost of such a survey at $90,000. And at least one official in the state attorney general's office, Assistant Attorney General Francis J. MacGregor, has maintained a high-profile denial of the validity of the Connecticut tribes' land claims. So far he has shown every intention of fighting them to the bitter end in the courts.[17]

Negotiated settlements of land and tax issues should always be attempted, because court action is a slow and expensive alternative. But in negotiations of such issues, Connecticut tribes—like those elsewhere in the country—should be armed with credible threats of court action. Such threats motivate the parties to negotiate, while court action remains an alternative should negotiations fail.[18]

Two 1980s cases reveal other kinds of Indian leverage in the policy process. They also have had important influences on the policy process itself. First was the federal recognition of the Mashantucket Pequots in 1983. In working through the steps of the settlement, Mashantucket Pequot Tribal Chairman Richard Hayward and his associates created their own ties with state officials and legislators. They were operating in a style that Hayward and others had developed even before they began pushing the settlement. They had earlier fanned out among the state offices to attract housing and other develop-ment money to the reservation rather than depend on the Indian Affairs Council or DEP to launch their development schemes.

The 1983 settlement created a formal duality in state policy: one policy for four of the tribes, another for the Mashantucket Pequots. The state lost regulatory authority over Mashantucket land and tribal operations, but otherwise is responsible for providing the same services to the Mashantuckets that it offers to the other reservations.[19] There is occasional confusion about this among members of the other tribes, who feel that the state regulations from which the Mashantucket Pequots are exempted because of federal recognition, should not ap-ply to their reservations as well. State officials, too, become confused by the formal duality when trying to sort out tax and jurisdictional regulations on these reservations.

There is also an informal duality: Hayward continues to use his contacts in the state apparatus to get things accomplished, largely independent of the Indian Affairs Council and the In-dian affairs coordinator. These contacts continue to be effec-tive in part because the Mashantucket Pequots have created a political entity as a going concern in the eyes of state officials. The multimillion-dollar bingo operation gets public attention, but the other developments—the housing, the roads, the gravel operation, and before them the hydroponic farm and the maple-sugar enterprise—are what reassure the keepers of the public purse and the political movers and shakers that they will not be embarrassed by supporting Mashantucket programs.

Mashantucket representatives still sit on the Indian Affairs Council and interact with the coordinator as other tribes do. But they have extra political leverage because of their savoir faire and their extensive tribal resources. There is also the po-tential to call in federal influence should problems develop between the Mashantucket Pequots and the state. Small wonder that other Connecticut tribes are well into their own federal recognition processes!

Finally, and by whatever means, the Mashantucket Pequots have managed to present a united political front to state and federal agencies. The continuing success of their tribal programs has a way of keeping factional disputes within manageable limits.

More recently it was the Schaghticokes who provided the catalyst for another important development in the state's Indian policy. A factional dispute erupted within the tribe in the spring of 1986. It was the latest of a series of conflicts between the two factions, and it involved allegations of misconduct and misappropriation by former members of the tribal council. Although certainly important to the tribe, it might have had little impact on policy had it not been picked up by a major state newspaper and given extensive, in-depth treatment.

The newspaper account suggested that the state was somehow negligent in policing the use of nonstate grant monies by the tribes.[20] A collective shudder passed through DEP and the governor's office; the governor's staff was already trying to clear away political damage done by other in-depth pieces on state operations such as highway-bridge safety inspections.

The state's reaction was typical of what both it and the federal government have always done in such situations: first it made sure the chief executive had nothing to do with it; then it told representatives of DEP to hold hearings to look into problems of state Indian policy.

The hearings got underway in June, 1986. The response from the Connecticut tribes was so overwhelming that five sessions were held that summer and fall. Predictably, the Indians were most concerned about tribal membership and state jurisdiction on Indian lands. And their positions on those issues were far from united. In part the disunity was the product of enlightened disagreement about best alternatives. But a more dominant cause was a fundamental confusion about existing regulations—confusion among Indians and DEP officials alike—that has been a persistent feature of Connecticut's Indian-policy process.

As a result of the hearings, the Indian Affairs Council and DEP staffers decided to seek a $92,000 appropriation to hire a permanent staff for the Indian Council. Presumably, the staff would consider options based on the hearings and would draft new regulations for the council's action. But the state's Office of Policy and Management, the behavioral and structural clone of the federal Office of Management and Budget, shot down the proposal as too expensive.

The next step was also fairly typical in such situations: DEP called for the creation of the special Indian Affairs Task Force to study Indian policy and make recommendations for change—at no cost to the state. This idea sailed through the Office of Policy and Management without a hitch and was approved by the Connecticut general assembly in the spring of 1986. The sixteen-member task force includes the tribal representatives now on the Indian Affairs Council, two representatives of the state legislature and the administrative departments, and one archaeologist.

The task force's mandate is to recommend policies to clear up the tribal membership and jurisdiction problems, as well as another persistent issue closely related to proper recognition of Indian identity: the treatment of Indian remains after they have been excavated. This last issue generated a good deal of emotion and interest among Indians during the 1980s.

The task force—on paper at least—promises to overcome persistent problems in the existing policy process. First, it convenes the major parties most directly involved in that process to discuss issues face to face. Ideally, there will be no more delays and confusion caused by cycling and recycling information through groups that seldom talk to each other directly. Second, the task force may be able to operate above the intense conflict that has hobbled the Indian Affairs Council's consideration of tribal membership and jurisdictional issues. The task force must confine itself to policy reformulation rather than settlement of individual cases. For example, even during the hearings in the summer of 1986 the DEP staff repeatedly had to admonish those testifying to confine their remarks to policy issues and to cease the emotional blasts at rival individuals and groups.

Avoiding such conflicts may be difficult, given the depth of the divisions among individuals and groups, and because the same tribal interests will be represented on the task force that presently influence the Indian Affairs Council. For example, the task force could face the same question of sovereignty that has confronted the Indian Affairs Council since the council was established in 1973: what body, under what conditions, has the authority to override the declared interests of a particular tribe?

The creation of the Connecticut Indian affairs task force suggests the following generalizations about Indian leverage in policy. First, raising hell in the media about state administrative incompetence is a fairly sure way to goad state officials into action. The factional controversy at Schaghticoke had been going on for some time, but things did not really happen in the governor's office or DEP until the series of articles appeared in the *Hartford Courant.* Specifics—particularly if they involve considerable sums of money—are crucial. Vague allegations or generalized "we-don't-get-no-respect" essays have little effect.

Second, except for the Indian affairs coordinator, state officials' knowledge of regulations pertaining to Indians is fragmentary and crisis-derived. The Indians' knowledge is also generally fragmentary and crisis-derived. Fortunately, this inspires them to keep clamoring rather than drop out in resigned frustration. By clamoring they keep up the pressure for policy clarification and reform.

A comparison of the two events suggests there are at least two major strategies for wielding political leverage. But they may not be equally effective: although getting the state's attention through crisis confrontation works, the alternative pursued by Richard Hayward and other Mashantucket representatives may be even more lucrative for the individual tribes.

State agencies have been more than willing to work with the Mashantucket Pequots to improve the reservation when tribal leaders approach officials personally, using connections carefully cultivated beforehand. The Mashantucket Pequots have had good results by operating outside of the existing policy channels.

Does this mean that all tribes should circumvent the Indian Affairs Council and the DEP bureaucracy? No. The council and Indian affairs coordinator have performed valuable functions, and DEP has remained generally supportive. Rather, experience suggests that, in addition to working through the council, the tribes should seek their own avenues of contact within the various state agencies, and whenever possible, they should use charm rather than hostile confrontation to get what they want. A politician or bureaucrat on the defensive may well cooperate, but only as much as is politically required, and only until the opportunity to get even presents itself.

But this suggestion is surely idealistic for the other four tribes, at least for now. It was not charm alone that won over state officials to the Mashantucket Pequots, but a good track record at getting things done and a knack for stifling public disclosure of intratribal friction. Either because they lack resources or because of internal political turmoil—or both—the other Connecticut tribes have not yet been able to build up a critical mass of reservation development and political influence equal to that enjoyed by the Mashantucket Pequots.

The two—development and political influence—are clearly interrelated and reciprocal. But which comes first? Federal recognition and successful settlement of land claims are ways of getting the means for reservation development. The tribes have already set off on those quests. Should they be successful, the next step will be to parlay those resources into visible projects that will demonstrate to politicians and officials that the tribe has its act together—that is, it wants to follow the path of the Mashantucket Pequots.

There is another path, of course. That is *not* to develop, but rather to preserve and protect present and future tribal lands.

Certainly tribes should be free to choose that option if they wish. The political influence with state officials may be harder to gain with such a goal—there would be nothing to see, nothing politicians could proudly point to as a product of their enlightened support. It may also be more difficult to unify the tribal factions behind a push for nondevelopment, particularly if some tribal members now lack the resources for the kinds of housing and other amenities they wish to have. Still, it looks as though Connecticut is in a mood to listen—to be educated. Furthermore, the existing policy regulations clearly provide support for that option if the tribes choose it.

Surely there is a state Indian policy. Surely there are some discontinuities between its ideal administrative intent and the realities of implementing it. And surely Connecticut's generally supportive stance is an extremely valuable component of the present policy process, even though "generally supportive" has often become synonymous with benign bemusement. But as angry as Indian critics become at state confusion and inaction, many of them realize that, as one put it, "Indians in other states would give their eye teeth for what we've got here."[21]

Afterword

By James D. Wherry

Today the Mashantucket Pequot Tribe has an on-reservation population of 110 persons and a membership of approximately 150. When one reflects on the tribe's recent history, the 1983 land-claim settlement and federal recognition stand out as important precursors that set the stage for the tribe's economic resurgence. Since this federal enactment, the tribe and its members have experienced great changes. This legislation provided for the settlement of the tribe's land claim, conferred federal recognition on the Mashantucket Pequot Tribe, and created a $900,000 trust fund to be used by the tribe to acquire land within a specific area defined by the act. Federal recognition has meant a substantial increase in on-reservation employment, the success of new economic development initiatives, and an increase in population, along with changes in the sociopolitical process and improvements to its infrastructure. Meanwhile, the tribe's land base has grown from 214 acres in 1983 to its current 1,638 acres. While the changes experienced by the Mashantucket Pequot Tribe following federal recognition have occurred elsewhere, few other reservations can attest to changes as dramatic.

Although the land-claim settlement stands out for its importance to the tribe, tribal leaders had already begun laying the organizational groundwork and experimenting with measures to develop the reservation economy. Well before the settlement act, tribal members began meeting to establish a more formal governmental structure. By 1974 these meetings had produced a tribal constitution. In 1976 the tribe elected Richard ("Skip") Hayward as the chairman of the Mashantucket Pequot Tribal Council. Under Chairman Hayward's enlightened leadership, the tribe in 1974 began planning the development of the reservation. Because no new housing had been added to the reservation during the entire twentieth century, and because employment for tribal members was needed, the reservation population had fallen to just thirteen by 1980. Thus the reorganized Tribal Council set the development of adequate housing and the attainment of economic self-sufficiency as the goals of the tribe.

The tribe's housing authority became the first and only Indian housing authority ever recognized by the Department of Housing and Urban Development (HUD) on an Indian reservation not yet recognized by the BIA. The bureaucrats at HUD were thrown into a quandary when they had to deal with an Indian tribe without either BIA or Indian Health Service (IHS) involvement. It was only through Chairman Hayward's tenacious efforts that the tribe's housing authority obtained recognition from Connecticut Governor Ella Grasso so that housing development could proceed. Finally, after many years of organizational efforts, the tribe's state-recognized housing authority obtained HUD funding for fifteen units of single family housing, which were completed in early 1981. By the time of the settlement act, the Mashantucket Pequots had had a decade of experimenting with economic development projects that included commercial swine production, firewood sales, maple syrup production, and a hydroponic greenhouse. This decade of activity also provided important organizational training for the tribe's elected leaders and helped make rapid development a viable possibility in the years following federal recognition in 1983.

Development Projects, 1975–1985

It has been and continues to be the overriding long-range goal of the Mashantucket Pequot Tribe to achieve self-sufficiency and independence. The policy that has been repeatedly re-affirmed by the Tribal Council for achieving this goal has always included economic development strategies intended to generate income for the tribe and jobs for its members. With varying degrees of success, a number of projects have been designed to meet this goal.

Garden Project. In an area of approximately 6.8 acres, trees, stumps, and rocks were removed during 1976 and 1977 with the voluntary assistance of tribal members. A variety of crops were grown during the 1977, 1978, and 1979 seasons. During those years vegetables were supplied to tribal members, and the surplus was sold for a modest profit.

Maple Syrup. In 1975 the tribe began experimenting with maple syrup production as a viable economic development project, and in 1976 acquired a maple syrup evaporator. Since 1977 tribal volunteers have collected the maple sap, boiled the sap to syrup, and bottled the syrup for market. Each year the Mashantucket Pequot maple-syrup operation produces modest returns for the tribe.

Wood Sales. Beginning in 1976, the Mashantucket Pequot Tribe conducted its first timber sale. Every year since then the Mashantucket Pequot Tribe has sold either timber or cord-wood. These sales have produced a steady, if modest, return for the tribe.

Swine Project. The tribe began a swine project on the reservation in May, 1978, purchasing fifteen hogs, with grain and feed to fatten them for market. In November, 1978, the tribe sold twelve hogs and butchered one for tribal members. Returns were modest, and the swine project was discontinued following this sale.

Greenhouse Project. With funding from HUD's Community Development Block Grant (CDBG) Program and the volunteer labor of tribal members, the tribe in 1980 and 1981 constructed a hydroponic greenhouse on the reservation. With assistance from a consultant, TAG Associates, the greenhouse was designed to produce lettuce hydroponically (that is, with the root systems suspended in a solution of water and chemicals rather than in soil). Leaf-lettuce production at the tribe's hydroponic greenhouse commenced in March, 1981, and continued through May, 1982, but production fell far short of the predicted 6,000 heads per week, and the operation was suspended in 1982.

Sand and Gravel Operation. During March, 1985, the Mashantucket Pequot Tribe opened a gravel pit on the reservation with buyers doing their own loading with their own equipment. On July 25, 1985, a local bank approved the tribe's request for a loan to acquire sand and gravel mining equipment that included a Koehring model-866D hydraulic excavator, a Trojan model-5500 rubber-tire front-end loader, and a Hungry Lion portable screening plant, enabling the tribe to mine with its own equipment.

Land Acquisition. When it was established in 1666, the Mashantucket Pequot Reservation comprised 2,000 acres. Over the centuries it was reduced to 213 acres. In 1976 the tribe filed a suit under the Trade and Intercourse Act of 1790 for the return of land taken in an 1855 sale. Negotiations with the state and landowners continued until, on June 9, 1982, the state passed the "Act to Implement the Settlement of the Mashantucket Pequot Indian Land Claims." Eventually, companion federal legislation was submitted to the United States Congress and signed into law on October 18, 1983. This legislation provided for the settlement of the tribe's land claim and conferred federal recognition on the Tribe. In addition, the act created a $900,000 trust fund, established for land acquisition and economic development. Importantly, the act provided that any land acquired from within the "Mashantucket Pequot Settlement Area" would automatically become part of the reservation. During 1984 the Mashantucket Pequot Tribe used the settlement fund to acquire 1,021 acres, expanding the tribe's land base to 1,234 acres. By 1989 further land acquisitions had increased the tribe's land base to 1,638 acres.

Housing. On approximately thirty acres of the reservation, the Mashantucket Pequot Indian Housing Authority has developed thirty units of housing financed by the U.S. Department of Housing and Urban Development. Twenty of these are single family units, and ten are multifamily units located in two apartment buildings. Outside observers have described this housing as some of the finest Indian housing in the country.

Water System and Bond Issue. During 1984 the Mashantucket Pequot Tribe secured grants from the Farmers Home Administration and the Department of Housing and Urban Development totaling $703,000, and a loan from the Farmers Home Administration of $27,700 for the development of the tribe's central water system. When completed in 1986, the system included a 100,000-gallon pedestal-ball gravity-fed standpipe and a series of interconnected water mains that provide fire protection and water pressure at any point in the system. The comparatively small $27,700 loan for this project was the first Indian tax-exempt bond issue in the country to be issued under the authority of the Native American Tax Status Act of 1982.

Health Administration Building. On September 25, 1985, the Mashantucket Pequot Tribe issued its second tax-exempt bond issue in the amount of $173,500. The proceeds of this issue were used to construct a Health Administration Building, which was opened on September 18, 1985. Out of this facility, the Mashantucket Pequot Health Department administers to the health needs of the Indians of New London County, Connecticut.

Community Services. During fiscal year 1985, the Mashantucket Pequot Tribe began to provide services to its members that included health and social services, adult education, a tribal clerk's office, road maintenance, and forestry. Beginning on October 1, 1985, services were expanded to include vocational training, cultural resources, community fire protection, and higher education grants.

Future Development Plans

Following the range of activities completed in the recent past, the tribe has mapped plans for the future.

Housing. Although ten additional units of housing were approved for the tribe in 1985, the Department of Housing and Urban Development was unable to fund the tribe's project during that fiscal year. Partly for that reason, funding for the tribe's next ten units of housing became available early in fiscal year 1986. Because of reductions in HUD housing programs, the tribe has also endeavored to seek funding from the Connecticut Department of Housing to support the tribe's next housing project. So far, discussions with Connecticut housing officials have been successful, and it is likely that funding to support infrastructure development will be made available. For the long term, tribal demographic trends suggest that additional housing will be required every two or three years.

Bingo. After much discussion during 1983 and 1984, the Mashantucket Pequot Tribal Council resolved to finance and run an on-reservation high-stakes bingo game. But following the announcement by the Mashantucket Pequot Tribal Council of their plan, the chief state's attorney, Austin J. McGuigan, threatened to prosecute the tribe if the council proceeded with its bingo plans. In response, the tribe's general counsel entered federal district court with a civil action requesting a summary judgment and an injunction to end McGuigan's threats. Once in court, the case moved beyond the question of bingo to a broader consideration of the applicability of state civil and criminal jurisdiction on the Mashantucket Pequot Reservation. Despite widespread belief that the tribe would gain a positive court ruling, bankers were hesitant to commit themselves to the tribe's $3.8 million loan request for Pequot Bingo. The tribe's bingo project was thereby stalled and remained so until the favorable court ruling in January, 1986.

Bingo operations finally began on July 5, 1986. With 10 percent of the United States's population within approximately one hundred miles of the Mashantucket Pequot Reservation, Pequot Bingo is one of the most successful Indian bingo operations in the country. In 1987, Mashantucket Pequot High-Stakes Bingo generated nearly $13 million in gross sales and netted over $2.6 million, yielding a return on sales of 20.7 percent. In 1987 the Pequot Bingo return on equity represented an extraordinary 248 percent. In its first twenty-eight months of operation, the bingo games attracted more than 400,000 patrons while grossing over $30 million in sales and paying over $13 million in cash and prizes. The bingo operation has generated in excess of $4.5 million in profits for the Mashantucket Pequot Tribe, profits that support essential governmental functions, create opportunities for employment, and make possible further, much needed, economic development.

Museum and Indian Research Center. For many generations, the Mashantucket Pequot Indians have been concerned about the misconceptions and distortions of Pequot history and culture that have gained widespread public acceptance. In school and popular publications, the picture presented of Pequot culture and history has been offensive to generations of Pequot leadership. Accordingly, successive tribal councils have established as a priority the correction of these misconceptions. As currently envisioned, the Mashantucket Pequot Museum and Research Center will serve two distinct audiences. The exhibit portion of this facility will be entertaining and educational, and will teach the general public about Pequot history. A special emphasis will be placed on debunking some of the more odious popular misconceptions of Pequot history and culture. The other portion of the facility will be designed to serve a scholarly audience. Primary documents and microfiche copies will be available for study. As funding is available, research fellowships may be awarded to scholars. The intent of these efforts will be to induce a scholarly re-

*Fig. 7. Mashantucket Pequot Tribal Chairman Richard ("Skip")
Hayward receiving the National Historical Presentation Award at
the White House from Secretary of the Interior Donald Hodel, November 18, 1988.*

evaluation of Pequot history and culture. In a very real sense,
this effort has already begun. The Tribal Council has committed a significant portion of its base allocation from the Bureau of Indian Affairs to a culture resource program to survey
the reservation for historic and prehistoric archaeological sites.
Capital for the project will be obtained from a Mashantucket
Pequot tax-exempt bond issue. A museum trust fund will be
established with a portion of the proceeds from each of the
tribe's enterprises. Eventually, the museum trust fund will receive enough funding for the interest to pay the museum

bond-issue debt amortization as well as all museum salaries and operating costs. Based on current analysis, it is estimated that roughly 40 percent of the museum operating costs will be derived from gate receipts. Thus this essentially educational project must be viewed as a sociocultural development project rather than an economic development project.

Community Building. As envisioned, the Mashantucket Pequot Community Building will house all of the tribal offices as well as community facilities that will include meeting and recreation rooms. The community building will also house the administrative offices of the tribe's enterprises. Since this facility will be the tribe's window on the world, the Tribal Council realizes that careful planning will be required in its design.

Business Acquisition. As a direct result of Congress passing the Native American Tax Status Act, new opportunities for business acquisition have been made available to Indian tribes. The Mashantucket Pequot Tribe's general counsel, the law firm of Tureen and Margolin, have become leaders in putting together acquisition terms that are favorable to the tribe while attractive to the seller. As an example of their efforts, Tureen and Margolin have drafted the terms for the acquisition of a huge cement plant by the Passamaquoddy Tribe of Maine. The key feature of this leveraged buy-out was that it required very little capital supplied by the Passamaquoddies. The Mashantucket Pequot Tribe has considered the acquisition of two concrete plants, along with eighteen cement trucks.

Jurisdiction. It has long been the goal of the Mashantucket Pequot Tribal Council to have an on-reservation law-enforcement program, but to have one, the tribe needs a law-and-order code and an agreement with the state defining concurrent civil and criminal jurisdictions. During 1985 the Mashantucket Pequot Tribal Council held one negotiating session with the Connecticut attorney general's office, which seemed willing to work with the Tribal Council to develop such an agreement. But because the Connecticut chief state's attorney (who is charged with the prosecution of criminal law in Connecticut) has remained unwilling to work with the Tribal

Council, negotiations have been stalled. Despite this delay, the Tribal Council plans to move ahead with the tribe's law-and-order code and work toward an agreement to resolve the issue of concurrent jurisdiction.

Conclusion

An integral step in the tribe's social and economic development strategy was the federal recognition achieved in 1983, which strengthened the tribe's ability to govern itself and thereby enhanced its potential for social and economic development. The Mashantucket Pequot Tribe is indeed alive and well more than 350 years after the Pequots' alleged demise in the Pequot War of 1637.

Notes

Preface

1. For Mason's account, see *A Brief History of the Pequot War* (1736), reprinted in *History of the Pequot War,* Charles Orr, ed.
2. John De Forest, *History of the Indians of Connecticut: From the Earliest Known Period to 1850* (1851), p. 58.
3. De Forest, pp. 420–421.

Chapter 2. A Capsule Prehistory of Southern New England

1. Southern New England, for the purposes of prehistory consists basically of the modern states of Connecticut, Massachusetts, and Rhode Island. However, it also includes coastal New York state, except for Manhattan and Staten islands, and extends to New Hampshire to include the Ashuelot River drainage and the Merrimack drainage as far north as Manchester, and the Great Bay area of the coast. It excludes the Hoosic River drainage of northwestern Massachusetts. Denise C. Gaudreau and Thompson Webb, III, "Late Quaternary Pollen Stratigraphy and Isochrone Maps for the Northeastern United States," in *Pollen Records of Late-Quaternary North American Sediments,* Vaughn L. Bryant, Jr., and Richard L. Holloway, eds. (Dallas: American Association of Stratigraphic Palynologists Foundation, 1985), pp. 247–280; and Thompson Webb, III, "The Appearance and Disappearance of Major Vegetational Assemblages: Long-term Vegetational Dynamics in Eastern North America," *Vegetatio* 69 (1–3) (1987):177–187.

2. The cultural terminology used in this essay is my own. I have found it helpful for communicating with people unfamiliar with the specialist literature. See fig. 1 for equivalencies. The essay represents my interpretation of the information on Southern New England's prehistory as was available to me in 1987.

3. Mary Lou Curran, "The Spatial Organization of Paleoindian Populations in the Late Pleistocene of the Northeast." Ph.D. diss., University of Massachusetts, Amherst, 1987; John R. Grimes et al., "Bull Brook II," *Archaeology of Eastern North America* 12 (1984):159–183; Roger W. Moeller, *6LF21: A Paleo-Indian Site in Western Connecticut,* Occasional Paper No. 2 (Washington, Conn.: American Indian Archaeological Institute, 1980); Mary Lou Curran and Dena F. Dincauze, "Paleo-Indians and Paleo-Lakes: New Data from the Connecticut Drainage," New York Academy of Sciences, *Annals* 288 (February, 1977):333–348; Dincauze and Curran, "Paleoindians as Generalists: An Ecological Perspective," *SAA Abstracts,* 48th annual meeting (Pittsburgh: Society for American Archaeology, 1983), p. 49.

4. David J. Meltzer and James I. Mead, "The Timing of Late Pleistocene Mammalian Extinctions in North America," *Quaternary Research* 19 (1) (1983):130–135; Dena F. Dincauze and Mitchell T. Mulholland, "Early and Middle Archaic Site Distributions and Habitats in Southern New England," New York Academy of Sciences, *Annals* 288 (1977):439–456.

5. R. Ervin Taylor, *Radiocarbon Dating* (Orlando: Academic Press, 1987); Raymond S. Bradley, *Quaternary Paleoclimatology* (Boston: Allen and Unwin, 1985); Robert E. Funk and William A. Ritchie, *Aboriginal Settlement Patterns in the Northeast,* New York State Museum and Science Service memoir No. 20 (1973), pp. 9–36.

6. Dena F. Dincauze, *The Neville Site: 8000 Years at Amoskeag,* Peabody Museum of Archaeology and Ethnography Monograph No. 4, (Cambridge, Mass., 1976); James A. Moore and Dolores Root, "Anadromous Fish, Stream Ranking and Settlement," *Ecological Anthropology of the Middle Connecticut River Valley,* Robert Paynter, ed., University of Massachusetts, Department of Anthropology Research Report no. 18 (Amherst, 1979), pp. 27–44.

7. Frederick Johnson, *The Boylston Street Fishweir,* Papers of the Robert S. Peabody Foundation for Archeology), vol. 2 (Andover, Mass., 1942); Maurice Robbins, *Wapanucket;* William A. Ritchie, *The Archaeology of Martha's Vineyard* (Garden City, N.Y.: Natural History Press, 1969).

8. Robbins, *Wapanucket;* Arthur C. Staples and Roy C. Athearn, "The Bear Swamp Site: A Preliminary Report," *Bulletin of the Massachusetts Archaeological Society* 30 (3–4) (1969):1–8; Dena F. Dincauze, *Cremation Cemeteries in Eastern Massachusetts,* Peabody Museum of Archaeology and Ethnography Paper no. 59 (Cambridge, Mass., 1968); Dincauze, "The Late Archaic Period in Southern New England," *Arctic Anthropology* 12 (2) (1975):23–24; John Pfeiffer, "The Griffin Site: A Susquehanna Cremation

Burial in Southern Connecticut," *Man in the Northeast* 19 (Spring, 1980): 129–133.

9. Kevin A. McBride and Robert E. Dewar, "Prehistoric Settlement in the Lower Connecticut River Valley," *Man in the Northeast* 22 (Fall, 1981): 37–66.

10. Lucianne Lavin, "Pottery Classification and Cultural Models in Southern New England Prehistory," *North American Archaeologist* 7 (1) (1986):1–14; Barbara Luedtke, "Regional Variation in Massachusetts Ceramics," *North American Archaeologist* 7 (2) (1986):113–135.

11. Kent Lightfoot et al., "Coastal New York Settlement Patterns: A Perspective from Shelter Island," *Man in the Northeast* 30 (Fall, 1985):59–82.

12. M. Pamela Bumsted, "VT-CH-94: Vermont's Earliest Known Agricultural Experiment Station," *Man in the Northeast* 19 (Spring, 1980):73–82; Ritchie, *Archaeology of Martha's Vineyard;* Lynn Ceci, "Watchers of the Pleiades: Ethnoastronomy among Native Cultivators in Northeastern North America," *Ethnohistory* 25 (4) (1978):301–317.

13. Lynn Ceci, "Maize Cultivation in Coastal New York: The Archaeological, Agronomical, and Documentary Evidence," *North American Archaeologist* 1 (1) (1979–80):45–74; and Ceci, "Method and Theory in Coastal New York Archaeology: Paradigms of Settlement Pattern," *North American Archaeologist* 3 (1) (1982):5–36.

14. Edward J. Kaesar, "The Archery Range Site Ossuary, Pelham Bay Park, Bronx County, New York," *Pennsylvania Archaeologist* (40) (1) (1970):9–33; Francis P. McManamon, James W. Bradley, and Ann L. Magennis, "The Indian Neck Ossuary." *Chapters in the Archaeology of Cape Cod* 5 (Boston: National Park Service North Atlantic Regional Office, 1986); William Cronon, *Changes in the Land* (New York: Hill and Wang, 1983).

15. Mary Rowlandson, "A Narrative of the Captivity of Mrs. Mary Rowlandson," in *Narratives of the Indian Wars (1675–1699),* Charles H. Lincoln, ed. (New York: Charles Scribner's Sons, 1913), pp. 118–136.

16. Kevin McBride, "Prehistory of the Lower Connecticut River Valley" Ph.D. diss. University of Connecticut, 1984. Nonarchaeologists interested in reading more about the archaeology of southern New England may consult the following titles, which will in turn lead further into the specialist literature: *Connecticut Archaeology Today,* Archaeological Society of Connecticut Bulletin No. 47 (1984); Robert E. Dewar, Kenneth L. Feder, and David A. Poirier, eds., *Connecticut Archaeology: Past, Present and Future,* Occasional Papers in Anthropology (Storrs: Department of Anthropology, University of Connecticut, 1983); Dena F. Dincauze, *The Neville Site: 8000 Years at Amoskeag;* William A. Ritchie, *The Archaeology of Martha's Vineyard: A Framework for the Prehistory of Southern New England;* Dean R. Snow, *The Archaeology of New England* (New York: Academic Press, 1980); James E. Truex, ed., *The Second Coastal Archaeology Reader: 1900 to*

the Present (Stony Brook, N.Y.: Suffolk County Archaeological Association, 1982).

Chapter 3. The Pequots in the Early Seventeenth Century

1. John W. De Forest, *History of the Indians of Connecticut,* pp. 59–61; Mary Guillette Soulsby, "Connecticut Indian Ethnohistory: A Look at Five Tribes," M.A. thesis, University of Connecticut, 1981; Dean R. Snow, "Late Prehistory of the East Coast," in *Handbook of North American Indians,* vol. 15, *Northeast,* Bruce G. Trigger, ed. (hereafter *Handbook*) (Washington, D.C.: Smithsonian Institution, 1978), p. 65; Ives Goddard, "Eastern Algonquian Languages," in *Handbook* 15:70–77; Bert Salwen, "A Tentative 'In Situ' Solution to the Mohegan-Pequot Problem," *An Introduction to the Archaeology and History of the Connecticut Valley Indian,* William R. Young, ed. (Springfield, Ill.: Springfield Museum of Science, 1969), pp. 81–88.

2. Dean R. Snow, *The Archaeology of New England,* p. 33.

3. Johannes de Laet, "New World, or Description of West-Indian," in *Narratives of New Netherland,* J. Franklin Jameson, ed., pp. 42–43; Oliver A. Rink, *Holland on the Hudson: An Economic and Social History of Dutch New York,* pp. 33–34.

4. Kevin A. McBride and Nicholas F. Bellantoni, "The Utility of Ethnohistoric Models for Understanding Late Woodland-Contact Change in Southern New England," *Bulletin of the Archaeological Society of Connecticut* 45(1982): 51; Kevin A. McBride and Robert E. Dewar, "Agriculture and Cultural Evolution: Causes and Effects in the Lower Connecticut River Valley," in *Emergent Horticultural Economies of the Eastern Woodlands,* William F. Keegan, ed., pp. 305–328.

5. This discussion of subsistence and settlements is based, in part, upon the following sources: Froelich G. Rainey, "A Compilation of Historical Data Contributing to the Ethnography of Connecticut and Southern New England Indians," *Bulletin of the Archaeological Society of Connecticut* 3 (1) (1956): 1–89; Charles C. Willoughby, "Houses and Gardens of the New England Indians," *American Anthropologist,* n.s., 8 (1906): 115–122; E. B. De Labarre and H. Wilder, "Indian Cornhills in Massachusetts," *American Anthropologist,* n.s., 22 (3) (1920):203–225; Bert Salwen, "Indians of Southern New England and Long Island Sound: Early Period," in *Handbook,* Trigger, ed., 15:160–176; William S. Simmons, "Narragansett," *Handbook* 15:190–197; William C. Sturtevant, "Two 1761 Wigwams at Niantic, Connecticut," *American Antiquity* 40 (4) (1975):437–444; Snow, *The Archaeology of New England.* See also John Josselyn, *An Account of Two Voyages to New England, 1638–1663;* Thomas Morton, *New English Canaan* (1637); G. Mourt, *A Journal of the Pilgrims at Plymouth* (1622), Dwight B. Heath, ed.; Roger Williams, *Key into the Language of*

America (1643), in *The Complete Writings of Roger Williams,* J. H. Trumbell, ed. (New York: Russell and Russell, 1968), vol. 1; Daniel Gookin, *Historical Collections of the Indians of New England* (1792); William Wood, *New England's Prospect* (1634); Peter A. Thomas, "Contrastive Subsistence Strategies and Land Use as Factors for Understanding Indian-White Relations in New England," *Ethnohistory* 23 (1) (1976): 1–18.

6. Cf. Frederic W. Warner, "The Foods of the Connecticut Indians," *Bulletin of the Archaeological Society of Connecticut* 37 (1972): 27–47; Eva L. Butler, "Algonkian Culture and Use of Maize in Southern New England," *Bulletin of the Archaeological Society of Connecticut* 22 (1948): 3–39; William A. Ritchie, *The Archaeology of Martha's Vineyard;* McBride, "Prehistory of the Lower Connecticut River Valley," Ph.D. diss.

7. See n. 6.

8. See Bert Salwen, "Indians of Southern New England and Long Island: The Early Period," in *Handbook,* Trigger, ed., 15: 164–165; Snow, *The Archaeology of New England,* pp. 77–79, fig. 2.11.

9. See, generally, McBride and Bellantoni, "The Utility of Ethnohistoric Models," pp. 53–54.

10. Kevin A. McBride, personal communication, August, 1987.

11. Kevin A. McBride, "The Development of the Household as an Economic Unit in the Lower Connecticut Valley," *Man in the Northeast* 28 (Fall, 1984): 39–49.

12. Cf. McBride, "The Development of the Household," p. 41; Salwen, "Indians of Southern New England," p. 166; Snow, *The Archaeology of New England,* p. 77.

13. Snow, *The Archaeology of New England,* p. 77.

14. Simmons, "Narragansett," in Trigger, ed., *Handbook* 15: 193.

15. Salwen, "Indians of Southern New England," p. 167.

16. Salwen, p. 167.

17. Salwen, p. 167; Catherine Marten, "The Wampanoags in the Seventeenth Century," *Occasional Papers in Old Colony Studies,* no. 2 (1970).

18. Morton H. Fried, *The Notion of Tribe* (Menlo Park, Calif.: Cummings Publishing, 1975); Elman R. Service, *Primitive Social Organization* (New York: Random House, 1962).

19. Marshall D. Sahlins, *Tribesmen* (Englewood Cliffs, N.J.: Prentice-Hall, 1968), p. 49.

20. R. K. Beardsley, P. Holder, A. D. Krieger, B. J. Meggers, J. B. Rinaldo, and P. Kutsche, "Functional and Evolutionary Implications of Community Patterning," in *Seminars in Archaeology,* R. Wauchope, ed., Memoirs of the Society of American Archaeology, No. 11 (1956), p. 133.

21. Morton H. Fried, *The Evolution of Political Society* (New York: Random House, 1967); Melvin M. Tumin, *Social Stratification* (Englewood Cliffs, N.J.: Prentice-Hall, 1967), p. 21.

22. Salwen, "Indians of Southern New England," p. 167; Snow, *The Archaeology of New England,* p. 77.

23. Cf. Marten, "The Wampanoags in the Seventeenth Century," p. 18; Rainey, "A Compilation of Historical Data," p. 33; Williams, *A Key into the Language.*

24. William S. Simmons, "Southern New England Shamanism: An Ethnographic Reconstruction," in *Papers of the Seventh Algonquian Conference,* W. Cowan, ed. (Ottawa: Carleton University, 1976), pp. 220–221.

25. Ibid., p. 223.

26. Salwen, "The Indians of Southern New England"; Francis Jennings, *The Invasion of America: Indians, Colonialism, and the Cant of Conquest;* Ted J. Brasser, "The Coastal Algonkians: People of the First Frontier," in *North American Indians in Historical Perspective,* Nancy O. Lurie and Eleanor Leacock, eds. (New York: Random House, 1971), pp. 64–91; Snow, *The Archaeology of New England.*

27. Marshall T. Newman, "Aboriginal New World Epidemiology and Medical Care, and the Impact of Old World Disease Imports," *American Journal of Physical Anthropology* 45 (3, pt. 2) (1976):669.

28. Cf. Mark N. Cohen and George J. Armelagos, *Paleopathology at the Origins of Agriculture* (New York: Academic Press, 1984).

29. Newman, "Aboriginal New World Epidemiology," p. 671.

30. Sherburne F. Cook, "The Significance of Disease in the Extinction of the New England Indians," *Human Biology* 45 (3) (1973):485–508; and "Interracial Warfare and Population Decline among the New England Indians," *Ethnohistory* 20 (3) (1972):1–24.

31. Arthur J. Spiess and Bruce D. Spiess, "New England Pandemic of 1616–1622: Cause and Archaeological Implication," *Man in the Northeast* 34 (Fall, 1987):71–83.

32. Snow, *The Archaeology of New England;* Jennings, *The Invasion of America.*

33. Cf. Paul A. Robinson, Marc A. Kelley, and Patricia E. Rubertone, "Preliminary Biocultural Interpretations from a Seventeenth-Century Narragansett Indian Cemetery in Rhode Island," in *Cultures in Contact,* William W. Fitzhugh, ed., pp. 107–130; Marc A. Kelley, T. Gail Barrett, and Sandra D. Saunders, "Diet, Dental Disease, and Transition in Northeastern Native Americans," *Man in the Northeast* 33 (Spring, 1987):113–125.

34. Snow, *The Archaeology of New England.*

35. Snow, *The Archaeology of New England,* pp. 34, 39.

36. Cf. Kim Lanphear, "Biocultural Interactions: Smallpox and the Mohawk Iroquois," M.A. thesis, State University of New York at Albany, 1983.

37. Morton, *New English Canaan,* p. 23.

Chapter 4. Native Wampum as a Peripheral Resource in the Seventeenth-Century World-System

1. David I. Bushnell, Jr., "The Origin of Wampum," *Journal of the Royal Anthropological Institute of Great Britain and Ireland* 36 (1906): 172–177; William N. Fenton, "The New York State Wampum Collection: The Case for the Integrity of Cultural Treasures," *Proceedings of the American Philosophical Society* 115 (6) (1971): 437–461.

2. These measurements are based on statistical analysis of 3,212 loose and belt wampum recovered from the Power House, Dann, and Rochester Junction sites dated ca. A.D. 1640–1687. The beads were measured by electronic calipers and recorded by computer as part of a larger research project in which more than 7,000 shell beads were examined from 31 Archaic to historic archaeological and ethnographic collections from western New York state housed at the Rochester Museum and Science Center. The project was funded by the Arthur C. Parker Fund for Iroquois Research.

3. Bushnell, "The Origin of Wampum," 172–177; William M. Beauchamp, "Wampum and Shell Articles Used by the New York Indians," New York State Museum *Bulletin,* No. 41 (1901), pp. 319–480; Lynn Ceci, "The Effect of European Contact and Trade on the Settlement Pattern of Indians in Coastal New York, 1524–1664," Ph.D. diss., City University of New York, 1977.

4. James S. Slotkin and K. Schmidt, "Studies in Wampum," *American Anthropologist* 51 (April, 1949): 223–236.

5. Lewis Henry Morgan, *League of the Iroquois* (1851; reprint, New York: Corinth Books, 1962); Elisabeth Tooker, "The League of the Iroquois: Its History, Politics, and Ritual," in *Handbook,* Trigger, ed., 15: 418–449.

6. Cf. H. Wright and M. Zeder, "The Simulation of a Linear Exchange System under Equilibrium Conditions," in *Exchange Systems in Prehistory,* T. K. Earle and J. E. Ericson, eds. (New York: Academic Press, 1977), pp. 253–273. Proto-wampum was recovered from a Hopewell burial mound, Geneseo Mound (ca. A.D. 200–700?) and a burial on the Alhart site C dated A.D. 1335–1510; the five columellas C-14 dated A.D. 875–1485 were recovered from the Tottenville, Pelham Bay Knolls, Port Washington, and Sebonac sites. The C-14 dating project was funded by the National Science Foundation, BNS 8511663.

7. Charles F. Wray and Henry L. Schoff, "A Preliminary Report on the Seneca Sequence in Western New York, 1550–1687," *Pennsylvania Archaeologist* 23 (2) (1953): 53–63. Measurements were made on postcontact wampum from the Richmond Mills, Adams, Tram, Cameron, Feugle, and Dutch Hollow sites. The 62-bead bracelet was removed from the Tram site, ca. A.D. 1570–1590. The 231-bead wampum belt (?) from the Feugle site ca. A.D. 1600–1620 was reconstructed from the bead pattern observed in a burial that also contained copper tubular beads, brass beads and finger rings, and 15 varieties of (384) glass trade beads.

8. Immanuel Wallerstein, *The Modern World-System,* vol. 1 (New York: Acadmic Press, 1974), pp. 4, 15, 348–401.

9. Eric Wolf, *Europe and the People Without History* (Berkeley, Calif.: University of California Press, 1982), pp. 3, 13; O. Zunz, ed., *Reliving the Past: The Worlds of Social History* (Chapel Hill: University of North Carolina Press, 1985), pp. 5–6.

10. William P. Cummings, R. A. Skelton, and David Quinn, *The Discovery of North America* (New York: American Heritage, 1972), pp. 93, 128.

11. I. N. Phelps Stokes, *The Iconography of Manhattan Island, 1498–1909* (New York: R. H. Dodd, 1915–1928), vol. 2, cartographic plates 22a, 45, 51, 52.

12. Henry C. Murphy, *Henry Hudson in Holland* (The Hague: G. D'Albani Bros., 1859). See also Oliver Rink, *Holland on the Hudson,* p. 24.

13. Jameson, ed., *Narratives of New Netherland,* pp. 22–24.

14. Simon Hart, *The Prehistory of the New Netherland Company* (Amsterdam, Netherlands: City of Amsterdam Press, 1959); Ceci, "The Effect of European Contact and Trade," pp. 161–167; Robert F. Berkhofer, Jr., "The North American Frontier as Process and Context," in *The Frontier in History: North America and South Africa Compared,* Howard Lamar and Leonard Thompson, eds. (New Haven, Conn.: Yale University Press, 1981), pp. 43–75. Cf. Wolf, *Europe and the People Without History;* Eleanor Leacock, "Relations of Production in Band Societies," in *Politics and History in Band Society,* Eleanor Leacock and R. Lee, eds. (New York: Cambridge University Press, 1982), pp. 159–170. Comparison of the *X* locations against modern charts for the same offshore areas (U.S. National Oceanic and Atmospheric Administration, U.S. Geological Survey) does not support earlier interpretations. If Block meant the *X* to show dangerous rocks or shoals, he would have had to mark hundreds of such symbols the length of the New Netherland coast.

15. Marc Lescarbot, *The History of New France* (Toronto: Champlain Society, 1907–1914), 2:339, 565; 3:157–158.

16. Lynn Ceci, "The Value of Wampum among the New York Iroquois: A Case Study in Artifact Analysis," *Journal of Anthropological Research* 38 (1982):97–107.

17. Berthold Fernow, ed., *Documents Relating to the Colonial History of the State of New York,* vol. 14 (Albany, N.Y.: Weed, Parsons and Co., 1883), p. 470.

18. Beauchamp, "Wampum and Shell Articles," p. 338; J. H. Trumbull, ed., *Natick Dictionary,* Bureau of American Ethnography Bulletin No. 25 (Washington, D.C.: Smithsonian Institution, 1903).

19. A. J. F. Van Laer, ed. and trans., *Documents Relating to New Netherland, 1624–1626* (San Mateo, Calif.: Henry E. Huntington Library, 1924), pp. 223–231. Jacob J. Eelkens, a trader on the Hudson River since ca. 1613, and occasional commander of the trade post upriver after 1614, kid-

napped and ransomed a "Sickenanes" chief for 140 fathoms of "Zeewan." Jameson, ed., *Narratives of New Netherland,* pp. 47, 86; Hart, *Prehistory of the New Netherland Company,* pp. 37, 54. (The six-foot fathom would contain approximately 330 [5.5 mm long] wampum beads.) Eelkens had also been involved with the ransom of Indians for "beads" earlier in 1620 near Long Island.

20. Ceci, "The Effect of European Contact and Trade," pp. 193–196; Edmund B. O'Callaghan, *History of New Netherland,* vol. 1 (New York: D. Appleton and Co., 1846), p. 139.

21. Jameson, ed., *Narratives of New Netherland,* p. 110.

22. Ibid., p. 113; William Bradford, *Of Plymouth Plantation, 1620–1647,* Samuel Eliot Morison, ed. (New York: Alfred A. Knopf, 1952), pp. 203, 219; Bernard Bailyn, *The New England Merchants in the Seventeenth Century* (Cambridge, Mass.: Harvard University Press, 1955), p. 13; John Winthrop, *Winthrop's Journal, 1630–1649,* J. K. Hosmer, ed. (New York: Charles Scribner's Sons, 1908), 1:129.

23. Ceci, "The Effect of European Contact and Trade," table 10.

24. Bradford, *Of Plymouth Plantation,* p. 203; W. Wood, *New England's Prospect* (1634), p. 61; Jameson, *Narratives of New Netherland,* p. 103; O'Callaghan, *History of New Netherland* 1:150; Ted J. C. Brasser, "Early Indian-European Contact," *Handbook of North American Indians,* Trigger, ed., 15:85.

25. Wallerstein, *The Modern World-System* 2:17; Curtis P. Nettles, *The Money Supply of the American Colonies Before 1720,* University of Wisconsin Studies in the Social Sciences and History, no. 20 (Madison, 1934).

26. Wood, *New England Prospect* (1634), p. 61; John Underhill, *Newes from America* (1638), in Massachusetts Historical Society *Collections,* 3d ser. 6 (1831):8–9.

27. Winthrop, *Winthrop's Journal* 1:189–190.

28. Trumbull, J. H., ed., *The Public Records of the Colony of Connecticut* (Hartford, 1850), 1:9, 13.

29. Underhill, *Newes from America,* pp. 3, 25.

30. Henry Steele Commager, "Nations Aren't Innocent," *New York Times,* June 27, 1985, op. ed.

31. Ceci, "The Effect of European Contact and Trade," table 10; Roger Williams, *Key Into the Language of America,* p. 174, in *The Complete Writings of Roger Williams,* J. H. Trumbull, ed. (New York: Russell and Russell Reprint, 1963), 1:174.

32. Bradford, *Of Plymouth Plantation,* p. 439.

33. Lion Gardiner, *Lieft Lion Gardener His Relation to the Pequot Warres* (1660), in Massachusetts Historical Society *Collections,* 3d ser., 3 (1833):136–160; D. Pulsifer, ed., *Records of the Colony of New Plymouth in New England, 1643–1651,* vol. 1 (Boston: William White Press, 1859), p. 249.

34. See, for example, William Cronon, *Changes in the Land* (New York: Hill and Wang, 1983), p. 97; Wilcomb E. Washburn, "Seventeenth-Century Indian Wars," in *Handbook*, Trigger, ed., 15:89–100.

35. See table 1 above. Williams, *Key Into the Language of America*, p. 174.

36. Jameson, ed., *Narratives of New Netherland*, p. 280 ff.; O'Callaghan, *History of New Netherland* 1:226 ff.; Fernow, ed., *Documents Relating to the Colonial History of the State of New York* 13:6; Lynn Ceci, "The First Fiscal Crisis in New York," *Economic Development and Culture Change* 28 (4) (1980):839–847; and Ceci, "Locational Analysis of Historic Algonquian Sites in Coastal New York," in *Proceedings of the Conference on Northeastern Archaeology*, J. Moore, ed., University of Massachusetts—Amherst, Department of Anthropology Research Report No. 19 (1980), pp. 71–91.

Chapter 5. The Pequot War and Its Legacies

1. The best scholarly accounts of the War are still Francis Jennings, *The Invasion of America: Indians, Colonialism, and the Cant of Conquest;* Neal Salisbury, *Manitou and Providence: Indians, Europeans, and the Making of New England, 1500–1643;* and Alden T. Vaughan, "Pequots and Puritans: The Causes of the War of 1637," *William and Mary Quarterly* 21 (April, 1964):256–269; and Vaughan's *New England Frontier: Puritans and Indians, 1620–1675.* Vaughan has produced three major interpretations of the Pequot War, modifying, revising, and refining his conclusions each time.

2. Richard Drinnon, *Facing West: The Metaphysics of Indian-Hating and Empire-Building*, p. 60. Alvin M. Josephy, Jr., suggests that the Pequot War had a longer impact than just on the colonial era in America. Josephy, *Now That the Buffalo's Gone: A Study of Today's American Indians*, pp. 31–75.

3. Josephy, pp. 31–75; Ronald Sanders, *Lost Tribes and Promised Lands: The Origins of American Racism* (Boston: Little, Brown and Co., 1978), pp. 326–340.

4. John Demos, *Entertaining Satan: Witchcraft and the Culture of Early New England*, pp. 341–345, 380–383.

5. Besides the citations in n. 2, there are other important historical treatments of the war: Richard Slotkin, *Regeneration Through Violence: The Mythology of the American Frontier, 1600–1860*, pp. 69–93; Roy Harvey Pearce, *Savigism and Civilization: A Study of the Indian and the American Mind*, pp. 19–35; Charles M. Egal and David C. Stineback, *Puritans, Indians, and Manifest Destiny*, pp. 104–140. Also, Peter Thomas, "In the Maelstrom of Change: The Indian Trade and Cultural Process in the Middle Connecticut River Valley, 1635–1665," Ph.D. diss., University of Massachu-

Notes to Pages 70–76 233

setts, 1979, pp. 55–63; Ceci, "The Effect of European Contact and Trade on the Settlement Pattern of Indians in Coastal New York, 1524–1665: The Archaeological and Documentary Evidence," Ph.D. diss., chap. 4; William John Burton, "Hellish Fiends and Brutish Men: Amerindian-Euroamerican Interaction in Southern New England, An Interdisciplinary Analysis, 1600–1750" Ph.D. diss., Kent State University, 1976, pp. 106–147; and William John Burton and Richard Lowenthal, "The First of the Mohegans," *American Ethnologist* 1 (1974):589–599; Carroll Alton Means, "Mohegan-Pequot Relationships, as Indicated by the Events Leading to the Pequot Massacre of 1637 and Subsequent Claims in the Mohegan Land Controversy," *Bulletin of the Archaeological Society of Connecticut* 21 (1947): 26–34. See also De Forest, *History of the Indians of Connecticut,* pp. 69–160. Although other works can be cited, these books and articles provide a helpful introduction to the Pequot War.

6. Laurence M. Hauptman, Pequot field notes, 1982–1987, in author's possession.

7. I should like to thank Dr. Jack Campisi as well as my colleagues Judah Adelson, Donald D'Elia, David Krikun, Carole Levin, and Gerald Sorin for their suggestions. The historical literature on genocide is immense. I have especially benefited by reading Isidor Wallimann and Michael N. Dobkowski, eds., *Genocide and the Modern Age: Etiology and Case Studies of Mass Death* (Westport, Conn.: Greenwood Press, 1987).

8. Kevin McBride, "Ethnohistory Project Enters 4th Year," *Wuskusu Yertum: The Newsletter of the Mashantucket Pequot Tribe,* March, 1987, p. 4; McBride, personal communication, October 23, 1987.

9. The general historical outline presented here is based on a composite of the writings of Jennings, Salisbury, and Vaughan previously cited.

10. For an intriguing analysis on the death of Oldham, see Jennings, *Invasion of America,* pp. 204–209.

11. John Underhill, *Newes from America* Massachusetts Historical Society *Collections,* 3d ser., 6 (1837):1–28. Underhill's account as well as Captain John Mason's *Brief History of the Pequot War,* Philip Vincent's *A True Relation of the Late Battell Fought in New England,* and Lion Gardiner's *Relation of the Pequot Warres* are conveniently found together in Charles Orr, ed., *History of the Pequot War.* See pp. 80–81 for Captain Underhill's quotation used in the text of this article.

12. See Salisbury, *Manitou and Providence,* pp. 222–224; Jennings, *Invasion of America,* pp. 220–227; Vaughan, *New England Frontier* (1979 ed.), pp. 144–152. For the enslavement of Pequots and dispersal to Bermuda, see Ethel Boissevain, "Whatever Became of the New England Indians Shipped to Bermuda to be Sold as Slaves," *Man in the Northeast* 11 (Spring, 1981):103–114. Sherburne F. Cook, in "Intertribal Warfare and Population Decline among the New England Indians," *Ethnohistory* 22 (Winter, 1973):6–9, insists: "If the initial population [of the Pequots] was

3,000 and 750 were killed, the battle loss was twenty-five percent of the tribe."
Although Cook mentions that a total of 180 Pequot prisoners were distributed as slaves to Indians and non-Indians alike and that the "Pequot tribe
disappeared as a political entity," he fails to mention that the Pequot Indians
had no right to use their name for a generation while others were deported
as far away as Bermuda. Therefore, I believe that a more substantial number
of Pequots were affected by the war than Cook suggests.

13. Quoted in Alden T. Vaughan, ed., *The Puritan Tradition in America,
1620–1730*, p. 66. For the Puritans' perception of the Indians, see the excellent article by William S. Simmons, "Cultural Bias in the New England Puritans' Perception of Indians," *William and Mary Quarterly*, 3d ser., 38
(January, 1981):56–72. See also Peter N. Carroll, *Puritanism and the
Wilderness: The Intellectual Significance of the New England Frontier,
1629–1700*, pp. 65–86.

14. Leo Kuper, *Genocide: Its Political Use in the Twentieth Century*
(New Haven, Conn.: Yale University Press, 1982), app. 1.

15. The most complete ethnohistory of the Mashantucket Pequots is the
tribe's federal acknowledgment petition written by Dr. Jack Campisi and
submitted to the BIA in 1982.

16. Hauptman, Mashantucket Pequot field notes, 1982–1987. I was an
honored guest at the tribe's Thanksgiving ceremony held on the reservation
on October 21, 1983, after the Mashantucket Pequot Tribe of Connecticut
had been awarded federal recognition (October 18, 1983). James Wherry,
"Mashantucket Now 1,539 Acres," *Wuskusu Yertum* (January, 1987), 1–3.

17. Interviews with Chairman Richard ("Skip") Haywood, May 5–7, 1982,
SUNY/New Paltz, New Paltz, N.Y., and November, 1982, Indian Rights Association Centennial Conference, Philadelphia; and with James Wherry, September 18, 1987, Mashantucket Pequot Indian Reservation, Ledyard, Conn.

18. Hauptman, Mashantucket Pequot Indian field notes, 1982–1987.

19. Ibid.; interviews Richard ("Skip") Hayward; Steven Rosenbush, "United
Way Wins Big: Benefit Bingo Nets $20,000," *The Day* (New London), De-
cember 2, 1986.

20. McBride, "Ethnohistory Project Enters 4th Year," pp. 3–7. James
Wherry, *Environmental Assessment Construction and Operation of a
Bingo Hall, Mashantucket Pequot Indian Reservation, Connecticut* (Led-
yard, Conn.: Mashantucket Pequot Tribe of Connecticut, 1985), pp. 11–14;
map in *Wuskusu Yertum* January, 1987, 4–5; interview with James Wherry,
September 17, 1987.

21. Hauptman, Mashantucket Pequot field notes, 1982–1987.

22. Boissevain, "Whatever Became of the New England Indians," p. 103.

23. Hauptman, Mashantucket Pequot field notes, 1982–1987.

24. 95 Stat. 852 (October 18, 1983). This act, the Connecticut Indian
Land Claims Settlement Act of 1983, created a $900,000 trust fund for land

acquisition and economic development. Importantly, the act provided that any land acquired from within the "Mashantucket Pequot Settlement Area would automatically become part of the reservation."

25. Susan Chira, "Pequot Indians Prevail in Battle Begun in 1637," *New York Times,* October 20, 1983.

Chapter 6. Indians and Colonists in Southern New England after the Pequot War

1. Vaughan, *New England Frontier: Puritans and Indians, 1620–1675;* Jennings, *The Invasion of America.* Earlier versions of this article appeared in *Man in the Northeast* and in James Merrill and Daniel Richter, eds., *Beyond the Covenant Chain* (Syracuse, N.Y., 1987).

2. Salisbury, *Manitou and Providence,* esp. p. 98.

3. Bailyn, *The New England Merchants in the Seventeenth Century,* pp. 26–32, 49–60; Thomas, "In the Maelstrom of Change: The Indian Trade and Colonial Process in the Middle Connecticut Valley, 1635–1665," Ph.D. diss., chaps. 4–6; Stephen Innes, *Labor in a New Land: Economy and Society in Seventeenth-Century Springfield,* chaps. 1–2.

4. Re wampum, see Lorraine E. Williams, "Ft. Shantok and Ft. Corchaug: A Comparative Study of Seventeenth-Century Culture Contact in the Long Island Sound Area," Ph.D. diss., New York University, 1972, pp. 22–27; Salisbury, "Toward the Covenant Chain," in *Beyond the Covenant Chain,* James Merrill and Daniel Richter, eds., chap. 4. Re land, see Nathaniel E. Shurtleff and David Pulsifer, eds., *Records of the Colony of New Plymouth* (hereafter *Ply. Recs.*) (Boston: W. White, 1855–1861), 2:58. Re labor, see *Winthrop Papers,* Allyn B. Forbes, ed. (Boston: Massachusetts Historical Society, 1929–47), 4:26, 495; 5:279–280, 341; John R. Bartlett, ed., *Records of the Colony of Rhode Island and Providence Plantations in New England* (hereafter *R.I. Recs.*), 10 vols. (Providence and Boston, 1850–65), 1:124; Nathaniel E. Shurtleff, ed., *Records of the Governor and Colony of Massachusetts Bay in New England* (hereafter *Mass. Recs.*) (Boston: W. White, 1853–54), 2:252, 3:134; Gookin, *Historical Collections of the Indians in New England* (1674), p. 111; John A. Sainsbury, "Indian Labor in Early Rhode Island," *New England Quarterly* 48 (3) (1975):380–381.

5. Wood, *New England's Prospect* (1634), pp. 69, 75, 87–88, 100; Williams, *A Key into the Language of America* (1643), in *Complete Writings of Roger Williams* 1:107, 126, 133, 184, 197, 236, 260; Bradford, *Of Plymouth Plantation,* pp. 87, 114; Josselyn, *An Account of Two Voyages to New England* (1675), pp. 105–106; Bert Salwen, "European Trade Goods and the Chronology of the Fort Shantok Site," *Bulletin of the Archaeological Society of Connecticut,* No. 34 (1966); Simmons, *Cautan-*

touwit's House, chap. 5; Williams, "Ft. Shantok and Ft. Corchaug"; Bert
Salwen and Susan N. Meyer, "Indian Archaeology in Rhode Island," *Archaeology* 31 (6) (1978):57–58.

6. *R.I. Recs.* 1:80–81, 82, 107–108, 113, 116, 117, 124–125; J. Hammond Trumbull, ed., *Public Records of the Colony of Connecticut* (hereafter *Conn. Recs.*) (Hartford, Conn.: Case, Lockwood, and Brainard,
1850–1890), 1:186; *Ply. Recs.* 10:144. See also Forbes, ed., *Winthrop
Papers* 4:65–67, 118–119; 5:347.

7. Salisbury, *Manitou and Providence,* pp. 147–152, 203–235; De Forest, *History of the Indians of Connecticut,* chap. 6; Vaughan, *New England Frontier,* chaps. 6–7; Williams, "Ft. Shantok and Ft. Corchaug,"
pp. 47–53, 95–115, 128–133, 151–181; Timothy J. Sehr, "Ninigret's Tac-
tics of Accommodation—Indian Diplomacy in New England, 1637–1675,"
Rhode Island History 36 (2) (1977):42–53; Ceci, "The Effect of European
Contact and Trade," pp. 215–221.

8. Neal Salisbury, "Red Puritans: The 'Praying Indians' of Massachusetts Bay and John Eliot," *William and Mary Quarterly,* 3d ser., 31 (1)
(1974):27–54.

9. Re land, see Massachusetts Archives (hereafter Mass. Archives),
30:15; Massachusetts Historical Society (hereafter M.H.S.), Photostats 6,
May 21, 1646; *Suffolk Deeds* (Boston, 1880–1906), 1:93, 205; Duane
Hamilton Hurd, ed., *History of Middlesex County, Massachusetts* (Phila-
delphia: J. S. Lewis, 1890), p. 609; *Mass. Recs.* 2:159; 3:73; Samuel G.
Drake, *Biography and History of the Indians of North America,* 11th ed.
(Boston: B. B. Mussey, 1851), pp. 108–109. Re adult labor, see Thomas
Shepard, "The Clear Sun-shine of the Gospel Breaking Forth upon the In-
dians in New-England" (orig. pub., 1648), Massachusetts Historical Society
Collections (hereafter *MHSC*), 3d ser., 4 (1834):59; Josselyn, *Account of
Two Voyages,* p. 115. Re child labor, see "New England's First Fruits"
(1643), in Samuel Eliot Morison, *The Founding of Harvard College* (Cam-
bridge, Mass.: Harvard University Press, 1935), p. 423; *Ply. Recs.* 10:251;
Mass. Recs. 4 (2):23.

10. Re land, see M.H.S. Photostats, October 21, 1659; *Mass. Recs.* 4
(1):102–103, 363; Don Gleason Hill, ed., *Early Records of the Town of
Dedham,* 6 vols. (Dedham, Mass., 1886–1936), 4:255–261, 268; Gookin,
Historical Collections, p. 62. Re shamans, see Gookin, pp. 20–21; John
Cotton [Jr.], *Journal* of his preaching to the Indians, and a Vocabulary of
Indian words with Indian meanings (1665–1678) (Cotton Papers, M.H.S.),
June 12, October 9, 1667. Re sachems, see Henry Whitfield, "The Light Ap-
pearing More and More Towards the Present Day" (1651), *MHSC,* 3d ser., 4
(1834):139–142.

11. Susan L. MacCulloch, "A Tripartite Political System among Christian
Indians of Early Massachusetts," *Kroeber Anthropological Society Papers*
34 (Spring, 1966); Elise Melanie Brenner, "Strategies for Autonomy: An

Analysis of Ethnic Mobilization in Seventeenth Century New England," Ph.D. diss., University of Massachusetts—Amherst, 1984, chaps. 5–7; passim.

12. Salisbury, "Red Puritans"; Simmons, "Conversion from Indian to Puritan," pp. 197–218; Burton, "Hellish Fiends and Brutish Men," pp. 212–234; James P. Ronda, "'We Are Well as We Are': An Indian Critique of Seventeenth-Century Christian Missions," *William and Mary Quarterly*, 3d ser., 34 (1) (1977):66–82; and Ronda, "Generations of Faith: The Christian Indians of Martha's Vineyard," *William and Mary Quarterly*, 3d ser., 38 (3) (1981):369–394.

13. Thomas, "In the Maelstrom of Change," pp. 184–186; Brenner, "Strategies for Autonomy," pp. 211–229.

14. De Forest, *History,* chaps. 5–6; Burton, "Hellish Fiends and Brutish Men," pp. 148–170, 212–234; Brenner, "Strategies for Autonomy," chaps. 5–7.

15. Bailyn, *New England Merchants,* pp. 54–57, 59–60, 75; Innes, *Labor in a New Land,* chap. 2; Samuel Hugh Brockunier, *The Irrepressible Democrat: Roger Williams* (New York: Ronald Press, 1940), chap. 14; Sydney V. James, "The Worlds of Roger Williams," *Rhode Island History* 37 (2) (1978):98–109; Neal Emerson Salisbury, "Conquest of the 'Savage': Puritans, Puritan Missionaries, and Indians, 1620–1680," Ph.D. diss., University of California, Los Angeles, 1972), chap. 5; Jennings, *Invasion of America,* p. 234; Richard S. Dunn, *Puritans and Yankees: The Winthrop Dynasty of New England, 1630–1717,* pp. 74–75.

16. Forbes, ed., *Winthrop Papers* 3:427, 431, 434–438 passim, 441, 446, 448, 451–458 passim, 490–491; Winthrop, *Winthrop's Journal: "History of New England," 1630–1649)* 1:227, 229; Bradford, *Of Plymouth Plantation,* p. 297.

17. Bradford, p. 297; Forbes, ed., *Winthrop Papers* 4:258–259, 418, 427–428, 431–433, 435, 443, 507; *R.I. Recs.* 1:139–140; Winthrop, *Journal* 2:6–7; Jameson, ed., *Narratives of New Netherland,* p. 276; *Ply. Recs.* 9:11, 19, 30; Salisbury, *Manitou and Providence,* p. 231; Thomas, "Maelstrom of Change," pp. 71–74.

18. *Jesuit Relations* (hereafter *JR*), 36:79–101 passim, 105–111; *Documents Relative to the Colonial History of the State of New York,* O'Callaghan and Fernow, eds. (hereafter *NYCD*), 9:5–7; *Ply. Recs.* 9:199–203.

19. *R.I. Recs.* 1:295–296.

20. *Ply. Recs.* 9:202.

21. Thomas, "Maelstrom of Change," chaps. 4–6; Howard Millar Chapin, *The Trading Post of Roger Williams, with those of John Wilcox and Richard Smith* (Providence, R.I.: Society of Colonial Wars in the State of Rhode Island, 1933); Francis X. Moloney, *The Fur Trade in New England, 1620–1676* (Cambridge, Mass.: Harvard University Press, 1931), pp. 43–44.

22. A. J. F. Van Laer, ed., *Van Rensselaer Bowier Manuscripts* (Albany:

State University of New York Press, 1908), pp. 483–484, 526; *Ply. Recs.*
9:172–173; Thomas, "Maelstrom of Change," pp. 178–180.
   23. *R.I. Recs.* 1:295; Chapin, *Trading Post,* pp. 22–23.
   24. Thomas, "Maelstrom of Change," pp. 215–239.
   25. Bailyn, *New England Merchants,* pp. 101–103; Darret B. Rutman,
Winthrop's Boston: Portrait of a Puritan Town, 1630–1649 (Chapel Hill:
University of North Carolina Press, 1965), chap. 4; David Grayson Allen,
*In English Ways: The Movement of Societies and the Transferral of
English Local Law and Custom to Massachusetts Bay in the Seven-
teenth Century* (Chapel Hill: University of North Carolina Press, 1981),
pp. 109–116, 125–131, 213–216; David Thomas Konig, "Community
Custom and Common Law: Social Change and the Development of Land
Law in Seventeenth-Century Massachusetts," *American Journal of Legal
History* 18 (2) (1974):138–148; Konig, *Law and Society in Puritan Mas-
sachusetts: Essex County, 1629–1692,* (Chapel Hill: University of North
Carolina Press, 1978), pp. 38–45.
   26. Thomas, "Maelstrom of Change," pp. 285–333; Innes, *Labor in a
New Land,* pp. 24–27, 33–34, 173–174; Vaughan, *New England Frontier,* pp. 223–224; Salisbury, "Toward the Covenant Chain," p. 65; *NYCD,*
O'Callaghan and Fernow, eds., 13:103, 107, 150, 162–163, 240; 14:
446–447, 465–467. Arthur H. Buffinton, "New England and the Western
Fur Trade," *Publications of the Colonial Society of Massachusetts* 18
(1915–16):177–183.
   27. Ceci, "The First Fiscal Crisis in New York," pp. 846–847.
   28. Salisbury, "Toward the Covenant Chain," pp. 65–70.
   29. John Demos, "Notes on Life in Plymouth Colony," *William and
Mary Quarterly,* 3d ser., 22 (2) (1965):264–286; Philip J. Greven, Jr., *Four
Generations: Population, Land, and Family in Colonial Andover, Massachusetts* (Ithaca, N.Y.: Cornell University Press, 1970), chap. 2; Kenneth A.
Lockridge, *A New England Town: The First Hundred Years, Dedham,
Massachusetts, 1636–1736* (New York: W. W. Norton, 1970), pp. 63–75;
T. H. Breen and Stephen Foster, "Moving to the New World: The Character
of Early Massachusetts Immigration," *William and Mary Quarterly,* 3d ser.,
30 (2) (1973):194–211; David Thomas Konig, "Community Custom and
Common Law," 148–177; and his *Law and Society in Puritan Massachu-
setts,* pp. 45–63; David Grayson Allen, *In English Ways,* pp. 216–218.
   30. Douglas E. Leach, *Flintlock and Tomahawk; New England in King
Philip's War* (New York: Macmillan, 1958), chap. 2; Jennings, *Invasion of
America,* pp. 278–297; Salisbury, "Red Puritans," pp. 36–37, 53; Cotton,
Journal, October 12, 1670, et seq.
   31. John Easton, "A Relacion of the Indyan Warre," in *Narratives of the
Indian Wars, 1675–1699,* Charles H. Lincoln, ed., pp. 9–11; Salisbury,
"Red Puritans," p. 53.

32. *NYCD* 3:255, 265; 13:528; 14:715–716; *Conn. Recs.* 2:397–398, 404, 406–407; A. J. F. Van Laer, ed., *Minutes of the Court of Albany, Rennselaerwyck and Schenectady* (Albany, N.Y.: University of the State of New York, 1926–32), 2:48–49; N[athaniel] S[atonatall], "A Continuation of the State of New-England" (1676), and "A New and Further Narrative of the State of New-England" (1676), in *Narratives of the Indian Wars*, pp. 68, 87–88, 97; Jennings, *Invasion of America*, pp. 313–316; Stephen S. Webb, *1676: The End of American Independence* (New York: Alfred A. Knopf, 1984), pp. 367–371; Salisbury, "Toward the Covenant Chain," p. 183, n. 41.

33. Williams, *Key into the Language of America*, p. 191.

34. Elisabeth Tooker, "The League of the Iroquois: Its History, Politics, and Ritual," *Handbook*, Trigger, ed., 15:423–434; Daniel K. Richter, "The Ordeal of the Longhouse: Change and Persistence on the Iroquois Frontier, 1609–1720" Ph.D. diss., Columbia University, 1984, pp. 21–26, 31–33; Richter, "War and Culture: The Iroquois Experience," *William and Mary Quarterly*, 3d ser., 40 (4) (1983):530–532; Francis Jennings et al., eds., *The History and Culture of Iroquois Diplomacy: An Interdisciplinary Guide to the Treaties of the Six Nations and Their League* (Syracuse, N.Y.: Syracuse University Press, 1985), p. 106 and passim.

Chapter 7. The Historical Archaeology of the Mashantucket Pequots, 1637–1900

1. Carol Kimball, "Placing the John Mason Monument on Pequot Hill," *New London Day*, November 13, 1986.

2. The four major accounts of the war are John Mason, *A Brief History of the Pequot War* (1736); John Underhill, *Newes from America* (1638); Philip Vincent, *A True Relation of the Late Battell Fought in New England* (1638); and Lion Gardiner, *Leift Lion Gardener his Relation of the Pequot Warres* (1660). These accounts have been conveniently collected and published in one volume; see Charles Orr, ed., *History of the Pequot War*.

3. Orr, ed., *History of the Pequot War*, pp. 105–106.

4. De Forest, *History of the Indians of Connecticut*, p. 133.

5. McBride, "Prehistory of the Lower Connecticut River Valley," Ph.D. diss.

6. John Winthrop, *Winthrop's Journal: "History of New England,"* 1630–1649, pp. 187–188, 194.

7. Letter of Israel Stoughton to John Winthrop, July, 1637, Massachusetts Historical Society *Collections* (1918), p. 285.

8. McBride, "Prehistory of the Lower Connecticut River Valley"; De Forest, *History of the Indians of Connecticut*, p. 133; Johan De Laet, *From the "New World"* (1625, 1630, 1633, 1640), in *Narratives of New Netherland*, J. Franklin Jameson, ed., p. 43.

9. Roger Williams, *Complete Writings of Roger Williams, 1632–1682,* 6:19; Orr, ed., *History of the Pequot War,* p. 220; letter of John Brewster to John Winthrop, Jr., June 18, 1636, *Winthrop Papers* 3:270–271.

10. Orr, ed., *History of the Pequot War,* p. 32.

11. Ibid., pp. 25, 17; letter of Stoughton to Winthrop, July, 1637.

12. Williams, *Complete Writings of Roger Williams* 6:25.

13. Letter of Edward Winslow to John Winthrop, May 22, 1637, *Winthrop Papers* 4:3–4.

14. De Forest, *History of the Indians of Connecticut,* pp. 30–31, 71, 133; Means, "Mohegan Pequot Relationships . . . ," pp. 26–34; Williams, *Complete Writings of Roger Williams* 6:19, 136; *Winthrop Papers* 3:220, 225.

15. Williams, *Complete Writings* 6:28.

16. Letter of Stoughton to Winthrop, July, 1637.

17. Williams, *Complete Writings* 6:136; letter of Jonathan Brewster to John Winthrop, Jr., June 18, 1636, in *Winthrop Papers* 3:270–271.

18. See William A. Starna's chap. 3 in this volume.

19. Letter of Richard Davenport to John Winthrop, August, 1637, in *Winthrop Papers* 3:248.

20. Williams, *Complete Writings* 6:87.

21. Ibid., 6:18; Orr, ed., *History of the Pequot War,* p. 27.

22. Williams, *Complete Writings* 6:67.

23. Vaughan, *New England Frontier: Puritans and Indians, 1620–1675,* rev. ed. (1979), pp. 340–341; Williams, *Complete Writings* 6:60–69, 84–89.

24. Williams, *Complete Writings* 6:67; "List of the Pequot Indians at Pequot Plantation about the Time of the Settlement 1646," Eva Butler MSS, Indians and Colonial Research Center, Mystic, Conn.

25. New London Land Records (1651–1660), 1:9, New London, Conn., City Hall.

26. Charles J. Hoadley, ed., *Public Records of the Colony of Connecticut* (Hartford, Conn.: Lockwood and Brainard Co., 1870) (hereafter cited as *Conn. Recs.*), 5:431.

27. *Acts of the Commissioners of the United Colonies* (September, 1658), 2:194, Connecticut State Archives, Hartford, Conn.

28. J. Hammond Trumbull, ed., *Public Records of the Colony of Connecticut prior to the Union with New Haven Colony,* 1:440.

29. *Conn. Recs.* 5:398, 431. "Order for the Establishment of the Pequot Reservation," Groton Land Records (1720–1721), 1:5, Connecticut State Archives, Hartford.

30. "Report of the Committee Concerning the Complaint of Robin," Indians, Series 1 (1647–1759), vol. 2, Doc. No. 6 (May 1721), Connecticut State Archives, Hartford, Conn.; "Order for the Establishment of the Pequot Reservation," Groton Land Records, 1:3, 5.

31. *Conn. Recs.,* 6:402–403; 7:324–325; 8:411; 9:446; 10:415, 548–

549; "Report of the Committee Concerning Robin," Connecticut General Assembly, Public Acts, 1855–1860, May Session, 1855, Connecticut State Library.

32. Letter of Governor Talcott to Colonel Adam Winthrop, *Talcott Papers,* Connecticut Historical Society *Collections* (1896), 5:397; *Conn. Recs.* 7:411–412; Ezra Stiles, "Memoirs of the Pequots" (1755), Massachusetts Historical Society *Collections* (1809), 10:101–102; and Stiles's "Additional Memoirs" (1762), Massachusetts Historical Society *Collections* (1809), 10:102–103.

33. *Conn. Recs.* 5:431.

34. Ibid., 7:411–412.

35. Untitled MSS., "Indians," series 1 (1647–1759), vol. 2, Doc. No. 117, 118a–118b, October, 1760, Connecticut State Archives, Hartford, Conn.

36. Francisco de Miranda, *Diary of Francisco de Miranda: Tour of the United States, 1783–1784,* William Spence Robertson, ed. (New York: Hispanic Society of America, 1928), pp. 90–91.

37. *Conn. Recs.* 7:411–412.

38. Ezra Stiles, "From Itineraries and Memoirs" (1760–1762), vol. 1, Ezra Stiles MSS., Beinecke Library, Yale University, New Haven, Conn.: Sturtevant, "Two 1761 Wigwams at Niantic," *American Antiquity* 40 (4) (1975), 437–444.

39. Stiles, "Additional Memoirs" (1762), pp. 102–103.

40. De Forest, *History of the Indians of Connecticut,* p. 444.

41. "Report of Committee Advising Construction of Three Houses on the Pequot Reservation," January 24, 1856, miscellaneous document, Connecticut State Archives, Hartford, Conn.

42. John Avery, *History of the Town of Ledyard, 1650–1900* (1901; reprint, Ledyard, Conn.: Ledyard Historical Society, 1986.

Chapter 8. The Emergence of the Mashantucket Pequot Tribe, 1637–1975

1. Jack Campisi, Pequot field notes, 1976–1986, in author's possession.

2. Vaughan, *The New England Frontier* (1965 ed.), p. 150; Boissevain, "Whatever Became of New England Indians," pp. 103–114.

3. De Forest, *History of the Indians of Connecticut,* p. 22; Shuetleff and Pulsifer, eds., *Records of the Colony of New Plymouth* 1:6.

4. Richard A. Wheeler, *The Pequot Indians—An Historical Sketch* (n.p.: 1887), p. 14.

5. Ibid., pp. 18–19.

6. Hoadley, ed., *Public Records of the Colony of Connecticut* (hereafter *Conn. Recs.*), 4:140, 280.

7. De Forest, *History of the Indians of Connecticut,* p. 423.

8. *Conn. Recs.* 5:431.

9. *Conn. Recs.* 6:256–257, 355–356, 364. Petition of Robin Cassasina-

mon, Indians, 1647–1789, 1st ser., 11:95, Doc. No. 6; Report of Committee
Concerning a Petition of Robin Cassasinamon of Mashuntuxett [sic] about
English encroachment upon the Indians' improved lands at Mashuntuxett
[sic]. . . . Indians, 1647–1789, 1st ser., 1722, vol. 1, p. 100, Connecticut
State Archives, Connecticut State Library, Hartford (hereafter CSA, CSL).

10. De Forest, *History of the Indians of Connecticut,* pp. 425–427;
Conn. Recs. 6:364, 402; CSA, 1:109–110.

11. *Conn. Recs.* 7:324–325.

12. *Conn. Recs.* 7:411–412.

13. *Conn. Recs.* 9:306.

14. *Conn. Recs.* 9:523–524.

15. *Conn. Recs.* 10:21.

16. *Conn. Recs.* 10:111–112.

17. *Conn. Recs.* 11:136–137.

18. *Conn. Recs.* 11:287–288.

19. *Conn. Recs.* 11:415, 547–549.

20. Wheeler, *The Pequot Indians,* p. 20.

21. De Forest, *History of the Indians of Connecticut,* p. 137.

22. *Conn. Recs.* 14:366–367.

23. Records of the State of Connecticut, 6 (1785):57. Connecticut State
Archives, Connecticut State Library, Hartford (hereafter cited as RSC).

24. *RSC* 8 (1793):42.

25. K. Deloss Love, *Samsom Occum and the Christian Indians of New
England* (Boston: Pilgrim Press, 1899), pp. 335–357.

26. Timothy Dwight, *Travels in New England and New York* 3:14.

27. De Forest, *History of the Indians of Connecticut,* p. 443.

28. De Forest, p. 441; Indian Archives, 11:30–31, CSA, CSL.

29. Groton Town Hall Records, 1800–1801:164–167, CSA, CSL.

30. Petition of Western Pequots, Benjamin George and other Pequot Indians at Groton, May 21, 1804, Indians, 1666–1820, 2d ser., 2:35, CSA,
CSL.

31. See for example New London County Court Records, 1801–1875,
CSA, CSL.

32. See petition of complaint filed by George Ayers in 1835, box 485,
CSA, CSL. See also table 2 above.

33. See table 3 above.

34. See table 3 above.

35. Ayer petition (1835). See n. 32 above.

36. New London County Court Records, 1801–1875; Indian Archives
2:21, both in CSA, CSL.

37. New London County Court Records, CSA, CSL.

38. Ibid.

39. Connecticut Statutes, 1854, chap. 26, pp. 615–617.

40. Connecticut Statutes, 1855, chap. 65, pp. 79–80.

41. Report of the Committee on the Sale of Western Pequot Lands, January 23, 1856; Pequot Petition protesting sale of land, April 1, 1856, both found in CSA, CSL.

42. New London County Court Records, CSA, CSL.

43. Petition of Celia Watson v. William Morgan, Overseer to Pequot Tribe of Indians in Connecticut, July 2, 1856; Petition and Decree Jabez Niles v. Ulysses Avery, Superior Court . . . , November 1, 1859, CSA, CSL.

44. Avery, *History of the Town of Ledyard, 1650–1900*, p. 260.

45. Eva L. Butler, "Some Early Indian Basketmakers of Southern New England," in *Eastern Algonkian Block-Stamp Decoration,* Frank G. Speck, ed., pp. 39–41.

46. Connecticut State Park and Forest Commission, *Report* (1935), CSA, CSL. See also "Judge Brown Enters Order Governing Pequot Indians," *Norwich Bulletin,* June 18, 1933. For Speck's estimate of population, see his field notes, American Philosophical Society, Philadelphia.

47. Connecticut State Park and Forest Commission, Minutes of meetings and reports, 1935–1940, CSA, CSL.

48. Connecticut State Park and Forest Commission, Minutes of Meeting No. 282, March 11, 1936, CSA, CSL.

49. Connecticut General Statutes, supplement, title 51, chap. 272.

50. Quoted in "Judge Brown Enters Order Governing Pequot Indians," *Norwich Bulletin,* June 18, 1933.

51. Ibid.

52. Connecticut State Park and Forest Commission, Meeting No. 282, March 1, 1936.

53. Connecticut State Park and Forest Commission, *Report* (November 1, 1935–June 30, 1936), p. 40, CSA, CSL.

54. Ibid.

55. Connecticut Department of Environmental Protection, Office of Indian Affairs, "Indian File," CSA, CSL.

56. Ibid.

57. Notebook of J. R. Williams, Connecticut Department of Environmental Protection, CSA, CSL.

58. Campisi, Pequot field notes, 1976–1986.

59. Ibid.

60. Mashantucket Pequot Tribal Minutes (September 21, November 2, 1975), Mashantucket Pequot Tribe of Connecticut, Ledyard, Conn.

61. Ibid. (December 29, 1975).

62. Ibid. (June 26, 1976).

63. Ibid. (February 7, April 25, July 31, 1976).

64. Campisi field notes, 1976–1986.

65. See Campisi, "The Trade and Intercourse Acts: Land Claims on the

Eastern Seaboard," in *Irredeemable America: The Indians' Estate and Land Claims,* Imre Sutton, ed. (Albuquerque: University of New Mexico Press, 1985), pp. 337–362.

Chapter 9. The Mystic Voice: Pequot Folklore from the Seventeenth Century to the Present

1. William Simmons, *Spirit of the New England Tribes: Indian History and Folklore, 1620–1984,* pp. 172–234.
2. Ezra Stiles, *Extracts from the Itineraries and Other Miscellanies of Ezra Stiles, D.D., LL.D., 1755–1794,* p. 83.
3. Nicolaes van Wassenaer, "Historisch Verhael" (1624–1630), in *Narratives of New Netherland, 1609–1664,* ed. Jameson, p. 87.
4. Roger Williams, *Letters of Roger Williams, 1632–1682,* p. 6.
5. Edward Johnson, *Johnson's Wonder Working Providence, 1628–1651* (1654), p. 164.
6. John Underhill, *Newes from America* (1638), p. 16.
7. John Mason, *A Brief History of the Pequot War,* p. 20.
8. Roger Williams, *A Key into the Language of America* (1643), "To the Reader."
9. *New England's First Fruits* (London, 1643), p. 11.
10. Ibid., p. 13.
11. Cotton Mather, *Magnalia Christi Americana: Or, the Ecclesiastical History of New-England* 2:381.
12. "The Indian Powow, or Deception Rewarded," in *New England Historical and Genealogical Register* 2 (1) (1848):44.
13. Experience Mayhew, "A Brief Journal of My Visitation of the Pequot and Mohegan Indians," p. 101.
14. Mayhew, pp. 124–126.
15. William S. Simmons and Cheryl L. Simmons, eds., *Old Light on Separate Ways: The Narragansett Diary of Joseph Fish,* p. ix.
16. Benjamin Silliman, "From Benjamin Silliman, L.L.D.," in William B. Sprague, ed., *Annals of the American Pulpit* (New York, 1857), 1:365.
17. "The Pequot of a Hundred Years," in *The Publications of the American Tract Society* 11 (New York, n.d.):1.
18. Ibid., p. 4.
19. William Apes, *The Experiences of Five Christian Indians of the Pequod Tribe,* p. 15.
20. Apes, pp. 46–47.
21. Benson J. Lossing, "The Last of the Pequods," in W. W. Beach, ed., *The Indian Miscellany* (Albany, N.Y.: J. Munsell, 1877), p. 460.
22. Charles M. Skinner, *American Myths and Legends* (Philadelphia: J. P. Lippincott, 1903), 1:129–131.
23. Loretta Murnane, "Linguistic Folk Lore" (Connecticut State Library,

1936), pp. 5–6. See also Richard M. Dorson, *Jonathan Draws the Long Bow* (Cambridge, Mass.: Harvard University Press, 1946), pp. 171–173.

24. Simmons, *Spirit of the New England Tribes,* p. 142.

25. Eva L. Butler, "Curse of Cuppacommock," from "Folklore" file, E. L. Butler MSS., Indian and Colonial Research Center, Old Mystic, Conn.

26. Frank G. Speck, "Pequot Indian Remnants," in *The Southern Workman,* February, 1917, p. 102.

27. Ibid., p. 103.

28. Moses P. Dailey, who claimed to be a full-blooded Pequot, died in Providence in 1915. Because of his knowledge of Indian medicinal techniques, he made a living as a nurse. His aunt, Dorcas Dailey, made and sold baskets in Narragansett ("Last of the Pequots a Resident of Providence," *Providence Sunday Journal,* November 2, 1913, Special Features, p. 5; "Moses P. Dailey, Last Pequot, Dead," *Providence Journal,* August 21, 1915, p. 4). Also see Frank G. Speck, "Notes on the Mohegan and Niantic Indians," in Clark Wissler, ed., *The Indians of Greater New York and the Lower Hudson* (New York: American Museum of Natural History, 1909), p. 184; Speck, *Decorative Art of Indian Tribes of Connecticut;* Speck, "Native Tribes and Dialects of Connecticut: A Mohegan-Pequot Diary"; and Speck, ed., *Eastern Algonkian Block-Stamp Decoration.*

29. Murnane, "Linguistic Folk Lore," p. 1.

30. Murnane, pp. 1–2.

31. Eva L. Butler, "Notes from Pequot Indians 1939 Chiefly Martha Langevin," from the "Medicine Men" file (1939), Eva Butler MSS., Indian and Colonial Research Center, Old Mystic, Conn. Without going into a point-by-point comparison, it is clear that this list of Pequot lore is very similar to that of twentieth-century Mohegans, Narragansetts, and Gay Head Wampanoags.

32. Simmons, *Spirit of the New England Tribes,* pp. 121, 124, 127.

33. Eva L. Butler, "The Mashantucket Home of the Pequot Indians," in the *Ledyard* (Conn.) *Directory* (1956).

34. Eva L. Butler, "Mashantucket," in *The Norwich Bulletin Magazine,* December 3, 1967.

35. Simmons, *Spirit of the New England Tribes,* pp. 143–144, 151–152, 157.

36. Richard Hayward, personal communication, December 5, 1986.

37. Alice Brend, personal communication, July 28, 1987.

38. Loretta Libby, personal communication, March 24, 1987.

39. Samuel Mason, "Expedition from New London to Woodstock, Conn., February 1699/1700," in *Massachusetts Historical Society Proceedings, 1866–1867* (1867), p. 477.

40. Simmons, *Spirit of the New England Tribes,* p. 272.

41. Theresa Hayward and Loretta Libby, personal communication, March 24, 1987.

42. Richard Hayward, December 5, 1986.

43. Libby, March 24, 1987.
44. Theresa Hayward, March 24, 1987.
45. Brend, July 28, 1987.
46. R. Hayward, December 5, 1986.
47. T. Hayward and L. Libby, March 24, 1987.
48. R. Hayward, December 5, 1986.
49. Simmons, *Spirit of the New England Tribes,* pp. 123–127, 162–171.
50. Helen Le Gault, personal communication, March 24, 1987.
51. Ibid.
52. Ibid.
53. Ibid.
54. Ibid.
55. Simmons, *Spirit of the New England Tribes,* pp. 134, 148–149.
56. Ernest W. Baughman, *Type and Motif-Index of the Folktales of England and North America* (The Hague: Mouton, 1966), p. 177.
57. Brend, July 28, 1987.
58. De Forest, *History of the Indians of Connecticut,* pp. 60–61.
59. Daniel G. Brinton, *The Lenape and Their Legends* (1884; reprint, New York: 1969), p. 30.
60. Speck, "Native Tribes and Dialects of Connecticut," pp. 216–217.
61. Speck, p. 216.
62. Roger Williams observed that the seventeenth-century Narragansetts considered the southwest to be the most sacred direction. The creator lived in that direction, corn and beans came from there, and souls migrated there after death. Robert St. George has written an important paper in which he argues that southwest/northeast comprised a major contrast in early historic-period New England Indian symbolism. On the basis of existing sources, it is difficult to know if or how these later Pequot-Mohegan legends derive from this earlier symbolism.
63. Le Gault, March 24, 1987.
64. Dorson, *Jonathan Draws the Long Bow,* pp. 189–190.
65. Brend, July 28, 1987.
66. T. Hayward, March 24, 1987.
67. R. Hayward, December 5, 1986.
68. Le Gault, March 24, 1987.
69. Brend, August 4, 1987.
70. Brend, July 28, 1987.
71. T. Hayward, March 24, 1987.
72. Simmons, *Spirit of the New England Tribes,* pp. 235–246.
73. Le Gault, March 24, 1987.
74. Brend, July 28, 1987.
75. R. Hayward, December 5, 1986.
76. Ibid.

77. Ibid.
78. Ibid.
79. Ibid.
80. Ibid.
81. Ibid.
82. Ibid.
83. Ibid.
84. Brend, July 28, 1987.
85. Ibid.
86. Ibid.
87. Brend, August 4, 1987.
88. Ibid.
89. Ibid.
90. T. Hayward, March 24, 1987.
91. Thomas Commuck, "Sketch of the Brothertown Indians," in *Collections of the State Historical Society of Wisconsin* (1859), p. 297.
92. Brend, July 28, 1987.
93. Following the delivery of this paper at the Mashantucket Pequot Historical Conference on October 23, 1987, several persons of Pequot and Narragansett descent who were in the audience told the author several new legends. The specifically Pequot legends are included here. The first, told by John Holder, a Mashantucket Pequot, concerns his great grandfather, Chief Silver Star (Atwood I. Williams, an Eastern Pequot), who died in the 1950s. The legend pertains to the 1920s or 1930s.

My great grandfather was Chief Silver Star. My mother told me the story. When he was in the field one day out in the woods working came a wolf and the wolf had red eyes. And he stared at it and knew it was the devil. Then the wolf just turned and ran back in the woods.

Phyllis Monroe, a Mashantucket Pequot, related the following legend regarding three blackbirds as omens of death:

Have you heard about the blackbirds on the reservation? My aunt when we moved back to the reservation they stayed at my house and three blackbirds took up residence in the tree outside. Just three of them. They would be there every morning. Skip [Hayward] came by to visit. One of my aunts had a bad heart. Skip came out to see my aunt and talked for a while. So Skip came out of the house. The three blackbirds followed him. He got in the tribal truck and started down the road. The three blackbirds followed him down Elizabeth George Drive down the cul-de-sac and came up. And when he got back to the house, they went back to the tree. The birds stayed there as long as I lived there. They're no longer there. I left and the birds left. When Skip's brother died we were on Amos George Drive. You know the trees that separate

Joann's house from the apartment complex. All of a sudden all these birds came flying out. And she said, "Oh, another death." There were three blackbirds and three deaths. There's something about those blackbirds.

Phyllis Monroe and Maxine Pinson related the following items regarding birth veils.

My mother was born with a veil and people came to her with dreams and what she said came true.

They sold veils to people on boats and, if they were going into a bad storm, the skin would shrivel up. Captains would buy the veils and stretch them out and they could tell if they were coming into a storm.

Some examples of white folklore about Pequots can be found in P. D. Ridge, *A Story of Pequot Swamp* (Southport, Conn., 1869). I am grateful to Professor Adam J. Hirsch for this reference.

Chapter 10. The New England Tribes and Their Quest for Justice

1. See Jack Campisi, "The Trade and Intercourse Acts," in *Irredeemable America*, Imre Sutton, ed. (Albuquerque, N. Mex., 1985), pp. 337–362.

2. Ibid., pp. 347–356, 359–361; Paul Brodeur, *Restitution* (Boston: Northeastern Press, 1985).

3. *Seneca Nation of Indians* v. *Christie*, 126 N.Y. 122 (1891).

4. *Tuscarora Nation of Indians* v. *Power Authority of New York*, 257 Fed. 2d 885, 2d Cir. (1958).

5. *Oneida Indian Nation, et al.* v. *County of Oneida, et al.*, 414 U.S. 661 (1974).

6. *Joint Tribal Council of the Passamaquoddy Tribe* v. *Morton* [CV 1960]: 8.

7. *Montoya* v. *United States*, 180 U.S. 266 (1901).

8. *Mashpee Tribe* v. *New Seabury Corp.*, Trial Transcript, 40:38–39.

9. For the decision in the case, see 447 Fed. Supp. 940 (1978) and 592 Fed. 2d, 1st Cir. (1979).

10. Rhode Island Claims Settlement Act, 94 Stat., 3498 (1978).

11. *Federal Register* (1978) 43 (172): 39361–64.

12. Ibid., p. 39363.

13. *Congressional Quarterly* 41 (April 1983):710–711.

14. I was directly involved in this process. 95 Stat. 852 (Oct. 18, 1983); Susan Chira, "Pequot Indians Prevail in Battle Begun in 1637," *New York Times*, October 20, 1983.

15. Cayuga, Oneida, and Pequot field notes, 1980–1983. I have worked as an applied anthropologist for all three American Indian nations.

16. Gay Head Wampanoag field notes, 1978–1985. I have worked as an

applied anthropologist for the Gay Head Wampanoag Indians throughout this period, and the narrative here is based upon my fieldwork.

17. Francis Jennings to John A. Shapard, Jr., October 30, 1986, copy of letter in my files.

18. I have copies of Levitas's and Simmons's critiques in my Gay Head Wampanoag files.

19. Simmons, *Spirit of the New England Tribes*, p. 258.

20. See United States Senate, Select Subcommittee on Indian Affairs, Hearings on S. 1452: *Indian Land Claims in the Town of Gay Head, Mass.,* 99th Cong., 2d sess. (Washington, D.C.: U.S.G.P.O., 1986).

Chapter 11. Connecticut's Indian Policy

1. This essay is based largely on my personal observations of the state's Indian policy process since 1967 and intermittent discussions with some of those actively involved in it since that time. My brief summaries of eighteenth- and nineteenth-century state policy and of the creation of the Connecticut Indian Affairs Council are based on Mary G. Soulsby's enlightening publication cited below and on documents she generously made available to me. I am also grateful to Mikki Aganstata, Trudie Lamb Richmond, Edward Sarabia, and James Wherry for taking time to discuss issues raised in this essay, though none of these persons should be held responsible for the analysis of conclusions offered here.

2. There were two explicit statements of this in the Constitution: agreements between the Indians and the federal government would be set forth in treaties that the Congress alone—not the states—had the power to ratify; and Congress—not the states—had the sole right to "regulate commerce" with Indian tribes, presumably including land transactions.

3. Irving Harris of the Schaghticoke tribe repeatedly referred to this problem of bureaucratic stereotyping in his energetic lobbying for Indian policy reform in the 1970s. See, for example, his quoted comments in the *Waterbury Republican,* January 18, 1973, p. 6.

4. This was explicitly noted in a postscript of a letter from Edward A. Danielczuck, supervisory investigator of the Welfare Department's Resources Division, to Irving Harris of the Schaghticoke tribe on May 27, 1971 (copy in author's files).

5. Mary G. Soulsby, *American Indians in Connecticut: Past to Present* (Hartford, Conn.: Connecticut Department of Environmental Protection, 1979), pp. 1–2.

6. Ibid., p. 8.

7. Ibid., p. 2.

8. Meskill, known as "Mean Tom" to his detractors, vetoed 173 bills that year. That record still stands.

9. Letter from State Representative John F. Mannix to Irving Harris, February 12, 1973. Copy in author's files.

10. Originally only four of the five tribes were to be represented; the Paugussetts had been left out of the legislation through a misunderstanding. The statutes were revised a year later to include the Paugussett representative as a voting member of the council. Soulsby, *American Indians in Connecticut,* p. 3.

11. Connecticut Statutes, 8, chap. 824 (1973), p. 381.

12. Ibid., pp. 381–384.

13. See Alvin J. Ziontz, "After *Martinez:* Civil Rights under Tribal Government," *University of California-Davis Law Review* 12 (1) (1979): 1–35. For the decision, see 436 U.S. 49 (1978).

14. The petitions had already been rejected by the leadership and members of the tribes as recognized by the state.

15. A reader of an earlier draft of this essay noted that the court's decision on the Paucatuck Pequot case did not explicitly concern the qualifications for membership of the petitioners, but rather the extent to which those already in the tribe were aggrieved by the action of a state agency. Thus, although the formal appeals process indeed must pass through the superior court system, that court has yet to rule on a membership petition, as far as I can determine.

16. Cf. Robert L. Bee, *The Politics of American Indian Policy,* p. 14ff.

17. MacGregor argues that the Trade and Intercourse Act of 1790 was never intended to apply to the Indians of Connecticut, but instead to the larger tribes along the new country's western frontier. Thus any claims by Connecticut tribes based on the violation of the 1790 act are without legal basis. According to newspaper accounts, his outspoken views on the issue of the tribes' legal basis so angered the Narragansetts of Rhode Island that they demanded that the Connecticut Attorney General's office dismiss him (*Norwich Bulletin,* April 12, 1987, p. 1).

18. Bee, *The Politics of American Indian Policy,* p. 118 ff.

19. Connecticut General Assembly, special act no. 82-31, June 9, 1982.

20. *Hartford Courant,* May 10, 1986, p. 1ff.

21. For notable contrasts, see Laurence M. Hauptman, *Formulating American Indian Policy in New York State, 1970–1986* (Albany: State University of New York Press, 1988).

Selected Bibliography

Archives/Manuscript Collections

American Philosophical Society, Philadelphia. Frank G. Speck MSS.
Connecticut State Archives. Connecticut State Library. Hartford.
1. Indians (1647–1789), 1st ser.
2. Indians (1666–1820), 2d ser.
3. Handwritten Petitions from Both the Overseer James Avery and the Members of the Pequot Tribes (1835, 1839).
4. New London County Court and Superior Court Records.
5. Groton Town Hall Records.
6. Reports of Connecticut State Park and Forest Commission, 1934–1941.
7. Papers Relating to Pequot Tribe; Court and Probate. Index of Papers.
Indian and Colonial Research Center, Old Mystic, Connecticut. Eva L. Butler MSS.
Mashantucket Pequot Tribe of Connecticut.
1. Tribal Records.
2. Federal Acknowledgment Petition (prepared by Jack Campisi) and submitted to the United States Department of the Interior (1982).
Massachusetts Historical Society, Boston.
Yale University, Beinecke Library.
1. James Noyes Pequot Indian Glossary MSS.
2. Ezra Stiles MSS.

Books/Booklets/Dissertations

Allen, David G. *In English Ways: The Movement of Societies and the Transferral of English Local Law and Custom to Massachusetts Bay in the Seventeenth Century.* Chapel Hill: University of North Carolina Press, 1981.

Apes, William. *The Experiences of Five Christian Indians of the Pequod Tribe.* Boston: J. B. Dow, 1833.

Axtell, James. *The Invasion Within: The Contest of Cultures in Colonial North America.* New York: Oxford University Press, 1985.

Bachman, Van Clef. *Peltries or Plantations: The Economic Policies of the Dutch West India Company in New Netherland, 1623–1639.* Baltimore: Johns Hopkins University Press, 1969.

Bailyn, Bernard. *The New England Merchants in the Seventeenth Century.* Cambridge, Mass.: Harvard University Press, 1955.

Bartlett, John Russell, ed. *Records of the Colony of Rhode Island and Providence Plantations in New England.* 10 vols. Providence and Boston, 1850–1865.

Beauchamp, William M. *Wampum and Shell Articles Used by the New York Indians.* New York State Museum Bulletin No. 41. 1901.

Bee, Robert L. *The Politics of American Indian Policy.* Cambridge, Mass.: Schenkman Publishing Co., 1982.

Bowden, Henry W. *American Indians and Christian Missions.* Chicago: University of Chicago Press, 1981.

Bradford, William. *Of Plymouth Plantation, 1620–1647.* Edited by Samuel Eliot Morison. New York: Alfred A. Knopf, 1952.

Bridenbaugh, Carl, ed. *The Pynchon Papers.* Vol. 1, *Letters of John Pynchon, 1654–1700.* Boston: Colonial Society of Massachusetts, 1982.

Burton, William John. "Hellish Fiends and Brutish Men: Amerindian-Euroamerican Interaction in Southern New England: An Interdisciplinary Analysis, 1600–1750." Ph.D. diss., Kent State University, 1976.

Carroll, Peter N. *Puritanism and the Wilderness: The Intellectual Significance of the New England Frontier, 1629–1700.* New York: Columbia University Press, 1969.

Ceci, Lynn. "The Effect of European Contact and Trade on the Settlement Pattern of Indians in Coastal New York, 1524–1665: The Archaeological and Documentary Evidence." Ph.D. diss., City University of New York, 1977.

Clifford, James. *The Predicament of Culture.* Cambridge, Mass.: Harvard University Press, 1988.

Connecticut Archaeology Today. Archaeological Society of Connecticut Bulletin No. 47, 1984.

Crosby, Alfred W., Jr. *The Columbian Exchange: The Biological and Cultural Consequence of 1492.* Westport, Conn.: Greenwood Press, 1972.

————. *Ecological Imperialism: The Biological Expansion of Europe, 900–1900.* New York: Cambridge University Press, 1986.

De Forest, John W. *History of the Indians of Connecticut from the Earliest Known Period to 1850.* Hartford, Conn.: W. J. Hamersley, 1851, 1853.

Demos, John. *Entertaining Satan: Witchcraft and the Culture of Early New England.* New York: Oxford University Press, 1982.

Denevan, William T., ed. *The Native Population of the Americas in 1492.* Madison: University of Wisconsin Press, 1976.

Dewar, Robert E., Kenneth L. Feder, and David A. Poirier, eds. *Connecticut Archaeology: Past, Present and Future.* Department of Anthropology Occasional Papers. Storrs, Conn.: University of Connecticut, 1983.

Dincauze, Dena F. *The Neville Site: 8000 Years of Amoskeag.* Peabody Museum Monograph No. 4. Cambridge, Mass.: Peabody Museum of Archaeology and Ethnography, 1976.

Drake, Samuel. *The Book of the Indians of North America.* Boston: Josiah Drake, 1853.

Drinnon, Richard. *Facing West: The Metaphysics of Indian-Hating and Empire-Building.* Minneapolis: University of Minnesota Press, 1980.

Dunn, Richard S. *Puritans and Yankees: The Winthrop Dynasty of New England, 1630–1717.* Princeton, N.J.: Princeton University Press, 1962.

Egal, Charles M., and David C. Stineback. *Puritans, Indians and Manifest Destiny.* New York: G. P. Putnam's Sons, 1977.

Fernow, Berthold, ed. *Documents Relating to the Colonial History of the State of New York.* Albany: Weed, Parsons, and Co., 1883.

Fitzhugh, William W., ed. *Cultures in Contact.* Washington, D.C.: Smithsonian Institution, 1985.

Gardiner, Lion. "Lieft Lion Gardener his Relation of the Pequot Warres" (1660). In Massachusetts Historical Society *Collections,* 3d ser., 3:131–160. Cambridge, Mass.: 1833. See also Orr, Charles, ed.

Gookin, Daniel. "Historical Collections of the Indians in New England." In Massachusetts Historical Society *Collections,* 1st ser., 1 (1792). Reprint, New York: Arno Press, 1972.

Greven, Philip J., Jr. *Four Generations: Population, Land, and Family in Colonial Andover, Massachusetts.* Ithaca, N.Y.: Cornell University Press, 1970.

Guillette [Soulsby], Mary. *American Indians in Connecticut.* Hartford: Connecticut Department of Environmental Protection, 1979.

Hart, S. *The Prehistory of the New Netherland Company.* Amsterdam, Netherlands: City of Amsterdam Press, 1959.

Hoadley, Charles J., ed. *Public Records of the Colony of Connecticut.* 11 vols. Hartford: Lockwood and Brainard, 1850–1890.

————, ed. *Public Records of the State on Connecticut.* Hartford: Case, Lockwood, and Brainard, 1894–1900.

————, ed. *Records of the Colony and Plantation of New Haven, from 1638 to 1649*. 2 vols. Hartford: Case, Tiffany, 1857.

————, ed. *Records of the Colony or Jurisdiction of New Haven from May, 1653, to the Union*. Hartford: Case, Lockwood, 1857.

Hubbard, William. *The History of the Indian Wars in New England . . .* (1677). Edited by Samuel G. Drake. 2 vols. Roxbury, Mass.: W. Elliot Woodward, 1865.

Innes, Stephen. *Labor in a New Land: Economy and Society in Seventeenth Century Springfield*. Princeton, N.J.: Princeton University Press, 1983.

Jameson, J. Franklin, ed. *Narratives of New Netherland*. New York: Charles Scribner's Sons, 1909.

Jennings, Francis. *The Invasion of America: Indians, Colonialism, and the Cant of Colonialism*. Chapel Hill: University of North Carolina Press, 1975.

Johnson, Edward. *Johnson's Wonder-Working Providence, 1628–1651*. 1654. Edited by J. Franklin Jameson. New York: Charles Scribner's Sons, 1910.

Josephy, Alvin. *Now That the Buffalo's Gone: A Study of Today's American Indians*. New York: Alfred A. Knopf, 1982.

Josselyn, John. *An Account of Two Voyages to New England, 1638–1663*. Boston: William Veazie, 1865.

Keegan, William F., ed. *Emergent Horticultural Economies of the Eastern Woodlands*. Center for Archaeological Investigations Occasional Paper No. 7. Carbondale: Southern Illinois University, 1987.

Konig, David T. *Law and Society in Puritan Massachusetts: Essex County, 1629–1692*. Chapel Hill: University of North Carolina Press, 1979.

Leach, Douglas Edward. *Arms for Empire: A Military History of the British Colonies in North America*. New York: Macmillan, 1973.

————. *Flintlock and Tomahawk: New England in King Philip's War*. New York: Macmillan, 1958.

————. *The Northern Colonial Frontier, 1607–1763*. New York: Holt, Rinehart, and Winston, 1966.

Lincoln, Charles H., ed. *Narratives of the Indian Wars (1675–1699)*. New York: Charles Scribner's Sons, 1913.

Love, W. Deloss. *Samson Occum and the Christian Indians of New England*. Boston: Pilgrim Press, 1899.

McBride, Kevin. "Prehistory of the Lower Connecticut River Valley." Ph.D. diss., University of Connecticut, Storrs, 1984.

McMullen, Ann, and Russell G. Handsman, eds. *A Key Into the Language of Woodsplint Baskets*. Washington, Conn.: American Indian Archaeological Institute, 1987.

Mason, John. *A Brief History of the Pequot War: Especially of the Memo-*

rable Taking of Their Fort at Mistick in Connecticut in 1637. Boston: S. Kneeland and T. Green, 1736. See also Orr, Charles, ed.

Mather, Cotton. *Magnalia Christi Americana: Or, the Ecclesiastical History of New-England, From its First Planting in the Year 1620, Unto the Year of Our Lord, 1698.* 1702. 2 vols. Hartford, Conn.: Silas Andrus, Roberts, and Burr, 1820.

Mather, Increase. *Early History of New England: Being a Relation of Hostile Passages Between the Indians and European Voyagers and First Settlers* (1677). Edited by Samuel G. Drake. Albany, N.Y.: J. Munsell, 1864.

Mayhew, Experience. "A Brief Journal of My Visitation of the Pequot and Mohegin [sic] Indians." In *Some Correspondence Between the Governors and Treasurers of the New England Company in London and the Commissioners of the United Colonies in America.* London, 1896.

Merrell, James, and Daniel K. Richter, eds. *Beyond the Covenant Chain: The Iroquois and Their Neighbors in North America.* Syracuse, N.Y.: Syracuse University Press, 1987.

Moeller, Roger, *6LF21: A Paleo-Indian Site in Western Connecticut.* Occasional Paper No. 2. Washington, Conn.: American Indian Archaeological Institute, 1980.

Morton, Thomas. *New English Canaan* (1637). Charles Francis Adams, Jr., ed. 1883. New York: Burt Franklin, 1967.

Mourt, G. *Mourt's Relation of a Journal of the Pilgrims at Plymouth.* D. B. Heath, ed. 1622. New York: Corinth Books, 1963.

New England's First Fruits. London, 1643.

O'Callaghan, Edmund B., ed. *Documentary History of the State of New York.* 4 vols. Albany, N.Y.: Weed, Parsons, 1849–1851.

O'Callaghan, Edmund B., and Berthold Fernow, eds. *Documents Relative to the Colonial History of the State of New York.* 15 vols. Albany, N.Y.: Parson, 1853–1887.

Orr, Charles, ed. *History of the Pequot War.* Cleveland: Helman-Taylor Co., 1897.

Paynter, Robert, ed. *Ecological Anthropology of the Middle Connecticut River Valley.* Department of Anthropology Research Report no. 18. Amherst, Mass.: University of Massachusetts, 1979.

Pearce, Roy Harvey. *Savagism and Civilization: A Study of the Indian and the American Mind.* Baltimore: Johns Hopkins University Press, 1953; rev. ed., 1965.

Rink, Oliver A. *Holland on the Hudson: An Economic and Social History of Dutch New York.* Ithaca, N.Y.: Cornell University Press, 1986.

Ritchie, William A. *The Archaeology of Martha's Vineyard: A Framework for the Prehistory of Southern New England.* Garden City, N.Y.: Natural History Press, 1969.

Robbins, Maurice. *Wapanucket.* Attleboro, Mass.: Massachusetts Archaeological Society, 1980.

Ronda, James P., and James Axtell, comps. *Indian Missions: A Critical Bibliography.* Bloomington: Indiana University Press, 1978.

Rutman, Darret B. *Winthrop's Boston: Portrait of a Puritan Town, 1630–1649.* Chapel Hill: University of North Carolina Press, 1965.

Salisbury, Neal E. *Manitou and Providence: Indians, Europeans, and the Making of New England, 1500–1643.* New York: Oxford University Press, 1982.

Shurtleff, Nathaniel, and David Pulsifer, eds. *Records of the Colony of New Plymouth.* 12 vols. Boston: W. White, 1851–1861.

Shurtleff, Nathaniel, and David Pulsifer, eds. *Records of the Governor and Colony of the Massachusetts Bay in New England.* 5 vols. Boston: W. White, 1853–1854.

Simmons, William S. *Cautantowwit's House: An Indian Burial Ground on the Island of Conanicut in Narragansett Bay.* Providence, R.I.: Brown University Press, 1970.

———. *Spirit of the New England Tribes: Indian History and Folklore, 1620–1984.* Hanover, N.H.: University Press of New England, 1986.

Simmons, William S., and Cheryl L. Simmons, eds. *Old Light on Separate Ways: The Narragansett Diary of Joseph Fish, 1765–1776.* Hanover, N.H.: University Press of New England, 1982.

Slotkin, Richard. *Regeneration Through Violence: The Mythology of the American Frontier, 1600–1860.* Middletown, Conn.: Wesleyan University Press, 1973.

Snow, Dean. *The Archaeology of New England.* New York: Academic Press, 1980.

Speck, Frank G. *Decorative Art of the Indian Tribes of Connecticut.* Anthropological Series 10. Memoirs of the Canadian Geological Survey 75. Ottawa, Ont.: Canadian Department of Mines, 1915.

———. *The Functions of Wampum Among the Eastern Algonkian.* Memoirs of the American Anthropology Association, no. 6, 1919.

———. "Native Tribes and Dialects of Connecticut: A Mohegan-Pequot Diary." *Forty-third Annual Report, Bureau of American Ethnology, 1925–1926.* Washington, D.C.: Smithsonian Institution, 1928.

———, ed. *Eastern Algonkian Block-Stamp Decoration: A New World Original or an Acculturated Art.* Trenton: Archaeological Society of New Jersey, 1947.

Stiles, Ezra. *Extracts from the Itineraries and Other Miscellanies of Ezra Stiles, D.D., LL.D., 1755–1794.* New Haven, Conn.: Yale University Press, 1916.

Thomas, Peter. "In the Maelstrom of Change: The Indian Trade and Cultural Process in the Middle Connecticut River Valley, 1635–1665." Ph.D. diss., University of Massachusetts—Amherst, 1979.

Thornton, Russell. *American Indian Holocaust and Survival: A Population History Since 1492.* Norman: University of Oklahoma Press, 1986.

Trelease, Allen W. *Indian Affairs in Colonial New York: The Seventeenth Century.* Ithaca, N.Y.: Cornell University Press, 1960.

Trigger, Bruce G., ed. *Northeast.* Vol 15, *Handbook of North American Indians.* Washington, D.C.: Smithsonian Institution, 1978.

Truex, James, ed. *The Second Coastal Archaeology Reader: 1900 to the Present.* Stony Brook, N.Y.: Suffolk County Archaeological Association, 1982.

Trumbull, J. Hammond, and Charles J. Hoadley, eds. *Public Records of the Colony of Connecticut.* 15 vols. Hartford, Conn.: Case, Lockwood, and Brainard, 1850–1890.

Underhill, John. *Newes from America* (1638). New York: Underhill Society of America, 1902. Also in Orr, Charles, ed.

Van Laer, A. J. F., ed. and trans. *Documents Relating to New Netherland, 1624–1626, in the Henry E. Huntington Library.* San Mateo, Calif.: Henry E. Huntington Library, 1924.

Vaughan, Alden T. *The New England Frontier: Puritans and Indians, 1620–1675.* Boston: Little, Brown, and Co., 1965. Rev. ed., New York: W. W. Norton and Co. 1979.

———, ed. *The Puritan Tradition in America, 1620–1730.* New York: Harper and Row, 1972.

Vincent, Philip. "A True Relation of the Late Battel Fought in New England Between the English and the Pequot Savages" (1637). Massachusetts Historical Society *Collections,* 3d ser., 6 (1837):29–43. See also Orr, Charles, ed.

Williams, Roger. *The Complete Writings of Roger Williams.* Edited by J. H. Trumbull. 7 vols. 1866. New York: Russell and Russell, 1963.

———. *A Key into the Language of America.* 1643. Edited by John J. Teunissen and Evelyn J. Hinz. Detroit: Wayne State University Press, 1973.

———. *Letters of Roger Williams, 1632–1682.* Edited by John Russell Bartlett. Providence, R.I.: Narragansett Club and Providence Press Publications, 1874.

Winthrop, John. *Winthrop Papers.* 5 vols. Edited by Allyn B. Forbes. Boston: Massachusetts Historical Society, 1929–1947.

———. *Winthrop's Journal: "History of New England," 1630–1649.* 2 vols. Edited by James K. Hosmer. New York: Charles Scribner's Sons, 1908.

Wood, William. *New England's Prospect.* 1634. New York: De Capo Press, 1968.

Young, William R., ed. *An Introduction to the Archaeology and History of the Connecticut Valley Indian.* Springfield, Ill.: Springfield Museum of Science, 1969.

Contributors

ROBERT L. BEE is Professor of Anthropology at the University of Connecticut at Storrs. He has authored numerous articles and books, including *The Politics of American Indian Policy* (1982).

JACK CAMPISI is Associate Professor of Anthropology at Wellesley College. He is the editor of two books on the American Indians of the Northeast. He has served as an expert witness in the Oneida Indian land claims case and is a consultant to many American Indian tribes, including the Mashantucket Pequot Tribe of Connecticut.

LYNN CECI was Associate Professor of Anthropology at Queens College of the City University of New York until her recent death. A specialist in coastal Algonquian cultures in the Late Woodland and early contact periods, she wrote numerous articles on the Indians of southern New England and Long Island. She was the Associate Editor of the *Proceedings of the 1986 Shell Bead Conference* (Rochester Museum of Science Center, 1986).

DENA F. DINCAUZE is Professor of Anthropology at the University of Massachusetts—Amherst. An environmental archaeologist specializing in the prehistory of New England, she has

259

published extensively in this area, including *The Neville Site* (1976).

LAURENCE M. HAUPTMAN is Professor of History, State University of New York, College at New Paltz, and is the author of numerous articles and five books, including *The Iroquois and the New Deal* (1981) and *The Iroquois Struggle for Survival* (1986). He has also served as a historical consultant for the Mashantucket Pequot Tribe of Connecticut.

ALVIN M. JOSEPHY, JR., a lifelong resident of Greenwich, Connecticut, is a former editor at *Time* and *American Heritage*. He has written numerous books on American Indians, including *The Patriot Chiefs* (1961), *The Nez Perce Indians and Opening up of the Northwest* (1965); *The Indian Heritage of America* (1968); *Red Power* (1971); and *Now that the Buffalo's Gone* (1982).

KEVIN A. MCBRIDE is Assistant Professor of Anthropology at the University of Connecticut, Storrs. A specialist in the archaeology of southern New England, McBride is the project director of the Mashantucket Pequot Ethnohistory Project, now in its sixth year.

NEAL SALISBURY is Professor of History at Smith College. He is the author of *Manitou and Providence: Indians, Europeans, and the Making of New England, 1500–1643* (1982), editor of *The Indians of New England: A Critical Bibliography* (1982), and he has written many articles on the American Indian history of colonial New England.

WILLIAM S. SIMMONS is Professor of Anthropology at the University of California, Berkeley. He is the author of five books and numerous articles, including *Cautanowwit's House* (1970); *Old Light on Separate Ways: The Narragansett Diary of Joseph Fish, 1765–1776* (1982); and *Spirit of the New England Tribes* (1986).

WILLIAM A. STARNA is Chairman and Professor in the Department of Anthropology at the State University of New York, College at Oneonta. He is coeditor of *Iroquois Land Claims* (1988) and *A Journey into Mohawk and Oneida Country, 1634–1635: The Journal of Harmen Meyndertsz van den*

Bogaert (1988). He has published extensively in the areas of Iroquois prehistory, ethnohistory, and public policy, and has served as a consultant to the Gay Head Wampanoag and Mashantucket Pequot Tribes.

JAMES WHERRY is the Mashantucket Pequot Tribe's Socio-Economic Development Specialist, a position he has held since 1984. An applied anthropologist, he previously worked for the Houlton Band of Maliseet in Maine. He is also a past recipient of the prestigious Praxis Award for his work as an applied anthropologist.

Index